POLITICAL INSTITUTIONS
IN ITALY

POLITICAL INSTITUTIONS IN ITALY

Maurizio Cotta and Luca Verzichelli

OXFORD
UNIVERSITY PRESS

OXFORD
UNIVERSITY PRESS

Great Clarendon Street, Oxford OX2 6DP

Oxford University Press is a department of the University of Oxford.
It furthers the University's objective of excellence in research, scholarship, and education by publishing worldwide in

Oxford New York

Auckland Cape Town Dar es Salaam Hong Kong Karachi
Kuala Lumpur Madrid Melbourne Mexico City Nairobi
New Delhi Shanghai Taipei Toronto

With offices in

Argentina Austria Brazil Chile Czech Republic France Greece
Guatemala Hungary Italy Japan Poland Portugal Singapore
South Korea Switzerland Thailand Turkey Ukraine Vietnam

Oxford is a registered trademark of Oxford University Press in the UK and in certain other countries

Published in the United States by Oxford University Press Inc., New York

First published 2007

British Library Cataloguing in Publication Data

Data available

Library of Congress Cataloging in Publication Data

Cotta, Maurizio, 1947–
Political institutions in Italy / Maurizio Cotta and Luca Verzichelli.
p. cm.
ISBN 978-0-19-928470-2 (alk. paper)
1. Italy–Politics and government–1994–2. Public administration–Italy. I. Verzichelli, Luca. II. Title.
JN5452.C674 2007
320.945–dc22
2006101526

Typeset by Laserwords Private Limited, Chennai, India

Printed in Great Britain
on acid-free paper by
Ashford Colour Press Ltd, Gosport, Hampshire

ISBN 978–0–19–928470–2

10 9 8 7 6 5 4 3 2 1

CONTENTS

LIST OF FIGURES

LIST OF TABLES

LIST OF BOXES

PREFACE

This book appears at an interesting moment for the Italian political system. Over the past twenty years the issue of a 'big institutional reform' has been more or less constantly on the agenda and has monopolized public debate for long periods. The need for a big reform, which would entail a major rewriting of the constitution, has been advocated by political actors of the left and right and by a large number of external observers as the ultimate cure for the many problems of the Italian political system. Yet, after the failure of many (bipartisan) attempts in the past and particularly of the last (partisan) attempt of Berlusconi's centre-right government, the general perception seems to be that this big reform is very difficult to achieve and is perhaps impossible given the fragmentation of its political actors. Some even think that it might not be the best cure as it is very difficult to compose all the different reform demands in a harmonious way. The failure (so far) of the big reform does not mean, however, that nothing has changed in the Italian institutional landscape of these years. In fact, quite on the contrary, significant changes have taken place in many different areas of the political system. Such changes affected both the institutional design of many 'pieces' of the state and the political practices that determine how they work. These changes, however, although often connected and interacting among themselves, rather than being guided by a central mind with a comprehensive design, have 'happened' under the impulse of non-coordinated factors. Whether this is a positive or negative feature could be the object of an interesting normative debate. This book engages in a more modest exercise, that of attempting to document these changes and to assess their effects (or at least those that have come to the surface so far). Given the somewhat haphazard and unsystematic nature of these changes, they have first of all to be documented one by one. However, it will be significantly more difficult to appraise their joint effects.

Is what in current parlance is called the 'second republic', really a *new republic*, i.e. a political and institutional system that is substantially different from that of the past? And what is its nature? Or is it, as some more sceptical observers propose after a season of great hopes for a major change, that things have gone back to what they were? We will not provide the answers to these questions, but we aim to offer some elements to the reader in an attempt to proceed in this direction. In particular we have tried to pay attention to the coexistence of the old and new in the structure and life of the institutions and to both the endogenous and exogenous factors of change.

This brings us to another theme which will deserve some attention in this book: that of the relationship between the Italian domestic political system and the international system. The importance of this relationship cannot be underestimated. Two sub-themes must be mentioned here: the first concerns the impact of the East–West international divide on Italian politics and particularly on the party system. The second concerns the relationship between Italy and Europe. Since the beginning Italy has strongly supported the process of European integration, fully trusting its positive role to compensate for domestic weaknesses. This process at the same time, particularly in recent years (with the completion of the single market, monetary union and the stability pacts), has forced the Italian political system to abandon some of its traditional and well-established instruments for solving difficult problems (large deficit spending, large public debt, clientelistic policies, etc.), or at least to reduce their use. These themes will be approached in the chapters where they are more relevant. The same occurs for other themes such as that of patronage and corruption which are often recalled in many analyses of the Italian political system, and have to be connected to different institutional aspects, from parties and party system, to local government and to the judicial institutions.

Purposes of the book

Three concerns have guided us through the preparation of this volume: the first one corresponds to the need to provide a comprehensive and accurate *description* of the institutional topics that are the common features of the present Oxford University Press series, without abstaining from focusing on a number of themes, paradoxes, and problems which seem particularly relevant in the Italian case.

The second concern has to do with the prospective readers: this is mainly an introductory and informative book for educational purposes. If our work has been done successfully, entry-level students of comparative politics should find this volume clear enough and helpful for their attempts to explore the unknown territories of Italian politics. At the same time, other readers—students and scholars with a greater knowledge of Italian history and politics—may have an additional tool to consider the state of institutional transformations in the country.

The third concern is mainly methodological: the Italian political system is often remembered for its peculiarities. To include this case in a series entitled Comparative Political Institutions means, to some extent, to make an effort to look *beyond* the country specificities and to enable the readers to produce implicit comparisons and evaluate the distance between the case in point and other sets of democratic institutions.

Concerning the more ambitious aim of the interpretative level, a note of caution must be sounded: the reader will not find any astonishing assertion 'repositioning' the current Italian political system in a given typology, or formulating a new definition of the Italian style of democracy. We believe this is not the ultimate goal of this book, which is devoted to simplification rather than to producing sophisticated analyses. On the contrary, the main purpose of this book is to stress and comprehend the reasons for the persistence and the adaptation of a number of institutional features, when faced by the challenges and the claims for change. Explaining why institutions are able to persist and under what conditions they are able to adapt without collapsing is a fundamental neo-institutional interpretation of contemporary politics and, in the end, a natural attitude of the empiricist student dealing with macro-institutional scenarios.

Plan of the book

Given the aims outlined above, we have decided to put some constraints on the time perspective adopted by this book. With the exception of the first chapter, the book focuses particularly on the most recent developments, that is, those which have occurred during the past fifteen or twenty years. However, in order to provide the reader with the tools for understanding this period of change, a synthetic introductory view will be supplied for each topic, covering a longer time span and in particular the post-war period of the republican age.

The reader will find some interpretative ideas guiding the analysis across the different chapters. We can here summarize three main themes which sound particularly relevant in our analysis. The first one concerns the changing equilibrium between centre and periphery, in a country which has historically adopted a centralistic model of administration, but is usually mentioned for its localism and its internal fragmentation.

The second theme concerns the great divide between governing parties and permanent oppositions which structured Italian politics for approximately forty years, making alternation in power impossible, but at the same time leaving a significant space for collusive agreements between the opposing sides.

The third theme can be sketchily presented as follows: Italy was and remains a crucial, but to some extent difficult, country of the Western democratic hemisphere. This geo-political position has guaranteed a quite fast pace of social and political growth, as well as strong links to a number of 'global' political phenomena. At the same time, a number of country-specific factors have determined significant feedbacks and resistances to innovations, which make a precise assessment of the institutional change difficult. In defining the architecture of this volume, we had to consider several elements of innovation, which are largely connected with the global and supranational processes. Among them are the modification of executive–legislative relations, the transformation of the core executive, the emergence of regulatory institutions and of a new public management approach, and the judicialization of politics. At the same time, we have tried to discuss the extent to which these global trends have had an impact upon the specific Italian reality and to which changes in the Italian political institutions have to be connected to country-specific factors.

In order to provide a comprehensive analysis, the volume is organized in nine chapters. As already mentioned the first chapter focuses on the long-term transformation of the Italian polity. The second chapter analyses the transformation of the parties and the party system, which have always been depicted as the crucial actors in the crystallized political system of the first republic and, to a large extent, have played a central role in shaping the new democratic regime. The third chapter provides a discussion of the electoral regimes and the main features of electoral behaviour in Italy, focusing in particular on the most recent transformations.

The two central chapters of the volume (4 and 5) deal with the key institutional actors of the parliamentary government, the executive and the legislature, whose destinies are unquestionably linked. Chapter 6 covers the evolution of the different tiers of local government in contemporary Italy, while the following two chapters illustrate the transformation of the administrative system (Chapter 7) and of judicial power (Chapter 8). These institutions seem particularly relevant for the explanation of current political change, given the factual relevance they have achieved over the past two decades.

A short conclusion is then presented, with the purpose of summarizing change and continuity across the different institutional sectors and to reflect on the reasons for the peculiar Italian sequence seen in the recent season of more accelerated changes after the previous one of institutional continuity.

ACKNOWLEDGEMENTS

This book has been slowly put together over a period of at least two years. Our teaching and professional duties are of course the main reason for this slowness. However, sometimes the drafting of the chapters had to be delayed in order to follow the developments of the Italian institutional setting, which in recent years has gone through important and sometimes unexpected changes. In some cases we had to 'wait and see', deliberately postponing the drafting of specific parts of the book. For instance, during the spring of 2006 we had to wait for the results of the general election and then for the important referendum concerning the proposal of a broad constitutional reform. Some may see it as somehow frustrating to spend all this time looking for institutional changes and then discovering so many evidences of continuity. But this is the real world of politics and if, as citizens and voters, we are allowed to have legitimate reasons for concern, as political scientists we cannot allow ourselves to be too surprised.

During this long period we have benefited from many suggestions and collaborations and other sources of help. Ruth Anderson, from Oxford University Press, was always very encouraging and supportive, combining in all her communications two messages—friendship and exhortation—that generally sound incompatible. Several colleagues, Italians and *Italianists* abroad, have been very generous with their comments and suggestions. In particular, we would like to thank our colleagues from the Centre for the Study of Political Change of the University of Siena (CIRCaP), the place where we spend most of our time, teaching Italian and non-Italian students.

One of our most active colleagues in Siena is Jean Blondel, a master of the profession and a great friend. His advice has always been very much appreciated, both for the substantive knowledge he can transmit and for his extremely enthusiastic approach to political science.

The concrete preparation of the book has proceeded along two routes. A first route links the University of Siena with the European Studies Centre of St Antony's College, Oxford, where Luca Verzichelli was a visiting Fellow during the academic year 2005/6. We are very grateful to Timothy Garton Ash, the Director of the Centre, for his hospitality, but also for having had the opportunity to meet him along with other scholars, in such a lively and stimulating environment where so many ideas and comments about the current developments of Italian and European politics are being voiced.

A second route links two more peripheral places, the coastline of Grosseto, in southern Tuscany, and the Robella hills in Piedmont, which are, however, two significant places for us and for our families. There, many friends and relatives not only provided us with substantial help, but also stimulated our work and patiently tolerated our non-attendance.

Chris Hanretty and Peter Levy have helped us with the editing of some chapters. Other crucial help has been provided in Siena by Alice Mackenzie, Silvina Cabrera, Marina Borgogni, and all the staff in our department.

Maurizio Cotta
Luca Verzichelli

1

The Italian Polity and its Long-Term Transformations

Overview

In this chapter we will briefly sketch the main features of the Italian polity and its long-term transformations. We will concentrate our attention on three aspects that seem particularly crucial for defining the environment within which the institutions and political processes that will be analyzed in later chapters are to be understood. The first aspect concerns the formation of the Italian polity and the shape the organization of the state originally acquired. The main question addressed here relates to the way in which the original centralized state, which resulted from the unification of regional states, developed into a regionalized and then a quasi-federal state.

The second aspect concerns the democratization of the political system. This process has, in the Italian case, proved difficult and discontinuous. We will briefly document how, following the apparently successful building of a liberal parliamentary regime, Italy experienced a democratic breakdown which led to a Fascist authoritarian regime and eventually to its collapse in the ruins of the Second World War. We will then see how the democratic consolidation achieved in the climate of international division of the two blocs system, and the 'partycracy' which ensued, were shaken after forty years of continuity by a dramatic political earthquake which brought about a deep renewal of electoral rules, of the party system, and of patterns of political competition.

As a third aspect we discuss the role played by the international environment and its changing equilibria, and in particular by the processes of supranational integration, in the shaping of the internal political processes and the working of institutions.

From the pluralism of regional states to a centralized state to a new tentative federal model

The unification of the country

In 2011 Italy will celebrate its one hundred and fiftieth anniversary as an independent state. It is thus older than many other states in the world and in Europe (such as Germany, Norway, the Czech Republic, etc.), but it is younger than France, Portugal, Spain, Sweden, and the United Kingdom. As a united and independent country it was shaped in the age of nationalism, when it was believed that any nation should have a state and every state should be a nation. It was built from a number of regional states and with parts carved out from the declining multinational empire of the Habsburg Monarchy.

The unification in 1861 of Italy—a name that, after the fall of the Roman Empire and of the old medieval kingdom of Italy,[1] had maintained only a geographical meaning and evoked feelings of 'nostalgia' of a golden time,[2] or a literary and artistic patrimony, but no political reality—was the result of the successful international manoeuvres of the Kingdom of Sardinia,[3] a relatively peripheral regional state but comparatively successful in its state-building, and of the failures of the other *ancien régime* states of the peninsula.

The timing of the process of unification, and the conditions under which it took place, had important consequences for the future developments of the Italian polity. With regard to the international arena, the late achievement of the 'large dimension' threshold when compared with the other major actors of the European and world scene, and the fact that this had been made possible only with decisive military help from France and the benign support of the United Kingdom, left the new country in the uneasy position of being the least of the big powers. This produced within parts of the political elites the recurrent feeling that Italy had to catch up with the more influential countries of Europe and that it 'deserved' a better place in the world. It was this feeling that induced Italian governments during the first eighty years following unification to take part in a number of colonial expeditions and in the two great wars of the twentieth century.

With regard to the internal order it can be said that the unification of Italy was more easily produced than implemented. The form it took, namely the annexation of the other Italian states to one of the existing regional states—the Kingdom of Sardinia—rather than a form of consensual unification into a new state (possibly with a federal character), had to do with a number of factors which cannot be discussed here at length. Fundamentally, however, it related to the fact that the Piedmontese kingdom had gained in the mid-nineteenth century a combined advantage vis-à-vis the other states of the peninsula. It was (probably as a result of its long struggle for survival against a stronger neighbour, France) a more powerful state in terms of its administrative and military capacities (Ziblatt 2006); it was more independent from some of the stronger and influential neighbours of the peninsula; and it was the only state which had maintained the liberal constitution that it had adopted, like the other Italian states, in 1848. The other more significant actors of the peninsula—the Grand Duchy of Tuscany, the State of the Church, and the Kingdom of Naples and Sicily—lagged far behind in terms of such resources. These features put the Kingdom of Sardinia, which geographically and culturally was at the periphery, in a central position when the game of nation-building opened in Italy as everywhere in Europe. Although there was originally no unity in the Italian 'national movement'—a significant republican wing led by Mazzini and Garibaldi would have preferred the independence and unity of Italy to be reached via a popular upheaval and the elimination of monarchical institutions—the Savoy monarchy, thanks to its military successes and its parliamentary institutions, was able to win the support of the moderate wing of the movement (and could count on a fairly solid allegiance of its internal public opinion), and gradually came to be widely accepted as the leader of the Italian national cause.

Unification was achieved for the major part in 1861 (which became the official birthday of the Italian state), but other areas of what was considered to be Italian territory were acquired only later: Venice and the Veneto in 1866; Rome (which entailed the eviction of the Pope from its centuries-old secular sovereignty) in 1870; the region of Trento, South Tyrol (Alto Adige for the Italians), Trieste and its territory, Istria, and part of the Dalmatian coast in 1918. As in most other European cases of nation-building, it was not always easy to determine where the borders of the Italian state should be. The concepts of natural, historic, and linguistic borders were used in conjunction or separately to justify the annexations achieved and those requested. Different criteria, but also different interpretations of the same criterion, would inevitably produce different borders and in some cases open conflicts of nationalities. The process of unification ultimately brought into Italy a substantial German-speaking minority in South Tyrol and Slavic minorities in the Friuli-Venezia Giulia region, but excluded significant regions that had historically belonged to the Piedmontese kingdom (including Savoy itself and the Italian-speaking area of Nice) and other Italian-speaking Venetian territories along the Dalmatian coast of the Adriatic sea. In both cases this created, at some point, problems (of a different nature) for the Italian state as a political community. Different policies towards the internal minorities were adopted during the twentieth century, from the Fascist attempts at forced assimilation to the elaborate system of autonomies gradually granted throughout the decades following the Second World War. With regard to Italian populations abroad no serious thought of recovery was given to the territories lost to France (except perhaps during the initial phase of the Second World War), but for some time territories populated by 'Italians' on the Yugoslav coast were discussed by some political forces as legitimate targets of recovery.

The displacement of the old states with their institutions and sovereign dynasties was easily accepted by the modernizing and liberal-minded elites, but left significant strata of the population nostalgic for the old order. This feeling was strengthened when the newborn state had to increase the tax burden to pay for unification. Internal opposition was significant, although never able to put unity in danger or to offer a realistic alternative; but its effects on the political life of Italy were not negligible and, at given points in time, could determine important features of political life. By far the most crucial component of this opposition was the Catholic one. It had its roots in the resentment both of the military occupation of Rome, the seat for almost two millennia of the Pope's temporal authority, and also of the severe secularization policies promoted by the liberal elites, which had entailed large-scale expropriations of religious properties. This opposition was all the more significant since the appeal of the church for large swathes of the population, particularly but not exclusively in the countryside, was strong. Catholic opposition to the new state was first defined in 1874 by a papal decree (the *non expedit*) which ordered non-participation in the political life of Italy at the national level. It took a long time before participation in elections was again permitted (with the Gentiloni pact of 1913) and a Catholic party was created and accepted by church authorities. The Partito Popolare (Popular Party) founded in 1919 immediately became the second largest party of the country (Kalyvas 1996). The story of the difficult relationship between the Italian state and the church had, however, further episodes that affected political life. The settlement of the disputes (which concerned problems of sovereignty and mutual recognition, but also significant financial aspects and problems of religious freedom, education, marriage regulations, etc.) was achieved only under the Fascist regime with the Treaty of 1929 and the *Concordato*. This ensured the regime a support which the liberal elite had not been able to achieve. This settlement was to be confirmed in 1947 by a very large majority in the Constituent Assembly of the new democratic regime and, with minor changes negotiated by the Craxi cabinet in 1984, still governs this crucial relationship. It must also be remembered that with the fall of fascism the reborn Catholic party, now called Democrazia Cristiana (DC, Christian Democracy), became rapidly the central actor of the democratic regime.

The process leading from the original intransigent opposition of the Catholic Church, which touched all three dimensions (polity, politics, and policies) of the new state, to the full incorporation of the Catholics into the system was a long and difficult one. For a long time this problem weakened the stability of Italian democracy.

Opposition came also from other directions. In southern Italy support for the Bourbon royal family persisted among part of the aristocracy and other sections of the elite, the clergy, and in the countryside. Episodes of violent resistance against the new authorities took place repeatedly and were repressed severely by the government, which dubbed their authors bandits.

The existence of these oppositions was perceived by the nation-builders as a threat not to be underestimated. In particular it contributed to making them reluctant to extend the suffrage, through fear that peasants, influenced by the church and by old allegiances, would challenge the liberal supremacy, as well as making them unwilling to grant some form of regional autonomy, in case this should unleash centrifugal forces too strong for the new state to control. Under the thin layer of liberal hegemony there were forces that might have endangered what had been achieved and had to be kept at bay, even if this required using means that contradicted some of the tenets of liberalism itself. Thus the liberal elites defended for a long time the restricted suffrage, shelved the regional reform they had originally envisaged, and did not hesitate to use repressive means against what were considered subversive manifestations (as happened in a particularly serious way in Sicily and Milan in 1898–99).

Italian society

While Italy was formed relatively quickly and without much serious resistance, 'making the Italians', as a former Piedmontese prime minister (Massimo d'Azeglio) once said, took longer and proved more complicated. This should not be a surprise: Italy is a geographically long and thin territory. Its northern part is strongly interconnected with the centre of Europe (Piedmont has had a long tradition of wars but also of economic and cultural relations with France and Switzerland, as has Lombardy with Germany and Austria, Trentino with Austria, etc.), but its southernmost part floats in the centre of the Mediterranean sea, very close to the northern coasts of Africa (and has had strong Arab influences over the centuries and a long Spanish domination).

As a result of this geographical position, legacies of the past, a long history of separate polities within its territory, and different paths of economic development, the society of Italy remained, after unification, strongly diverse internally. Although the literary language had been standardized long before, this did not mean that all elites would use Italian as their main tongue (in Piedmont they preferred to use French). And most of the populace used a vast array of dialects which to a great extent did not facilitate communication between different groups. A Piedmontese peasant would understand nothing spoken by a Sicilian peasant, but also probably very little spoken by a Venetian or Genoese fisherman. Degrees of literacy, patterns of economic and social life, styles of family, social relations, and religious life, etc. all varied significantly across Italy.

In the north, in Piedmont, Lombardy, and Veneto, there were thousands of small municipalities dotting the countryside with their parishes and local authorities; in the south a much smaller number of large communes existed, where the authority resided in a large agglomeration, geographically and psychologically much more distant from a large part of the population. Patterns of land ownership were also rather different. A great number of small independent farmers coexisted alongside a number of large properties in the north; sharecroppers had a major role in central Italy; in the south latifundia prevailed together with day labourers (Zamagni 1998).

If Italy, in the aftermath of its unification, could be globally considered an economically backward country, compared with Britain, France, Belgium, and Switzerland, its internal landscape was in fact rather diversified. Piedmont and Lombardy had a long tradition of textile, mechanical, and military industries which were not matched in the centre and south. To an extent unification made the differences even larger. Protected industrialization starting in the Kingdom of Naples was to a great extent damaged by the creation of a larger internal market and by the competition with northern industries.

The take-off of the process of industrialization during the last decades of the nineteenth century increased rather than smoothed the differences. Milan, Turin, and Genoa became the poles of a thriving industrial triangle with important international projections, while the south of Italy was left behind. The *questione meridionale*, the problem of the economic and social south/north disparity, became thus a long-term leitmotiv throughout the history of Italy.

The features of the new state

The way in which Italian unification had been attained determined some of the features of the new polity. The creation of the new Kingdom of Italy consisted, in fact and from a legal point of view, in a series of (successive) annexations of the other states and regions of the peninsula to the Kingdom of Sardinia. The pre-existent state changed only its name, keeping its royal family, its constitution (the *Statuto Albertino*), its parliament (which was simply enlarged), its bureaucratic apparatus, and, for some years, its capital, which remained in Turin. The annexations were sanctioned through significantly manipulated universal male suffrage plebiscites which gave an overwhelming majority in favour of unification. Given the peripheral character and limited size of the incorporating state, the old structure had to be extended and with time inevitably underwent changes. But the principle of administrative centralization was strictly implemented. The new regions were therefore largely ruled by Piedmontese bureaucrats for some years. Only during the twentieth century was there a large 'southernization' of Italian bureaucracy, with proportionally greater numbers of civil servants being recruited from southern regions.

The national nature of political elites also increased only gradually: until 1876, under the *destra storica* (the conservative sector of the liberal elite), about half the ministers originated from the north-western area, while the south was rather under-represented. In 1889, Crispi was the first head of government to originate from a southern region (although he had been an émigré in Piedmont). The liberals, however, became with time a truly national political elite well rooted (at least in the upper and middle classes) in all parts of Italy. The territorial cleavage resurfaced, however, after the First World War when a combination of factors—the turmoil following the end of a bloody and costly conflict, the crisis of the liberal elite which had been internally split on the war issue, the new electoral system, and the delayed effects of the extension of suffrage—led to a new political landscape which saw the liberal elites still strong in southern Italy, but practically wiped away in northern and central Italy, where the new political forces—the Socialists and the Christian Democrats of the Partito Popolare—had succeeded in securing the votes of the greatest part of the electorate. This territorial divide appeared again, but in a weakened form, after the Second World War in the elections of 1946, but was completely bridged in the following elections when another type of divide pushed it to the background. The re-founded Christian Democratic Party became in 1948 a truly national party, able to win considerable support in all regions (only overcome by the Communist Party in the regions of the centre—Emilia, Tuscany, and Umbria).

From 1861 to 1946 the constitution of Italy was the *Statuto Albertino*, the charter granted to its territories by the then king of Sardinia, Charles Albert of Savoy. This document was still based on the principles of constitutional monarchy: popular sovereignty was not even mentioned, and with regards to the executive it simply said that the cabinet nominated by the king was 'responsible' and did not specify either its responsibility vis-à-vis the parliament, or the need for a confidence vote. The parliament was bicameral, with an elected Chamber of Deputies and a Senate with members nominated by the king within a list of twenty-one selected categories (such as high state officials, military officers, judges, former ministers, property owners, etc). The bill of rights included in the *Statuto* was minimal. In practice, however, and without any formal change, the constitution permitted the experimentation of a parliamentary regime, whereby cabinets had to have a parliamentary majority in the lower chamber. This, however, did not mean that the king would refrain completely from interfering with the choice of prime ministers and ministers (Cotta and Verzichelli 2003). Until the emergence of fascism, Italy functioned fundamentally as a parliamentary monarchy but still with significant restrictions on the freedom of political dissent and some significant degree of government manipulation of elections (particularly in the south through the prefects). Interestingly, the *Statuto* was maintained during the Fascist period—albeit emptied of its meaning—and after the fall of the authoritarian regime, some of the transition actors (in particular the monarchy) made attempts to bring it back to life. These attempts were, however, defeated by the majority of the parties, which wanted to make a clean break with the past and to assert their role also as constitution-makers.

Under the *Statuto Albertino* territorial decentralization was limited. Below the national level only the province and the municipality existed. The province, conceived very much along the French model of the *département* and headed by a prefect, was in fact a very important instrument by which the central power could govern and control the periphery. As for municipalities they had an elected council but the mayor was initially nominated by the prefect. Only in 1888 were the councils (or directly the voters in small villages) given the power to elect the first citizen. But all these democratic bodies remained under the control of the prefect, who had the power and the duty to check the legality of their acts and could always disband them if they violated any rule or were seen as unable to govern effectively.

Requests for greater decentralization were voiced from time to time, but were rejected or delayed. As noted, the fear of losing control of a hostile periphery was the original reason for rejecting the regionalization of the country. A more favourable attitude was present in the new democratic parties, especially in the Partito Popolare, but its programmes of reform were quickly shelved when the democratic crisis opened the way to an authoritarian regime, which had no interest in decentralization and also erased some progress of the past (such as the democratic election of mayors).

Windows of opportunity for a revision of the centre–periphery balance opened recurrently, occurring at moments of serious crises and turning points in the political system. The three points in time to be mentioned are the years of the transition from fascism to democracy and of the making of the new constitution; the centre-left alliance; and finally the years of crisis in the 1990s.

The fall of fascism meant also its models of governance were brought into disrepute. The centralization that it had not only maintained but even increased was more easily challenged. To this should be added that the liberal elite, which had been responsible for putting in place the original model of centre–periphery relations, had also more or less disappeared and that the parties now on the rise were more ready, by having been part of the opposition in the past and in some cases also for their specific ideological platforms, to rebalance these relations to the advantage of the periphery. The new constitutional design, while refusing to go to the extreme of a federal solution and to abandon the old administrative scheme based on prefects, gave a fully constitutional rank to locally elected authorities and added regions to provinces and municipalities. The adoption of a general regionalization scheme had to do also with the fact that special regional autonomy was the solution adopted to face secessionist drives, which had become apparent in some peripheral areas of the country (Aosta Valley, Sardinia, Sicily, South Tyrol, Friuli-Venezia Giulia) at the time of the military defeat and of the collapse of the Italian state that had followed it (see Chapter 6).

Pressures from below (mainly in the peripheral regions), limited ability to resist from above and the ideological propensity of significant parts of the national elites produced a favourable mix of conditions for such a significant change in the institutional design of the polity. This situation was, however, bound to change very rapidly and to lead to a delay in the implementation of regionalization. Once special regional autonomy was granted to the few regions listed above, and with the dominant preoccupation of the population being then focused on economic reconstruction and international tensions (both themes in the field of competence of the central government), mobilization from below for regional autonomies virtually disappeared. As for the governing elites, their enthusiasm for decentralization cooled rapidly for a variety of reasons: as they had changed their role from opposition to government, the advantages of centralization had increased for them, the necessities of reconstruction seemed to require centralized action, and, finally, in the political landscape that had emerged with the return to democracy, implementing the regional scheme would have meant granting significant powers to a number of regions of central Italy which would be governed by the Communist opposition. The danger of cutting Italy in half was at that time perceived as a serious one.

The window of opportunity for regionalization thus closed very rapidly, to be opened again only twenty years later. After the years of the 'economic miracle', demands for a more flexible administration had increased and the implementation of regions had become in the 1960s one of the requests of the Socialist Party, which had entered into the centre-left coalition with Christian Democracy. It had also become more acceptable to the latter party, which had now consolidated its power and, being less afraid of the Communist threat, could conceive of leaving some regions in the hands of the opposition. Moreover, in the many regions where the national governing parties would be in power, some extra positions of influence would thus be available for them: a precious resource for managing the internal competition among factions. With the 1970 elections of regional councils ordinary regions came thus into life. As a result of this delayed implementation, they had, however, to deal with a central state administration which had been by then fully reconstructed and had become used to perform the duties that the constitution had assigned to regional governments. The transfer of functions and resources was thus far from easy and took more than a decade (Putnam 1993). What is more the control over financial resources remained strongly concentrated in the hands of the central state.

A new challenge to the territorial balance of the polity began to appear, and with truly new contours, at the end of the 1980s and in the 1990s gained a real significance. It was raised by a new political movement, the Lega Nord (Northern League), which, launched from the economic heart of Italy, the regions of Lombardy, Veneto, and Piedmont, gained an unexpected electoral success with its calls either for a federal transformation of Italy or for a secession of these regions. The secessionist call was, as we have seen, not totally new (it had been voiced before in some peripheral areas); what was unprecedented were the regions it now came from: the richest and industrially most advanced areas of Italy, regions which nobody before had thought could become the centre of a secessionist movement.

The seriousness of the issue was therefore also unprecedented. The electoral success of the League coincided to a large extent with (and was one of the causes of) the dramatic decline of the DC, precisely in those regions of the north which had been among its strongholds. It meant a territorial segmentation of the country, with the League in the ascendant in the north, the post-communist party defending its strongholds in the centre (but weakened in the north), and the DC on the defensive in the south. When the collapse of the DC and the other governing parties came about, between 1993 and 1994 (see Chapter 2), the League obtained a pivotal role in the new bipolar system, and the request for a devolution of authority to the regions gained momentum. The effect of competition was such that the word federalism (which had had no space in Italian political discourse for a very long period) entered in the daily political lexicon, and more or less all the parties included some form of it in their programmes.

At the same time there was a broad pressure from below which involved both regions and municipalities. The direct election of city mayors after the reform of 1993 and the increasing national political visibility gained by the first citizens of the largest cities (Rome, Naples, Milan, etc.) also stimulated an increased activism at the regional level. This led first to a reform of the regional electoral system, then, in 1999, to a constitutional revision by which the direct popular election of the head of the regional executive was introduced and the regional councils were given the power to rewrite the regional statutes without the control of the national parliament.

The close electoral competition between left and right coalitions led the left—then in power—first to promote a large devolution of administrative powers to the regions (through the so-called 'Bassanini laws'), then to anticipate the federal reform proposed by the right by adopting a broad constitutional amendment (see Chapter 6). The reform, passed in great haste and with a small majority, transferred major powers to the regions. The model adopted was essentially that of cooperative federalism according to which on a very large series of matters the national parliament maintained the right to define the general principles valid for the whole country, within which the regional councils would have the power to legislate freely.

When the right, having succeeded in bringing the League back into the coalition, won, after the regional elections, the national ones in 2001, it was its turn to adopt the federal reform it had promised. As a great deal had been accomplished by the reform of the left, the right concentrated its efforts on granting exclusive powers to the regions in the fields of health care, education, and local police, on the reform of bicameralism, and on the strengthening of the premier. Passing this reform, to which other topics were also attached, making it a very broad rewriting of the constitution, took the whole legislature and created many dissensions, which in the end weakened the cohesion of the centre-right, antagonized the opposition and frightened a large part of the electorate. The consequence was that in the 2006 referendum, required by the constitution to confirm the reform passed by parliament, a majority of the participants voted against, thus invalidating the reform (62.3 per cent of voters, with a rate of participation of 52.3 per cent).

At the end of this process the institutional structure of the state had changed significantly at the constitutional level, but important aspects of the reform are still unfinished and their implementation remains contentious. The constitutional design now clearly states that the country is no longer a centralized unitary state but is based on four levels—the state, the regions, the provinces, and the municipalities. Two of these levels, the state and the regions, have legislative powers, but the distribution of the competences between the two levels remains poorly defined and concurrent competences still predominate. After the failure of the 2005 reform introduced by the Berlusconi government, the transformation of the second chamber into a federal chamber is still unaccomplished, and proposals for a reshaping of the Constitutional Court in order to take into account the federal transformation of the country are still on the table.

As regards the practical implementation, the amount of resources administered by regions has increased significantly and the spheres of intervention of sub-national authorities have become very substantial for the day-to-day life of citizens. At the same time, however, the traditional centralism of the state has been hard to overcome. Regions have remained to a large extent dependent on the central state for financial resources; this has produced a lengthy and complicated process of negotiation between the two levels for the transfer of funds (see Chapter 6). More generally the government and the central bureaucracy, and also the national parliament, have been slow to adapt to the transfer of functions and, as a consequence, conflicts of competences have burgeoned, bringing to the Constitutional Court an increasing number of cases. The equilibrium between centre and periphery is thus still not fully stabilized.

Democratization with interruptions and new reforms

When Italy was created, the practice of parliamentary government had already been more or less accepted in its predecessor state—the Kingdom of Sardinia—with the only limitation being that the monarchy maintained a significant influence on the selection of the prime minister and of some crucial ministers, and that suffrage was still severely restricted. This first step in the democratization process had been achieved earlier than in Austria, France, Germany, Portugal, and Spain. In fact only Britain and Belgium had in the 1860s or 1870s a more strongly established parliamentary system. It may then be asked why, given this favourable beginning, the process of democratization encountered a severe interruption during the first part of the twentieth century?

We have already pointed to some weaknesses of the Italian political system. The first and foremost was probably the large Catholic opposition following the conquest of Rome by the new state. More than in the nature of opposition activities (which were not particularly disruptive), the relevance of this factor lay in the fact that it weakened the legitimacy of the Italian state and seriously limited the possibility for liberal elites to win greater popular support. It thus induced them to take a more defensive attitude towards democratization. Another negative factor which probably played a crucial role was that the liberal elite did not develop a seriously articulated party organization in the country until just before the advent of fascism, when it was too late. This was probably a result of the fact that the governing party did not face a significant electoral competition for long and that it could count upon the state bureaucracy (the prefects) to manipulate electoral consent in the periphery.

Without a true party organization and with limited popular support, in the last years of the nineteenth century the governing elites had to face the growth of the Socialist Party and the mobilization of the Catholics. Parliamentary tactics of alliances and reformist policy making at the elite level, and repression or manipulation at the mass level were the only instruments available against this opposition. Giolitti, repeatedly prime minister and one of the dominant figures of the liberal elite, was the leading actor of this game. Through skilful policy concessions he managed, in the years before the First World War, to enlist the parliamentary support of the Socialists and of the Catholics once they appeared in parliament. In fact as long as suffrage was restricted these tools seemed effective in preserving the liberal hegemony. They had, however, some negative side effects: in particular they helped create a gap between moderate and radical socialists, and thus in the end making the Socialist Party less able to play a constructive role in the phase of democratization; and it strengthened the illusion among liberal elites that their hegemony could be preserved without a properly organized popular base.

The election of 1913, the first after the great extension of male suffrage, which had finally been accepted in 1912, seemed at first to confirm the correctness of this policy. The Liberals, having formed an electoral alliance with the Catholics (the so-called Gentiloni pact), maintained their majority in the Chamber of Deputies: their hegemony appeared assured. After the parliamentary co-option of the Socialists, managed by Giolitti, the electoral co-option of the Catholics was to be the final piece of that construction. Yet what had seemed to be an effective tactic soon unravelled and what was perceived as a very strong hegemony gave way in a few years to a major regime crisis and to the seizure of power by an outsider, Mussolini, and his newly created movement. To explain this we have to take into account a series of new developments which had, rather quickly, created an entirely different landscape from that of the past. During the First World War and the years immediately afterwards the internal unity of the liberals was increasingly challenged on matters of international and internal strategy. Neutrality versus intervention in the First World War, and a softer or a more repressive attitude towards working-class protests and the socialist movement were the crucial points. The Socialist Party too became increasingly factionalized and, after a first split in 1912 of part of the moderate wing, the radical faction gained the upper hand. As for the Catholics, having gained a greater awareness of their potential political strength, they became less inclined to accept the liberal hegemony.

At the end of the First World War the transformation of the political system accelerated dramatically. The enormous human and material costs of the war, the fact that the country did not seem to reap all the expected benefits of the victory, the problems of the demobilization of the war machine and of the conversion of the economy, and the waves of the

Bolshevik revolutions in Russia and in other parts of Europe, generated in Italy, as in many other European countries, new challenges for which the existing political system was not prepared.

In a few years the traditional governing elite of Italy experienced a rapid political decline following its electoral defeat in the most advanced parts of Italy and following a growing internal fragmentation. The rise of the new mass parties (Popular Party and Socialists), which together came to have a majority of the seats in the parliament elected in 1919, and the development of nationalist movements also spurred this decline. The political system had entered into a process of deep restructuring which led to a significant decline in its ability to perform effectively (Farneti 1978), at a moment when Italian society increasingly required the political system to solve its problems. With a parliament more or less equally split between the old and the new parties, the latter were not yet ready to take over a governing role both because of their ideological differences and, particularly in the case of the Socialists, because of their still uncertain loyalty to the liberal state and to the monarchy. On the other side, the old political class, with a more reduced parliamentary weight, had lost much of its freedom of manoeuvre. Moreover, the difficulty in understanding the other half of the parliament and its new party logic, the end of the life cycle of the great leader Giolitti, and internal fragmentation diminished greatly its previous ability effectively to dominate the political process. A succession of short-lived and uncertain cabinets was one of the first consequences. At the same time a significant radicalization of society was taking place: great strikes and occupations of industrial plants fuelled the opposite hopes and fears of the revolution. The economic elites and significant parts of the middle classes lost their confidence in the ability of the parliamentary class to face the threat of a Soviet-style revolution. The ineffectiveness of the institutional scene coupled with the mobilization and radicalization of society led to a progressive shift of the political centre of gravity from democratic institutions to the streets and non-democratic powers. This explains how the Fascist Party (PNF), which had won no more than 35 seats out of 535 in the elections of 1921, could gain, within a few months, a crucial role in the political game and obtain in October 1922 the position of head of the government for its leader. If, until then, the crucial legs on which political power had rested were parliament, monarchy, and state bureaucracy, it was now street politics and violence, great economic interests, and the monarchy that provided the triangle of forces that could subjugate parliamentary politics and pave the way for the dictatorship.

Mussolini's ascent to power was a clear example of the new politics: on one side there was the display of force and violence by the Fascist Party organizations culminating in the 'march on Rome' of October 1922; on the other side, the 'constitutional' process whereby the king nominated Mussolini head of government and a parliamentary majority (where the Fascists were only a tiny minority) gave him a confidence vote. In fact, until the end of 1924, talks continued among the opposition groups in parliament, with the purpose of putting together a coalition that would vote down Mussolini. The truth is that, in spite of the fact that the elections of 1924 had been conducted with a very disproportional electoral system and with significant recourse to violence and manipulation, the Fascists still lacked a true majority in parliament and had to rely on the support of other groups. Since, in the end, a coalition of the opposition never emerged because of internal dissension, we do not know what would have been the consequences of a parliamentary vote. Given the fact that the parliamentary arena had been already significantly weakened, it is possible that Mussolini would in any case have made recourse to violent means to overcome a parliamentary defeat. As the events developed he was able to exploit for its advantage a parliamentary legitimacy, which had not been effectively challenged by divided and frightened democratic parties, thus combining both old and new political resources.

With the passing of years, and through a process which included evolutionary change and ruptures, Mussolini was able to consolidate the new regime, progressively freeing it from the constraints of the old order, and to shape a new political construction which (regrettably) was bound to be one of the most influential 'inventions' of the twentieth century. The role of the leader was absolutely central in this construction. Mussolini was the head of the government throughout the whole period of the regime, while the official position of chairman of the PNF, the only party allowed to exist after 1925, was left to someone else. This solution did not disguise the fact that Mussolini was the real leader of the party, but at the same time it enabled him to play a role that went beyond the party itself. In fact the party, albeit playing an important part in the working of the regime, was never an independent factor vis-à-vis the leader. It was an instrument for mobilizing support among the masses and for exerting pressure on the other institutions and actors that could not be completely 'fascistized'. Its membership increased very significantly with the passing of time, particularly when being a member became a prerequisite for a career in public administration.

How to classify this regime in the panorama of non-democratic regimes has been the object of intense discussions. If we leave aside the term dictatorship, which is too vague, the debate is whether it should be considered a totalitarian or an authoritarian regime. The regime's own self-definition points to the former (which it obviously took as a positive term), as does the importance of its mass mobilization efforts. Mussolini's regime shared with Soviet Russia and Nazi Germany the gamut of totalitarian forms of mobilization (parades, marches, mass meetings, etc.), yet if we stick to the features of the totalitarian regime according to the most accepted definition (Linz 1975) Italian fascism lacked some of its crucial elements. More specifically it had not been able, or willing, to eliminate any other centre of influence in society that had potential political resources. While all forms of political opposition were crushed by fascism without much difficulty, the regime was much more prudent in its handling of other state and social actors. Monarchy, Catholic Church, army, state bureaucracy, and big capital had in different ways supported or tolerated the advent of fascism, seen as a lesser evil than the feared proletarian revolution and the impotence of parliamentary government. They even felt sympathy for some aspects of fascism, although it was combined with a dislike for other aspects. In any case these actors could not be fully identified with the fascist movement and were viewed with some suspicion by Mussolini who feared the possibility of a betrayal by them. The regime adopted towards them a mixed strategy of persuasion, co-option, penetration, and to an extent coercion. Veiled menaces were from time to time voiced; but fascism in the end never dared to attack them directly or dismantle them. The *fascistizzazione* of Italian society was therefore not completed. Maybe longer survival would have enabled the regime to reduce their autonomy, or maybe not; in any case the alliance with Nazism in the war sealed the fate of fascism. As Mussolini feared, some of these actors in fact played a significant role in the fall of the regime, when defeat in war became catastrophic and the regime was seriously weakened. They demonstrated that they had not been completely destroyed.

The legacies of fascism were multiple. It is pretty obvious that, given its authoritarian nature, fascism repressed freedoms and thus delayed significantly the process of creation of a freer society, which had begun with some difficulties during the previous regime. It would take a good number of years after its end before the illiberal aspects of the penal code or of police laws would be dismantled. The influence of the regime was, however, not only limited to the repressive aspects. For both external and internal reasons, it was significant also with regard to many other dimensions of social and economic life. The time span of fascism coincided with the phase when the question of social protection had become an important item on the political agenda; with the economic crisis of 1929 and the need to face its consequences, fascism had to respond to these challenges as did any other regime. To this should be added that the regime had its own reasons for developing instruments of consensus building and used these opportunities for this purpose. In fact some of the first institutions of the Italian welfare state—such as social pensions (Ferrera 1985)—were developed during this period. State ownership of industrial and particularly of banking firms became also a very significant component of the Italian economy during this period.

The crisis of fascism and transition to democracy

The decision by Mussolini to join the war launched by Nazi Germany for the domination of continental Europe came as a result of increasing international isolation, following Italy's attack and conquest of Ethiopia in defiance of the League of Nations, and of the fear that a German victory would have left a neutral Italy in a difficult position. But when the war effort proved much costlier than expected and the easy early victories of the Axis were followed by stalemate and defeats, the cost/benefit balance for the regime was drastically altered. Instead of rapidly 'sitting at the table of victory', as Mussolini had put it, Italy had to face the loss of its colonies and, even more seriously, the invasion by Allied troops of part of its territory (July 1943). The effects on the coalition explicitly or implicitly supporting the regime were extremely negative. Some of these actors, which had already been opposed to the war (such as the church) or at best lukewarm in their support (such as the monarchy and part of the army) became at that point ready to abandon Mussolini. The monarchy was the centre of a conspiracy to bring down the dictator, which involved the high commands of the army, the top levels of state bureaucracy, and even some components of the Fascist Party itself. The church and economic circles provided an external support. The downfall of Mussolini sealed the end of the Fascist regime, which was identified so much with his person, but opened a very difficult transition process. The transition to democracy was complicated by the fact that it began under conditions of war and with the country divided by the war front. While the south was occupied by Allied troops, the north and the centre had been invaded by German forces as soon as Italy changed sides after the armistice with the Allies (8 September 1943). In fact the whole state machine collapsed, leaving the country in an extreme state of uncertainty.

After the coup, which opened the way to a monarchical government headed by Marshal Badoglio, the top-ranking military officer, the political landscape broadened and other competitors entered the transition game. While the monarchy would have been happy with some semi-authoritarian solution preserving the *Statuto Albertino* and continuity with the past, political parties, both the old ones which had returned to life after the exile or imprisonment of their leaders and the new ones that were being formed, had different plans. With few exceptions they were suspicious of the monarchy and wanted to take control of the transition process. In their turn parties had to overcome their past conflicts and the reciprocal lack of trust that had plagued the last years of democracy, but also the persistent differences in their ideological platforms. The ability of all the actors to converge in spite of their differences was obviously a crucial factor for the success of the transition. The lessons of the past, the need to defeat the German occupiers, who were being fought also by an active resistance movement, and the pressures of the Allied nations probably contributed to overcoming the differences (Pasquino 1986). A first important compromise, reached in 1944, postponed the most divisive questions (among which was the problem of the monarchy and the constitution) to a later stage and enabled the formation of a cabinet by the king with the support and participation of all the major parties. From 1944 to 1946 a grand coalition of all anti-fascist forces governed the transition. If not without internal conflicts, this did provide for a large consensus on the crucial decisions of the transition. Particulary important among these descisions was that of electing a Constituent Assembly for the writing of a new constitution and leaving to a popular referendum the decision on the maintenance of the monarchy or the creation of a republic. An important political event of this period was the ascent in December 1945 of the Christian Democrat Alcide de Gasperi to the position of head of government, thanks to the central position of his party between the left and the right of the coalition. For the next thirty-five years Christian Democracy would always control that position.

In June 1946, while a referendum decided for a republican state, the first fully competitive elections for twenty-five years inaugurated the Constituent Assembly. This crucial institutional step in the transition to democracy had also a very important political meaning. It revealed for the first time the electoral weight of the different parties, and there were some surprises. The heirs of the liberal political class which had dominated the politics of pre-fascist Italy were reduced to a minor party (with its strongholds only in the south). Contrary to the expectations of the left, Christian Democracy was by far the leading party in most regions. The Socialist Party (PSIUP, then PSI) was the leading party of the left but only by a very reduced margin, and the success of the Communist Party (PCI), which gained almost as many votes, deprived the former of its hope to be clearly the leading force of the left. Other parties such as the Partito d'Azione or Democrazia del Lavoro, which had had a significant role during the resistance fight and the transition (each had supplied a prime minister), were found to have almost no following among the electorate. Finally, on the extreme right, the Uomo Qualunque (Front of Common Men), a party proposing a strong critique of the alliance of anti-fascist parties and of the left, obtained some success. This rang an alarm bell for the DC which, by its alliance with the left parties, now found itself exposed to competition from the right.

The new democracy and the problem of the opposition

The two years between the elections of 1946 and 1948 were crucial for the design of the institutional setting of the new democracy, and also for the shaping of the political conditions that would affect its practical implementation. Important aspects of this first mould were in fact to last for a long time. During this period parties were engaged in the writing of the new constitution, in the solution of the serious problems left by the war, and in political positioning in view of the future battles for electoral support and power. All this took place in a context heavily influenced by the changing state of international relations in Europe.

In the writing of the constitution the accord between the largest parties continued by and large to persist in spite of the differences in their ideological platforms. This led to a series of compromises which watered down many of the strongest and more innovative solutions proposed, but enabled in the end a large consensus on the constitution. Even if, for a large part of the left, the ideal political and institutional model was that of the Soviet Union, it came to accept a Western type of democracy with a parliamentary form; but proposals from the centre or the right to strengthen the executive were rejected and the same happened to schemes for an asymmetrical bicameralism. In the end the constitution was approved almost unanimously.

In the field of political relations important changes were taking place during this period, and coupled with internal developments Italian politics rapidly altered. Among the left, the competition between the PSI and PCI turned quickly to the advantage of the latter, thanks to its more developed organization in society, its internal discipline, and the strong international linkages with one of the victorious powers, the Soviet Union, but also because of the split that took place in the PSI on matters of international alignments (neutralism or alliance with the West) and of relations with the PCI. The consequence was to be a long-term predominance of the Communists on the left. At the centre of the party system the DC had to choose between the alliance with the left and a more independent course. Increasing competition from the right and the fear of losing votes in that direction, the radicalization of the largest party of the left, but also the appearance of a moderate Western-leaning left induced the leadership of the party to opt for a dissolution of the original alliance with the PCI and PSI.

The whole range of positions was significantly influenced by the new problems of international alignments. The growing internal division among the anti-fascist parties was a replica of the division that became increasingly manifest among the victors of the Second World War. Contrary to what happened in Germany, where the territorial division between western and eastern Germany drastically separated the two internal camps, in Italy they remained part of the same political system. This meant, however, that to the traditional internal cleavages a further one was added, that of international allegiances. The strong link between the internal and the international political spheres thus became a characteristic feature of Italian politics. The freezing in Europe of two antagonistic international blocs with opposing political, economic, and social systems made the cooperation in government between political parties linked to the two camps impossible. The Communist takeover in Czechoslovakia (1948) put the finishing touch to this, and the first regular election after the approval of the constitution (18 April 1948) was fought successfully by the coalition led by Prime Minister De Gasperi, on the choice for the West, Christian values, market economy, and multi-party democracy. The left, dominated by the Communist Party, fought on a platform stressing national pride and neutrality between the blocs, but could not dispel the image of subordination to the Soviet Union and its model. The legacy of this was a long-term exclusion of the largest opposition party from government, an exclusion which came fully to an end only in 1996, when the party had already some years previously changed its identity and become the party of the Democratic Left.

Stabilization and its weaknesses

The new democracy thus began to function in a somewhat paradoxical situation. On one hand it had a constitution approved with a very large consensus by the 'anti-fascist coalition'; on the other, this coalition had disappeared to give way to a new overarching division between pro-Western and pro-Eastern parties. The strong links between the largest opposition party and the Communist Party of the Soviet Union, with all this potentially implied in terms of international alliances, and political, economic, and social models, made the possibility of an alternation in government a risk too high to be accepted by the other parties and by a large majority of the voters. The consolidation of democracy was then conditioned to the exclusion from national power of the opposition. What would have happened had an electoral victory of the PCI occurred is obviously difficult to imagine (in terms both of actions and of reactions); for our purposes it is sufficient to know that on the basis of this fear a coalition with the PCI was excluded for a long period by parties of the centre-left, thus precluding any chance of this party gaining power. This type of consolidation meant also that one party, the DC, gained a permanent governing role, and in the end was voted for and held responsible, more for its ability to preserve democracy than for the quality of its policies.

A new crisis and reconsolidation?

The lessons of the early years proved strong and durable, and became part of the identities of the parties, shaping the deep orientations of the electorate and patterns of competition. This produced a paradoxical mix of stability and instability: the same parties were ensured a permanent or quasi-permanent governing role that could not be challenged by the opposition, but the likelihood of conflict between them, owing to their ideological differences and to this 'forced cohabitation', was always high. The specific coalition equilibrium within this group of parties was continuously under renegotiation, and this determined a high rate of government instability. In the end, however, after tensions, reciprocal accusations, and long cabinet crises, the same parties (and to a large extent the same ministers) returned together (Verzichelli and Cotta 2000).

After a long period of continuity, the political system underwent in the early 1990s a rapid and serious crisis, which at its peak induced some commentators even to have doubts about the survival of democracy. The crisis struck at the heart of the political architecture which had dominated the life of the previous decades. In a very short time there was a total collapse of the parties that had governed Italy for more than forty years, and a deep renewal of the political forces and of their relations took place.

A broad set of actors and dimensions of the political system were affected by the crisis. Political elites and their composition and recruitment patterns, the party system in terms of its elements and the relations between them, electoral rules and patterns of electoral behaviour, relations between institutions (in particular between the head of state and the government), the role of neutral powers (judiciary, central bank) in the political process, all underwent a significant transformation. At the heart of the thunderstorm, with all its dramatic emotions, was the *mani pulite* ('clean hands'), the judicial prosecution of a large section of the political class and of some important figures in the entrepreneurial world linked to them, and the media campaign that went along with it.

If it is not too difficult to gauge the short-term effects of the crisis—70 per cent of members of parliament lost their seats, an unprecedented number; major parties disappeared, others were deeply transformed and new ones were formed; competition patterns were changed from a multipolar to a bipolar mode; voters shifted their allegiances to new parties; the head of state gained a much more powerful role vis-à-vis the cabinet, etc.—the causes are more debatable. The corruption of the political elites and the widespread illegal financing of parties were obviously crucial factors. They are not enough, however, to explain such a deep crisis. There is neither strong proof nor good reason to believe that the level of corruption was in absolute terms significantly greater than in the past. It seems more reasonable to suggest that a combination of other factors turned something that in the past had been accepted and 'digested' into something which accelerated a crisis. Scandals had happened before, but they had remained isolated events involving few and generally second-ranking politicians. The fact that in 1992 a judicial case, not too dissimilar from those of the past, snowballed into a generalized attack on the heart of the political class had to do with the greater independence and political militancy acquired in recent years by the judiciary, with the media which played up the issue, and also with the deep disenchantment of the public and of the entrepreneurial class vis-à-vis the politicians, which pushed them to provide strong support for the judicial action. All these elements had, to an extent, their own internal explanations, but must also be linked, to a significant extent, to the weakening and the serious loss of prestige of the traditional governing elites. The point is that some of the crucial political resources on which these elites had counted in the past had been dramatically depleted—both the ideological and symbolic ones derived from their role in the defence of democracy and of the Western model against the threat of the communist left, and the material ones derived from their ability to distribute goods via clientelistic micro-policies and patronage (Cotta and Isernia 1996; Cotta and Verzichelli 1996). The international fall of communism and the transformation of its national branch had made the first justification almost useless and the second had been seriously curtailed, on the internal side, by the enormous growth of the public debt, which ate increasingly into the financial resources available in the budget for distributive purposes and, on the external side, by the constraints deriving from European integration which put more stringent limits to lax budgetary policies and state aids. If one adds that the governing elites had shown throughout the 1980s a limited ability to respond with innovative middle-range policies to some of Italy's most serious problems (from the reform of the pension system, to that of state administration, labour law, etc.), we have a situation that invited external actors to challenge those who governed the country.

In these years new challengers did in fact appear. The old establishment was challenged on one side by the League, the new party of the economically advanced north, on another side by the movement for the reform of the electoral system, and on a third side by the judiciary. In different ways the three challengers produced serious wounds in this enfeebled body. The League was able to erode the electoral support of the DC in the richest and most dynamic regions of Italy, which had been among its strongholds, thus transforming it into a party of the backward south only. The reform movement, with its proposal of a majoritarian electoral system, was able to demonstrate that public opinion, if given the chance, would not follow the suggestions of the politicians to leave to them alone the control of institutional reforms, but would vote massively to decide directly a reform that was to change the mechanism on which traditional parties had thrived. Finally, the decision of the judiciary not to stop at the lowest levels of the political ladder, but to prosecute also the leaders (as persons who could not ignore the illegal dealings of the money-men of the parties), destroyed what remained of the credibility of the political class.

Yet if the challengers were extremely successful in their destructive role, none of them was in the end able to reap the political fruits of the crisis. The suddenness of the collapse of the old parties opened a very wide empty political space and none of the challengers, because of its specific limits, could alone hope to take the place of the old parties, nor could they build, given the diversity of their appeal, a coalition of the innovators. The appearance of an entirely new actor—Silvio Berlusconi and his Forza Italia party, created just in time for the elections of 1994—and the renewal of the left and of the old right animated a strong left–right competition, which destroyed the hopes of the Lega to become the leading party of the north, the hopes of the leaders of the referendum movement to create a centre party of some weight, and the hopes of the leading figure of the judicial action, Di Pietro, to guide a movement for 'clean politics'.

With the elections run under the reformed electoral system, a new political order has begun to develop, within which the three original challengers have lost much of their initial strength. The institutional reform movement, its leader Segni, and the party that originated from it have disappeared from the scene; the judiciary has continued a long duel with Berlusconi but has had to submit itself to a reform it very much disliked. And the League has had to accept a junior role in coalitions.

The new political order has acquired, over recent years, some more stable features, while other aspects remain still more uncertain. Among the former the most important ones concern the new structure of the party system, characterized by the facts that all parties have now become fully accepted players of the government game, that competition centres around two broad left and right coalitions, that the leader of government is selected before elections by each coalition and thus commands a more eminent role in the cabinet, and that the government has gained a greater durability and more power in parliament. Among the less stable of features one can mention the electoral system, which was changed in 1993, then in 2005, and is again at the centre of debate, the federal structure of the state which has not yet reached a fully defined equilibrium, the form of bicameralism, and the institutional relationship between government and parliament for which reform proposals are repeatedly offered by both political sides. Also underway is a lively debate about reducing political fragmentation through the conglomeration of parties on the left and on the right. In this landscape a further significant question mark lies in the fact that a major party, Forza Italia, maintains a very personalistic character; it remains to be seen what would happen to it (and as a consequence to the centre-right camp) if it lost its leader.

Italy on the international scene

The least of the big European countries

When Italy as a unified country made its appearance on the international scene its political elites soon realized that the space was already crowded and that to gain a role among the big powers was difficult. To come to terms with this situation was not easy and took quite a long time. Obstacles to this were the nationalist and colonialist ambitions shared by significant components of the elite and of public opinion. The unification of Italy in 1861 was for a long time seen as incomplete by a large part of public opinion, as long as important regions totally or predominantly inhabited by Italians—the Veneto, Rome, Trentino, Friuli-Venezia Giulia, Trieste, and the Dalmatian coast—were under the rule of other countries. On the other side it was felt that Italy 'deserved', as most other European countries, a colonial empire. Colonies were seen at that time both as a 'status symbol' of international power and as a relief for internal problems of overpopulation. The two goals meant that, for a long period of time, Italian foreign policy leaned repeatedly against the status quo in and outside Europe (Chabod 1951) and induced, until the end of the Second World War, the less prudent side of Italian political elites to take sides with those in Europe who were willing to challenge the existing order and also to pursue recurrent attempts to conquer a colonial empire. The extreme and most disastrous case of this policy was the decision by Mussolini to join forces with Hitler in his attempt to transform the European order.

The complete disaster of the Second World War drastically reduced these ambitions or, to be more precise, persuaded the ruling elites that Italy's position in Europe and the world could be improved not by unilateral and conflictual attempts to turn the European order upside down, but rather by participating in multilateral and peaceful efforts to construct institutions of supranational governance.

In this new perspective the need to be considered part of the 'first league' has resurfaced from time to time, albeit in much less dangerous ways, as with the efforts to gain admittance to (or to avoid being excluded from) some of the 'elite clubs' of the international arena—the G5 (now G8), the Security Council of the United Nations, etc. More recently the willingness of Italy to take an active part in international peacekeeping operations probably has something to do with this need to demonstrate its status.

Atlantic integration and European destiny

The defeat in the Second World War left Italy to face the international system in the most unfavourable position ever. The difficult condition of being a loser (in spite of the late change of allegiance), the perspective of significant territorial losses (concerning not just the colonial empire but also parts of the Italian territory), the geo-political position of the country on the border between East and West, the internal divide between democratic parties and communists, and the fears for the stability of democracy determined rather quickly a clear orientation of the Christian Democratic elite and of its minor allies towards a more stable preference for international integration.

The first and decisive choice in this direction was to enter into the North Atlantic Treaty Organization (NATO). This choice had a double meaning for Italy. It was a way to ensure the external security of the country (and to reduce defence expenditures), and also to coalesce around the leadership of the DC and to strengthen the internal front of the political forces opposed to communism. This choice and the developments which followed assured a clear position for Italy within a solid system of collective security and contributed towards establishing a strong relationship with the leading country of the Western world. This relationship, which also had significant economic advantages, proved particularly important for the governing elites. The recurrent renewal by top government leaders of their allegiance for the Atlantic alliance with trips to Washington was a way to show those at home that they had the support of the Western superpower. At the same time it did not preclude some room for manoeuvre in the economic foreign policy of Italy where significant trade interests were at stake for the country, for example in the Middle East, particularly concerning oil (and the state oil company ENI), and even in the Soviet Union (for the car manufacturer Fiat). Domestically, with the world (and Europe in particular) divided into two opposing blocs and Italy being a member of the Western alliance, it became unthinkable to conceive of entry into government of the Communist Party as long as it remained closely linked to the Soviet Union. The government/opposition divide was thus stably crystallized. It would take the end of the Soviet Union and the consequent regeneration of the Italian Communists into the less conspicuous Left Democrats to erase that division fully.

For some time, membership of NATO was the crucial element shaping Italy's international position, but it was soon complemented by another form of international commitment in the European Economic Community (EEC). When proposals for supranational integration began to develop in Europe, especially under the impulse of France, with the aim of solving some of the problems left open by the Second World War (and in particular the problem of German rearmament), the Italian government quickly saw the need to join in these efforts in order to avoid the risks of isolation, and was generally inclined to push for stronger delegation of power to integrated authorities in order to prevent the interests of other countries predominating. The pro-European position adopted by the governing elites had originally to face the strong rejection of the opposition parties and lukewarm support from public opinion; but the economic success of the common market progressively encouraged a change of attitude among the public, which by the 1970s was expressing an overwhelming support for an integrated Europe (Ammendola and Isernia 2005).

The Atlantic alliance and European integration became thus the two main instruments through which Italy took part in the international system and successfully pursued the two primary goals of security and economic progress. They also became crucial elements in the internal legitimation of the governing elites. The opposition, which had been hostile to both, had in the end to come to terms with them. The European side was easier to accept. When, after the Czechoslovak repression of 1968, the links with the Soviet Union became an increasingly negative asset, the PCI discovered the importance of pursuing Europeanization by joining the international (but predominantly European) federation of socialist parties after having failed to develop a Euro-communist family. The integration of Europe also became increasingly accepted by the opposition as a counterweight to NATO, and finally even NATO came to be recognized, although less enthusiastically, as an unavoidable component of Italian international commitments.

By the 1980s the consensus on Europe was predominant both at the mass and at the elite level. Europe has become a positive symbol for almost all the components of the political system (Cotta *et al.* 2005). It has provided stable international anchoring and a source of legitimacy. For public opinion at large the possibility of compensating the fragility and ineffectiveness of the domestic institutions with something that did not have the same defects was probably a crucial factor. It was clear also that for the Italian economy integration in a wider European market had been a major opportunity for growth.

That European integration could have costs as well as advantages did not come to the surface of public debate for a long time. As some have suggested, this problem, which obviously existed, was dealt with when it manifested itself via a less visible strategy of delay in the implementation of European rules (Giuliani 1996). Unanimous public favour for Europe remained intact.

The important steps of the late 1980s and 1990s towards the full integration of the European market and a common currency had necessarily even stronger effects upon the Italian system. The combined effects of the rules introduced to complete the European market and to prevent obstacles to the free circulation of goods, of the transfer to the supranational level of the monetary policy, and of the budgetary constraints (particularly severe for a seriously indebted country such as Italy) implied by this decision, have produced important consequences for Italy. On the institutional level they have promoted an increased role within the cabinet for the Treasury vis-à-vis the other ministers because of the need to keep a stronger control upon expenditures. At the policy level they have contributed in a decisive way to initiate and sustain extensive programmes of privatization and for the dismantling of a large part of the entrepreneurial state, and later on to promote a reappraisal of some crucial aspects of the welfare state—in particular pension policies. Among the consequences of all this we must also reckon the decreased ability of parties to use patronage as an instrument of political influence. Because of this new situation parties have had to face more difficult choices than in the past. On one hand, the traditional position, taken by Italy and sustained in recent years by a broad consensus, requires continuation along the lines of a strong Europeanism; on the other hand, however, the costs of some European decisions and their impact upon the political exchange between politicians and voters are becoming more visible. It is probably as a result of this that some unprecedented positions of Euro-scepticism and even Euro-phobia have begun to be voiced (Conti 2006). So far, however, this has led more to rhetorical expressions than to more substantial decisions.

Conclusion

The past two decades have seen important changes in the three dimensions of the Italian polity discussed in this chapter. A combination of internal and external factors—among which the end of the cold war and the acceleration of the European integration process have played a particularly important role—have produced:

1. a significant transformation in the relations between centre and periphery with a strong redistribution of competencies from the central state to the regions;
2. a serious crisis of democracy followed by its reconsolidation and a deep restructuring of the party system and of some central democratic processes; and

3. a more profound Europeanization of the Italian political system and of its policies, but also a more open debate on the benefits and costs of European integration and a more active position on the international scene.

If in many aspects the pace of change has been faster than in the past, this does not mean that the weight of the past has vanished. Indeed many of the current problems—from the dissatisfaction with the working of democratic institutions to the financial and fiscal crisis, from the often tense relations between government and opposition to the deficient bureaucratic performances, from the inability to solve some crucial policy problems to the failure in curbing corruption or the excesses of political patronage—are rooted in the historical legacies of the Italian polity. Moreover some of the recent changes are still incomplete and in some cases their full implications remain difficult to fathom and their future durability is uncertain.

At the same time new important challenges have emerged in this period. Many of them cannot be classified as country specific. They are rather the fruits of supranational and global processes of change, and they entail complex processes and solutions, involving formal and informal institutions, actors from the local and the supranational arenas, and a sometimes attentive but increasingly segmented and volatile public opinion. Three seem particularly important for the future of the Italian polity: the ageing of the population, the dramatic increase in (legal and illegal) immigration, and international economic competition.

The ageing of the population, connected with a demographic transformation which has turned a traditional Catholic country into the least prolific in Europe, has obvious and extremely serious implications for the costs of the welfare state and consequently for the social pact between classes and generations crafted in the course of recent decades. The solution to this problem, common to all European countries, is made even more complicated in Italy because of the legacy of an impressive public debt, which eats into the resources available, together with the external constraints of the European Stability and Growth Pact.

The large flow of immigrants, to a great extent illegal and from different continents, raises serious and unprecedented problems for the political community and its institutions. This phenomenon, which is for Italy relatively new (and is in part linked to the previous one), adds to the political agenda the issue of the integration of the newcomers within a political community which had achieved, with some difficulties, a satisfactory degree of linguistic, cultural, and socio-economic homogeneity. To make things more difficult this is happening at a time when, given the new phenomena of religious fundamentalism and political radicalism of some of these immigrants, old recipes for integration seem often not to work.

Finally the increasing globalization of the markets challenges the ability of the traditional Italian economic structure to keep pace with international economic competition. This challenge concerns not only private economic actors and their readiness to increase their degree of innovation and competitiveness, but also the Italian state, its government, bureaucratic apparatus, local administrations, and their ability to provide the regulatory and fiscal environment, as well as the old and new infrastructures that are more favourable for sustaining the modernization of the economy.

The ability of Italian political institutions to face these three challenges will be a crucial test in the coming years.

KEY TERMS

- Atlantic alliance
- authoritarianism
- centralization
- democratization
- Europeanization
- fascism
- federalism
- nationalism
- nation state
- regionalization
- transition
- unitary state

GUIDE TO FURTHER READING

Acquarone, A. (1965) *L'organizzazione dello stato totalitario* (Turin, Einaudi).

A comprehensive historical analysis of the building of fascism.

Clark, M. (1996) *Modern Italy 1871–1995* (London, Longman).

Classic, straightforward account of Italian political and social history from unification to the crisis of the mid-1990s.

Cotta, M., Isernia, P., and Verzichelli, L. (eds.) (2005) *L'Europa in Italia. Elites, opinione pubblica e decisioni* (Bologna, Il Mulino).

A study of the impact of European integration on elite discourse and public opinion in Italy.

Foot, J. (2003) *Modern Italy* (London, Palgrave).

A description of the Italian political landscape in historical perspective.

Ginsborg, P. (2003) *Italy and its Discontents: Family, Civil Society and State, 1980–2001* (London, Penguin).

Another historical account, focusing on recent developments in Italian politics and society.

Ziblatt, D. (2006) *Structuring the State: The Formation of Italy and Germany and the Puzzle of Federalism* (Princeton, Princeton University Press).

Provides an insightful analysis of the process of unification and of its role in determining the centralistic structure of the Italian state.

NOTES

1 In the Middle Ages the Holy Roman Emperors received also the title of King of Italy, but effectively controlled only a limited part of its territory.

2 . . . *Ahi serva Italia*! ('. . . oh, enslaved Italy!'), wrote Dante and Machiavelli.

3 The official name of Kingdom of Sardinia should not hide the fact that this state had as its centre the region of Piedmont and, until 1861, Savoy. The island of Sardinia was acquired in 1720 and thanks to it the Duke of Savoy (this was the ruling dynasty of Piedmont) gained the much coveted title of king. Hence the somewhat misleading name of this state.

2

The Republic of Parties: From Deadlock to Bipolar Alternation

Overview

The features of individual parties and of the party system as a whole have traditionally received a great deal of attention from observers of Italian politics. They have been judged to offer an especially crucial lens for understanding some of the peculiarities of the political life of the country. The presence for a very long time of the strongest communist party of Western Europe in a permanent opposition role, a large but highly factionalized Christian Democratic party holding the keys of government for more than forty-five years, the weakness of the Socialist party(-ies), the fragmentation of the party system and the high level of ideological distance between its extreme forces, and the large penetration of parties in society and the economy: these and other aspects have made the study of parties particularly intriguing for observers of Italy.

This chapter, after a brief presentation of the historical background, will analyze in more detail the post-Fascist period, discussing the ideological and policy profiles and the organizational features of the main parties, and how their relations have concurred to shape the party system and its structure. After covering the party system born after the Second World War and lasting until 1992 and comparing the polarized multipartism model proposed by Sartori (1976) with other interpretations, the chapter will analyze in more detail the 1992–94 crisis, the foundation of new parties, the reshaping of old ones, and the birth and consolidation of a significantly different party system. Special attention will be given to the strikingly new features (by Italian standards) of one of the main new parties (Forza

Italia) and to the structure and functioning of the *Poli*, the two new electoral and parliamentary coalitions: on the centre-left, the Ulivo (Olive Tree), which became in 2006 the Unione, integrating this time also the extreme left, and on the centre-right, the Casa delle Libertà (House of Freedoms).

From a delayed start to a strong *partitocrazia*

During the first democratic attempt, which came to a dramatic end with the consolidation of the Fascist regime, the development of organized parties in Italy had been incomplete. The first party system, that of the period of restricted suffrage (1861–1913), had been dominated by parliamentary parties, which were little more than loosely connected cliques of notables and had almost no organized roots in the country. Only the Socialist Party could in fact be considered, some years after its foundation in 1892, a sufficiently established mass party, but it was kept for a long period on the margins of the political system and never managed during that period to be admitted into the government. Its influence was also significantly weakened by a tendency to internal divisions, with its reformist and maximalist wings fighting internecine wars.

The extension of suffrage in 1912, the First World War, and the change in 1919 to a proportional representation (PR) electoral system opened the way to the second party system, which, however, did not even have the time to consolidate itself because of the rapid breakdown of the democratic experiment and the transition to fascism (1922–5). This new party system (see Tables 2.1 and 2.2) saw the ascendance of another mass party, the Christian Democratic Partito Popolare, which, having been founded in 1919, could take part in only two truly competitive elections, those of 1919 and 1921. Apart from the Socialists and the Popolari, the remaining part of the political landscape was still occupied, until the rise of fascism, by weakly organized notable parties and independent personalities. This party system was thus characterized by a deep divide between old and new parties, between parties of notables and organized parties; this was also to a significant extent a divide between parties with an electoral following in southern Italy and those which had gained a foothold in the more developed north of the country.

TABLE 2.1 The four Italian party systems

	Period	Main parties	Type of parties	Type of party system
I	1861–1913	*Destra storica* (Conservatives) *Sinistra storica* (Liberals) *Radicali* (Left Liberals)	Notable parties	Unipolar
II	1919–24	Liberals Socialist Party (PSI) Popular Party (PPI) Fascist Party (PNF) Nationalists	Elite parties and mass parties	Atomized
III	1948–94	Christian Democracy (DC) Communist Party (PCI) Socialist Party (PSI) Italian Social Movement (MSI)	Mass-integration parties and catch-all parties	Polarized multipartism; tripolar competition
IV	1994–	Forza Italia (FI) Democratic Left (PDS-DS) National Alliance (AN) Popular Party/Margherita (PPI, DL) Communist Refoundation (RC) Northern League (LN)	Cartel parties, Leader's party (FI) Personalization of leadership	Moderate but fragmented multipartism; bipolar competition

Note: For a full description of party names and acronyms, see Table 2.2.

TABLE 2.2 Party acronyms and names

Acronym	Italian name	English name	Timing	Party orientation
		Historical parties		
DC	Democrazia Cristiana	Christian Democracy	1943–93	Christian Democratic party
MSI	Movimento Sociale Italiano	Italian Social Movement	1948–94	Neo-fascist party during the first republic
PCI	Partito Comunista Italiano	Italian Communist Party	1921–91	Communists
PLI	Partito Liberale Italiano	Italian Liberal Party	1946–94	Right liberals
PNF	Partito Nazionale Fascista	National Fascist Party	1919–43	Fascist (Mussolini's party)
PPI	Partito Popolare Italiano	Popular Party	1919–25	Christian Democratic party
PR	Partito Radicale	Radical Party	1963–	Radicals and libertarians
PRI	Partito Repubblicano Italiano	Italian Republican Party	1897–94	Republicans (left liberals)
PSDI	Partito Socialista Democratico Italiano	Italian Social Democratic Party	1948–94	Reformist, moderate socialists
PSI	Partito Socialista Italiano	Italian Socialist Party	1892–94	Socialists
		Parties born during the 1990s and then dissolved		
AD	Alleanza Democratica	Democratic Alliance	1994–95	Party of institutional reforms
CCD	Centro Cristiano Democratico	Christian Democratic Centre	1993–2001	Post DC party joining the centre-right
CDU	Unione Cristiano Democratica	Christian Democratic Union	1995–2001	Split from PPI when the latter joined the centre-left in 1995
DE	Democrazia Europea	European Democracy	2000–1	Christian Democratic list running alone in 2001

Table 2.2 continued

Acronym	Italian name	English name	Timing	Party orientation
PPI	Partito Popolare Italiano	Popular Party	1994–2000	Post-DC party
Rete	La Rete	The Network	1992–94	New-left party originating from a split of the DC and joining the centre-left alliance in 1994
RI	Rinnovamento Italiano	Italian Renewal	1996–2000	Centre-left liberal movement then joining DL
		Parties of the current party system		
AN	Alleanza Nazionale	National Alliance	1994–	Rightist party born from MSI
AS	Alternativa Sociale	Social Alternative	2004–	Extreme right party founded in 2004
DC	Nuova Democrazia Cristiana	New Christian Democracy	2006–	New small Christian Democracy party joining the centre-right camp in 2006
DL	Democrazia Liberale/Margherita	Liberal Democracy (Daisy)	2001–	Moderate centre-left Christian Democrats and left liberals
DS (formerly PDS)	Democratici di Sinistra	Democratic Left	1991–	Post-communist/socialist party
FI	Forza Italia	—	1994–	Centre-right Christian Democrats and liberals
IdV	Italia dei Valori	Italy of Values	1998–	Pro-justice party founded by the former clean-hands prosecutor Antonio Di Pietro
LN	Lega Nord	Northern League	1992–	Regionalist movement

continues

Table 2.2 continued

Acronym	Italian name	English name	Timing	Party orientation
MPA	Movimento per le Autonomie	Movement for Autonomy	2004–	A southern autonomistic movement founded in 2004 and joining the centre-right camp in 2006
MSI-FT	Movimento Sociale Fiamma Tricolore	Social Movement Tricolour Flame	1994–	Nostalgic neo-fascist split from the MSI refusing to join AN
NPSI	Nuovo Partito Socialista Italiano	New Italian Socialist Party	1996–	Party of former PSI supporters joining the centre-right camp
PdCI	Partito dei Comunisti Italiani	Party of the Italian Communists	1998–	Split from RC in 1998
RC	Rifondazione Comunista	Communist Refoundation	1991–	Post-communist
RnP	Rosa nel Pugno	Rose in the Fist	2006–	List including SDI and PR in 2006
SDI (formerly SI)	Socialisti Democratici Italiani	Italian Social-Democrats	1994–	Largest part of the old PSI, joining the centre-left camp
SVP	Südtiroler Volkspartei	People's Party of South Tyrol	1945–	Christian Democratic party of South Tyrol, today in the centre-left coalition
UDC	Unione Democratici Cristiani di Centro	Union of Centrist Christian Democrats	2001–	Christian Democratic party joining the centre-right, formed by CCD (1993) and CDU (1995)
UDEUR	Unione Democratici per l'Europa	Union of Democrats for Europe	1999–	Post-DC party included in the centre-left
Verdi	Federazione dei Verdi	Federation of Greens	1987	Ecologist party

This party system quickly proved unable to face the challenges of the troubled times following the First World War and the Soviet revolution and to provide a stable support for cabinets capable of excluding the anti-system forces. However, in spite of only embryonic development, some of its features would persist and consolidate in the post-Fascist period. The decline of the secular right and of the centre parties (Liberals, Republicans, Radicals), the growing importance of a Christian Democratic party able to challenge the former parties in the competition for the support of the middle classes, but also to make serious inroads among the working classes and the peasants, the difficulty of the Socialist Party to keep its reformist and revolutionary wings under the same roof, the significant territorial differences in the strength of parties: all these aspects would return to the surface after the fall of fascism and contribute to shaping the new party system.

The democratic interruption contributed to some important innovations. In particular, it should be mentioned that the special conditions of the transition from authoritarianism to democracy affected significantly both the role of parties in political life and the shaping of the new party system. The breakdown of the Fascist regime, as a result essentially of its military defeat and occupation by Allied forces in the south of the country, and the subsequent collapse of the state (and in particular of its central administration and the army) when the delicate change of alliance from Germany to the United Nations led in 1943 to the division of Italy and its complete occupation by foreign troops, prevented the success of the monarchy's attempt to steer the transition from fascism into the new order. Between 1943 and 1945 the reborn parties progressively gained control of the process that would lead in 1946 to the first competitive elections for a Constituent Assembly and the writing of a constitution between 1946 and 1948 (Pasquino 1986). A stronger role for the parties in the new state was thus established; at a time when the state was bankrupt they had taken the lead in the rebuilding process.

The parties which appeared after the fall of fascism seemed at first bound to reproduce the pre-Fascist landscape. Except for a few minor new entries (the left liberals of the Action Party, the rightist Uomo Qualunque, the Monarchist Party), there were again Communists, Socialists, Christian Democrats, and Liberals. The cabinets between 1944 and 1946, based on the common agreement of all the anti-fascist groups, reflected an equal representation of parties. It took the first free election of 1946 to define the political weight of the parties in a more realistic way and to give the first shape to the party system. Some crucial features of the party system, which would structure Italian politics for the next forty years, began at that point to become evident. The division of the left, with the Communist Party challenging the old Socialist Party for leadership in this area, and the growth of the Christian Democrat party Democrazia Cristiana, becoming from its position at the centre of the political spectrum the largest party, and confining the old Liberal party to a minority position, deserve, in particular, to be mentioned. But it was the general election of 1948 that crystallized the new party system. Under the impact of internal and international factors the anti-fascist cooperation between the most important parties, which had dominated the transition years, increasingly gave way to a robust competition between them. The electoral campaign of 1948, fought just after the Communist coups in Hungary and Czechoslovakia, at a time when international tensions in Europe were mounting and the division of Europe into two hostile blocs was becoming clear, produced a bipolar shaping of the party system along the communism/anti-communism divide. With the Socialist Party divided by this cleavage—the smaller wing, the Social Democrats, siding with the Western camp and the larger one running on the same ticket with the PCI (the Popular Front)—the left fell under the hegemony of the Communists. On the other side was the DC, which, counting upon the support of the strong Catholic Church and its widespread network of lay organizations, and because of its religious appeal, managed to have the support of voters from all social classes. Among all parties, it was the one in the best position to be a bulwark against the 'danger of communism'. As a consequence, the DC almost monopolized the other side of the political cleavage. There were other small moderate parties of centre-left (Republicans and Social Democrats) and centre-right (Liberals) and small parties of the extreme right (the neo-fascist Movimento Sociale and the Monarchist Party), but none could be considered a serious challenge to the DC.

The election of 1948 set the seal on the end of the anti-fascist coalition. The clear victory of the DC and its allies and the defeat of the leftist Popular Front created the conditions for the long-term hegemony of the Christian Democrats and for the stabilization of a difficult democracy.

The fact that the communism/anti-communism cleavage, with all its international implications, had become the dominant cleavage of Italian politics (rather than the left-right one), had important consequences for the party system and in general for the working of the Italian political system. It meant first of all that the left itself would be divided by this cleavage for the next forty-five years, with the Social Democrats and later also the Socialists preferring on the national arena an alliance with the DC rather than with the PCI.[1] It meant also that, for a long time, the PCI, because of its strong links with the Soviet Union, would be seen by a majority of the voters and by most of the other parties as an anti-system party (Sartori 1976), and therefore not suitable to be considered as a governing partner. As a consequence alternation in government was impossible. The DC was thus permanently in power and, as after 1948 it never attained a majority in parliament, it always needed to build a coalition with some of the small parties of the centre-right and centre-left and later also with the Socialist Party, once this party decided to detach itself from the alliance with the Communists. With the extreme right party also excluded from government, because of its openly declared nostalgia for the past regime, this situation enabled only a 'peripheral alternation' (Sartori 1976) of the small centrist parties in government.

This party system has been defined as a case of an 'imperfect two-party system' (Galli 1966), a definition which stressed, in particular, the dominant role of the two main parties and the impossibility of an alternation in government. With greater analytical precision Sartori (1976) characterized it as a 'polarized multipartism'. According to this model, with the existence of two anti-system parties (PCI and MSI), a wide stretched ideological space, and the presence of three poles (left, centre, and right), the Italian party system was characterized by the fact that governing coalitions were always formed around the centre pole and opposition was bilateral (from the left and from the right). Moreover competition was centrifugal rather than centripetal, thus putting the democratic centre under pressure, and making the opposition, with no chance of access to government, irresponsible. The latter feature applied in the end also to the government: as it could not be displaced without putting democracy at risk, it was difficult to keep it accountable. Sartori suggested also that the centre would be progressively eroded by the extreme parties, a trend which would create serious problems for the governability and stability of the system.

This pessimistic view was for some time confirmed by the growth of the Communist Party, which reached its peak in 1976, making it impossible for the old majorities to sustain a cabinet. At the same time, as others have noticed (Farneti 1985), the PCI, in order to overcome the exclusionary attitudes of the political system, was progressively moderating its position and loosening its links with the Soviet Union. The width of the political space was thus being reduced and in fact it was even possible, albeit for a short period (1976–79), to reach an agreement between governing parties and the PCI to provide a common parliamentary support for a DC cabinet. After this episode the parliamentary cooperation between governing parties and Communist opposition undoubtedly increased. As La Palombara noticed (1987), this produced a somewhat paradoxical difference between a still persistent anti-communist prejudice (and rhetoric) at the electoral level and the extensive bargaining going on within the parliamentary institutions. It is true, however, that the growing moderation of the political competition was not enough to reshape the party system in a more fundamental way: in particular, the 'permanent opposition parties', the PCI on the left and the MSI on the right, remained excluded from the governmental game and an alternation did not materialize.

Given these features of the party system the competition between the two main parties was a sort of 'position war' with each of the parties digging deeper trenches in society. The Communist Party, which had always had the most developed membership organization with a strong network of party sections and cells, developed also a wide range of associations in the fields of culture, sport, and leisure activities with the purpose of creating a sort of self-sufficient social environment for its supporters and sympathizers. The DC was, at first, much weaker from the organizational point of view, but compensated for this disadvantage with the support of religious organizations on one hand and with the control of the state and its bureaucracies on the other. After the 1950s its leadership made a deliberate effort to develop a stronger and more independent membership organization (see Figure 2.1). This organizational development, coupled with the failure to establish a strong central leadership, opened the way, with the passing of time, to an increasing fragmentation of the party: strongly organized factions came to dominate its internal life. In a way, while the competition for power between government and opposition parties had been frozen, that within the main party in power acquired a greater role. The electoral system allowing preferential voting (see Chapter 3) gave an electoral dimension also to the competition between party factions. With

FIGURE 2.1 **Selected trends in party membership in Italy, 1945–2005**

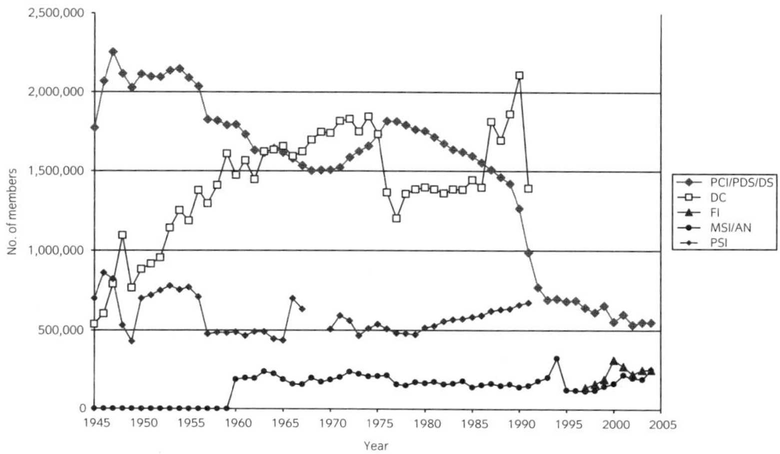

Source: Istituto Cattaneo.

the leaders of the factions having gained a prominent political role the chairman of the party was more a *primus inter pares* than the true leader.

This party system based on seven main parties—two big ones (DC and PCI), one medium-sized (PSI), and four small ones (PSDI, PRI, PLI, and MSI)—plus a few other less relevant ones remained fundamentally stable for almost forty-five years.

There were of course changes over time, but in the end it proved very difficult to change the fundamental features of the system (see Figure 2.2). Probably the greatest challenge to the existing equilibrium came in 1976 when the PCI, thanks to an exceptional electoral growth, seemed close to overtaking the DC as the leading party. The defensive reaction of the Christian Democrats, to include the Communist Party in the parliamentary majority sustaining the government and thus involving it in responsibility for the difficult decisions stemming from the economic crisis and the terrorist threat, together with other factors, contributed in fact to stopping the growth of the strongest opposition party. During the 1980s the PCI would be back in opposition, its electoral support would start declining,

FIGURE 2.2 **Electoral trends in the first republic: shares of votes at lower chamber elections, selected parties, 1948–87**

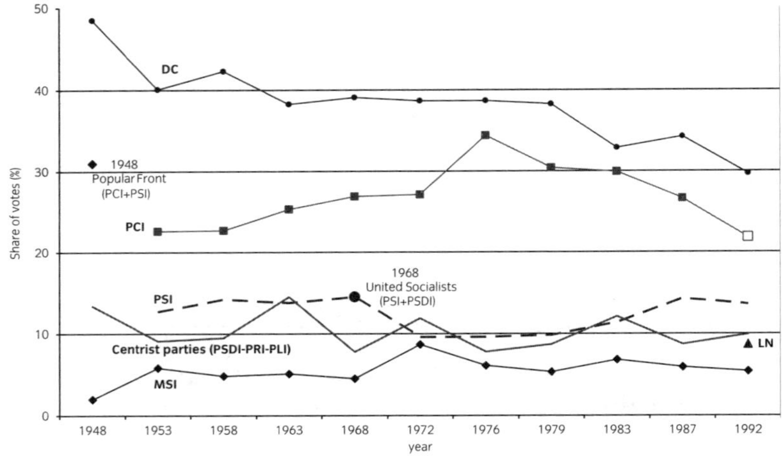

Note: The centrist parties include the PRI, PLI, and PSDI. However, since the PSDI joined the PSI in 1968, for that year the figure includes only the PRI and PLI. The figure for the PCI in 1992 includes both the electoral result of the PDS (16.1%) and that of the RC (5.6%). See Table 2.2 for the meaning of party acronyms.

and the most dynamic factor would become the Socialist Party under the new leadership of Bettino Craxi.

If the communism/anti-communism divide (with its strong international overtones) has dominated electoral alignments and the cabinet-building processes, other cleavage lines, to some extent cross-cutting the first one, have also contributed to characterizing the Italian party system. The left/right cleavage has obviously had an important role in the definition of party identities and in the policy-making processes. That this cleavage line has been significantly overshadowed by the first is shown by the above-mentioned fact that a part of the left (at first the PSDI and PRI, then also the PSI) has systematically preferred to support the Christian Democratic cabinets rather than enter into an alliance with the Communists. To this we could add the fact that the largest party—the DC—has never defined itself as a party of the right or as a bourgeois party, but rather as an 'interclass' party of the centre, and that among its internal factions one or two have had a left identity and strong links with an important sector of the trade unions. The other important cleavage was the clerical/anti-clerical one. The importance of the state–church conflict in the history of Italy is well known: as a result of the traditional strength of the Catholic Church in Italian society and its original opposition to liberalism, and of the fact that national unification took place against the opposition of the papal state (see Chapter 1) and entailed its conquest, together with systematic expropriations of church properties, the conflicts both on issues of principle and on practical matters have been significant. This and the weight of a confessional party have contributed to characterizing many parties (particularly of the left, but also of the right, such as the Liberals) with anti-clerical traits. This divide has come to the fore whenever the discussion has involved school matters or themes such as marriage regulations or abortion, producing alliances which have cut across the traditional governing ones. However, neither of the two cleavages was ever able to produce a stable governmental majority as long as the Christian Democratic party survived.

The party system has been characterized also by significant territorial variations in the strength of parties (see Chapter 3). This is particularly evident for the largest parties. The Christian Democrats have been particularly strong in Lombardy, Veneto, Trentino, Friuli, and part of Piedmont, regions which were traditionally defined as 'white', and in the south (especially Abruzzo, Sicily, Puglia, and Basilicata). The PCI has had its strongholds in the 'red' regions of Emilia, Tuscany (with the exception of the white province of Lucca), and Umbria. Other regions have had a more balanced distribution of forces. This territorial distribution confirms that party alignments have been dictated predominantly not by the class factor, since in some of the regions with the largest industrial working class the left has been weaker rather than stronger, but by a more complex mix of cultural and institutional traditions. The peculiar territorial distribution of the DC must be noted: its large following both in the most advanced and in the less advanced regions of Italy, making it the only fully national party, was undoubtedly a key element of its political success. A possible explanation for this lies in the fact that the DC was able to bring together in the 1940s both the traditions of the organized Catholic movement and also, thanks to its anti-communism and then its governing role, those of a great part of the conservative right (with its strongholds in the south). With the deep differences between north and south this meant also that within the largest Italian party significant organizational and cultural differences existed. The main opposition party, the PCI, had on the contrary far greater difficulties (except perhaps at the height of its success in the 1970s) in extending its following outside its core regions.

The party system we have briefly sketched and its basic characteristics has demonstrated a significant ability to persist over time in spite of the enormous socio-economic and cultural changes the country underwent in the forty years after the end of the Second World War (see Chapter 1). This has meant that certain critical features of the political system—above all the way in which governments have been made and broken (see Chapter 4)—have also remained basically unaltered. This, however, should not lead us to underestimate the amount of change that has taken place within this framework. Aside from fluctuations, which at each election have produced some variations in the micro-equilibria of the system, it must be stressed that some more additive transformations have also taken place. The first to be mentioned is the gradual electoral shrinking during the 1980s of the two largest parties—the DC and the PCI—from the peak joint percentage of 73.1 per cent in 1976 to 60.9 per cent in 1987 and the rise of the other parties. The other is the significant decline of the organizational force of all the traditional parties (Katz and Mair 1995). Although this was not accompanied by a loosening of their grip on the power centres of the state and also of important sectors of the economy—notably the public radio and television company RAI, the large industrial holdings such as ENI, IRI, ENEL, etc. (see Chapter 7), and approximately three-quarters of the banking system—it has meant an increasing distance of the parties from the common people and has possibly provided the basis for growing dissatisfaction (Morlino and Tarchi 1996).

Within the stable mould of the party system a significant weakening of the main parties and of their capacity to represent society effectively has thus taken place.

The crisis of the first republic and the first steps of a new party system

Between the end of the 1980s and the beginning of the 1990s a combination of factors produced what can be defined as an unexpected implosion of the traditional party system and the beginning of a new phase for Italian politics. The factors which caused this political earthquake were more than one and probably only their combination could produce it. The first shock was the fall of the Berlin Wall, which opened a difficult phase of transformation for the Communist Party, leading eventually to a change in the party name and also to a split of its left wing. This event affected not only the main opposition party but also its antagonist: the role of the DC as the bulwark against the danger of a victory of the Communist Party seemed after that event to have become less justified. The problem of the identity of the 'permanent' governing party was thus also put on the agenda. It is perhaps no accident that during this period the DC started being challenged in its electoral strongholds of northern Italy by new parties of territorial identity. In a very short time span the Venetian and Lombard Leagues (then fused into the Northern League), from being a minor phenomenon of political folklore, became a significant threat to the traditional electoral alignments in the richest and fastest developing part of Italy, achieving a significant number of local seats in the administrative elections of 1990, and then conquering 8.6 per cent of the vote and about eighty parliamentary seats in the 1992 general election.

The Northern League introduced into the Italian political system both new themes (territorial identity, secession, federalism, and anti-fiscal protest) and a radically different language, substituting the sophisticated and subtle jargon typical of the skirmishes of a static party system with a rather rude 'popular' language with vernacular and often vulgar expressions.

This period also saw an increasingly open challenge to the incumbent political elites by a significant part of the entrepreneurial establishment and by the media which, more outspokenly than in the past, denounced political corruption and criticized the indecisiveness of the political class before the problems of the country. At the same time, during this period, the idea that the political system required also an institutional reshaping gained a wider acceptance, together with the disillusionment regarding the ability of the governing class to produce the changes needed. It must be remembered that the growing consensus on the need to reform the main rules of the political game marked a significant change from the mood prevailing in the 1970s, when the constitution of 1948 had been exalted as the basis for a rapprochement between the DC and PCI (since both parties had cooperated in its making) after the political tensions of the previous years and was thus perceived as untouchable. As for the electoral system, after the failed 1953 attempt by the DC to add to it a more majoritarian element, it had also become a political taboo. But, after the failure of the Communist–Christian Democratic entente of the late 1970s, the theme of institutional reform (concerning both the constitution and the electoral system) had been put on the agenda in the 1980s by some leading politicians themselves (in particular by the Socialist leader Craxi and by the Christian Democrat De Mita). In the end, however, their efforts had met with failure owing to the opposing preferences of the main parties. This left a space for a popular initiative to change at least the electoral law. Public opinion had become more open to criticisms of the existing electoral law. With its proportional mechanism it was judged incapable of offering to the voter the possibility of making a clear choice for the government since it left ample room for manoeuvre to the parties in the building of coalitions after the results were known. The second aspect under attack was the preferential vote seen as a factor of fragmentation within parties and as a source of corruption (with the candidates of the same party actively competing for campaign resources from organized groups and special interests). The proposals for a referendum on the electoral system, promoted by a composite alliance of 'marginal leaders' (from the Christian Democrat Mario Segni to Radicals, left intellectuals, and religious associations) and supported by a large part of the press, mobilized a popular support sufficiently large to be admitted. A first referendum to reduce the number of preference votes was held in 1991 and, in spite of the opposition of the leaders of the governing coalition (who had encouraged the voters to 'go to the beach' in order to prevent attainment of the 50 per cent quorum, constitutionally required for an abrogative referendum to be valid), it obtained a resounding success.[2] This result would soon open the way to a second referendum on the central mechanisms of the electoral law. The collection of the 500,000 signatures required was immediately successful and the new referendum was tabled for 1993 after the general elections of 1992.

After the 1991 referendum a second important institutional step in the process of change was the electoral results of 1992. The two main elements to be underlined are the decline of the DC, which lost about 4 per cent in comparison with 1987 and for the first time fell below the 30 per cent threshold, and the rise of the Lega Nord, which obtained 8.7 per cent of the national votes, becoming the fourth party. The Socialist Party was still on the rise, while the PDS, the main successor of the Communist Party, had a very poor score. If we take a closer look, we find even more significant signs of change: in the regions of northern Italy, where it has its strongholds, the Lega became the second party, seriously challenging the leading position of the DC. As for the DC, while in the south its following remained constant, in the northern regions the losses were extremely serious. Given the economic and social importance of the northern regions (which had been traditionally a crucial electoral base for the DC), these results meant that the party was losing touch with the most dynamic part of the country and becoming increasingly a 'southern' party. The territorial cleavage (which in the past had been bridged by the DC) was again coming to play a critical political role, as in the 1920s when the then hegemonic political force—the Liberals—had lost the north and maintained its following only in the south (Cotta 1994).

After the election of 1992 the whole crisis began to unravel with growing speed. The other factor which at this point started to play a crucial role was the judicial campaign against corruption. While instances of judicial prosecution for cases of corruption involving politicians had not been rare in the past, they had never had more than an individual impact on the persons concerned. But at the beginning of the 1990s the mood of public opinion and of the media had become much more militant on this question. The action of the judiciary rapidly generated a strong movement of support which enabled its transformation into a sweeping indictment of a large part of the leading strata of the governing parties. No sanctuaries were left unaffected this time: one after another the parties were beheaded in front of large and enthusiastic television audiences.

At the same time the new referendum campaign for the change of the electoral system gained momentum, showing the disaffection of public opinion with the existing configuration of the party system and the desire for change. The popular vote in 1993 was a shattering 'yes' for the abolition of the old PR system, seen as the crutch of the old party system. Parliament had no option but to introduce a predominantly plurality system, as asked by the voters.

It is interesting to note how weak before the new challengers and how incapable of reacting proved the Italian *partitocrazia*, the oligarchic system of parties which had seemed all powerful only a short time before. The whole process of change was unexpectedly accelerated and quite suddenly the emperor appeared naked! During these crucial months, between June 1992 and January 1994, the traditional governing parties were at the same time under a multi-pronged political attack (from the Lega, from the referendum movement, from public opinion and the media) and their top leadership was taken to court for illegal financing and corruption. Parties thus faced the difficult task of renovating their identity, their political appeal, and at the same time their leaders. This proved extremely problematic and resulted in a situation where crucial resources slipped out of the hands of the party politicians. Particularly relevant is the fact that the government progressively fell into the hands of technocrats. The process reached its zenith in April 1993 when the leadership of the government was given by the President of the Republic to the head of the Central Bank with the mandate of having a new electoral law approved. The attempts at self-renewal of the old parties substantially failed, producing internal splits and an exodus of top and middle-ranking leaders. The DC in particular went through a difficult attempt to rethink its identity, which ended up in January 1994 in a party split, with the right wing leaving to form a new party, the Centro Cristiano Democratico, or CCD (Wertman 1994). As for the PSI, having lost Bettino Craxi—its dominant leader for more than a decade—it proved unable to recover, and the rapid succession of leaders showed the depth of its crisis.

In a very short time an earthquake had occurred that would leave the old Italian party system deeply shattered and open the way to a new political era.

The new party system after the crisis

The anticipated dissolution of parliament and the calling of new elections in 1994, decided as soon as the new electoral law required by the result of the referendum was drafted, triggered a deep restructuring of the party system. With new rules and a renovated set of players the electoral game of 1994 took a very special turn compared with the past. The new political landscape was characterized by an unexpected innovative mix of old parties trying to redefine their identity in order to escape from the problems of the past and of new parties trying to exploit the crisis of the old ones.

Of the old parties the best placed was probably the former Communist Party, at this time the Party of the Democratic Left (PDS), which had undergone its rejuvenation earlier than the others (with a change of name and emblem and a split of its left wing) and had not been too greatly affected by the judicial problems. Its main competitor on the left—the Socialist Party—was put completely out of play by the corruption charges and the leadership crisis which ensued and which completely destroyed the political capital it had gained during the 1980s. Under a by then predominantly majoritarian electoral system (see Chapter 3), the main problem for the Party of the Democratic Left was whether it would be able to overcome the traditional diffidence of centre voters and convince them to vote for left candidates. At the same time, however, it had to face new competition on its left as a consequence of the split that had led to the creation of a party—Communist Refoundation or Rifondazione Comunista (RC)—still loyal to the ideological tradition and proud to use the communist denomination and symbols. At the other extreme of the political spectrum, the MSI, also unaffected by judicial problems, was ready, after having refurbished its image into that of the more moderate Alleanza Nazionale (AN), to exploit the opportunities opened up by the crisis and to escape from its position of marginalization.

The crucial political question concerned that part of the political spectrum which had been previously occupied by the DC and its centrist allies. To what extent would the two main Christian Democratic successor parties (Partito Popolare Italiano or PPI and CCD) be able to defend and regain the old votes of the DC? In the north, the Lega had proved, in the general election of 1992 and in the local elections of 1993, to be a particularly strong competitor. In the south, AN was showing that it was able to make inroads into the electorate of a shattered DC. A little more to the centre-left there was another new party, Alleanza Democratica (AD), originally guided by the leader of the referendum movement Mario Segni, but now deprived of its most popular leader, and having at the centre of its agenda the transformation of the institutions.

A few months before the general election of 1994 the political landscape displayed a clearer situation on the left, where a broad alliance, guided by its largest party, the PDS, and including Rifondazione, the Greens, Alleanza Democratica, and other minor groups, showed that in a majoritarian competition, as had happened in the elections of mayors, it had a strong chance of prevailing over the more fragmented centre and right camps. This situation, however, was soon drastically changed by the appearance on the scene of a new actor, who was bound to affect the structure of the party system deeply. Silvio Berlusconi, probably the richest man in Italy, who in the 1980s, also thanks to the support of the Socialist leader Craxi and of some Christian Democrat wings, had challenged the monopoly of state television creating a media empire, launched his own political movement, Forza Italia, named after the battle cry of the supporters of the national football team. At the centre of its political platform was an appeal to all centre and right streams of opinion to oppose the now possible rise to power of the post-communists, to defend the market economy from state encroachments, and to reduce taxation. Also among the goals of the media tycoon there was obviously that of protecting his media empire against the threat of the left to introduce limitations to the television channels controlled by his company.

In a situation where, given the fragmentation of the party system (which had significantly increased as a result of the splits in the largest parties and the birth of new ones) and the requirements of the new electoral system, the building of large alliances was a crucial aspect of the electoral campaign, Berlusconi and his movement proved strikingly successful in rallying a great part of the centre and the right in a new cartel. The PPI, the main successor party of the DC, together with the Patto Segni—the movement founded by the most influential promoter of the anti-proportional referendums of 1991 and 1993—were reluctant to enter into an agreement with the Lega, which had been strongly critical of the old DC, and even more so with the rightist Alleanza Nazionale, but equally unprepared to support the left alliance. Berlusconi, then, after some attempts to come to an agreement with these parties, opted for an alliance with the two rising parties of this period, the Lega and Alleanza Nazionale. Since these two parties, one in favour of strong decentralization and the other with a more centralistic and *étatiste* platform, were not ready to accept a formal alliance between themselves, Forza Italia built two different alliances, one in the North with the Lega and one in the centre and south with Alleanza Nazionale.

The party system thus came to be articulated around three poles: a left pole dominated by the post-communist party, a centre pole made up of the main post-Christian Democratic party plus the new party of Segni, and a right pole with Forza Italia, the Lega, and Alleanza Nazionale plus the other small post-Christian Democratic party, the CCD. It was clear pretty soon that the competition was to be dominated by the duel between Berlusconi and his alliance on one side and the left on the other. The electoral results gave a new shape to the party system: the centre pole was seriously defeated, the left failed in its attempt to win access to the government for the first time since 1947, while the right scored an unexpected but sufficiently clear victory. The elections were a great success for Berlusconi and his newborn party. And for the first time the centre was no longer dominant.

The new party system combined legacies of the past and important innovations. With regard to individual parties, all of the traditional ones which had been the main actors of the 'first republic' had changed their names and redefined their identity, and most had faced serious splits. The PDS showed once again that for the heirs of the communist tradition it was difficult to win votes at the centre of the political spectrum. Alleanza Nazionale had a good showing in the south, but its growth was stopped by the birth of new competitors for the centre-right vote. The Popolari, the main successors of the DC, had a poor showing. Of the new parties, Alleanza Democratica and the Patto Segni, born in the wake of the electoral referendum, failed to become significant players. Also the Lega faced its first, albeit limited, downturn: in the north part of its electorate was captured by Forza Italia. By contrast Forza Italia was a surprising success, becoming, from its first election, the strongest party in Italy in terms of popular votes.

With regard to the structure of the party system (see Figure 2.3) the result of the election made it apparent that the left alone was not able to win a parliamentary majority; only through an alliance with part of the centre would its chances have been realistic. The centre in its turn could overcome the hurdles of the new electoral system and survive as a significant parliamentary force only if it agreed to enter into a coalition with either the left or the right; in neither case, however, would it be, as it had been in the past, the dominant force. As for the right, it had been proved that it could win a majority provided that it was able to bring into its camp the right wing of the old DC and to form and maintain an alliance with both the Lega and Alleanza Nazionale.

Contrary to what had been expected by some of the promoters of the referendum for electoral reform, the traditional fragmentation of the Italian party system was not reduced. In fact it even increased (Table 2.3). At the same time, however, the party system acquired a more clearly bipolar structure. Contrary to the situation in the past, when everything hinged around the central party, the DC, and no alternation in government was

FIGURE 2.3 Party system and coalitions, 1994–2006

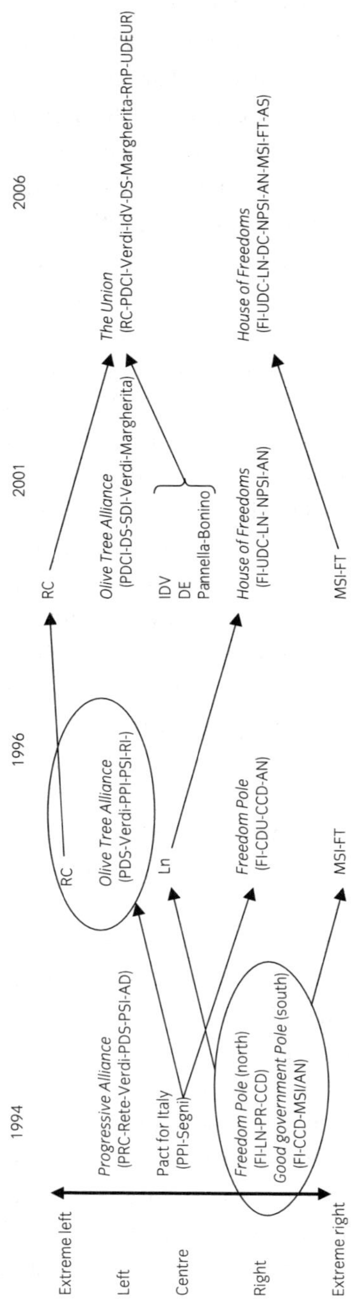

Note: See Table 2.2 for the meaning of party acronyms.

TABLE 2.3 Indexes of fragmentation of the party system

	Effective number of parties (lower chamber)	Sum of the two largest parties (percentages, elections to the lower chamber)
1948	2.9	69.5 (DC+ Popular Front)
1953	3.5	62.7 (DC+PCI)
1958	3.4	65.0 (DC+PCI)
1963	3.6	63.6 (DC+PCI)
1968	3.6	66.0 (DC+PCI)
1972	3.6	65.8 (DC+PCI)
1976	3.1	73.1 (DC+PCI)
1979	3.4	68.7 (DC+PCI)
1983	4.0	62.8 (DC+PCI)
1987	4.1	60.9 (DC+PCI)
1992	5.7	45.8 (DC+PDS)
1994	5.7	41.5 (FI+PDS)
1996	6.2	41.7 (PDS+FI)
2001	5.2	46.1 (FI+DS)
2006	5.1	52.0 (L'Ulivo*+FI)

* In reality, the sum of the two largest parties in 2006 was lower, since the list of L'Ulivo was a federation of two parties (DS and DL). If we take the figure for the senate, where DS and DL ran separately, the sum of the votes of the two largest parties (FI ad DS) was 40.8 per cent. The effective number of parties, a measure that considers both the number and the size of parliamentary parties, has been calculated following the Laakso and Tagepeera index:
$ENF = \frac{1}{\sum (s_i)^2}$ where s_i is the proportion of parliamentary seats of party i.

possible, the new party system was now dominated by bipolar competition between left and right (or, better, between centre-left and centre-right coalitions). It is true that a central pole of parties existed in these elections and in some of the following ones, that some parties of the left and of the right coalition have continued to define themselves as 'centre parties', some of them even moving from one side to the other of the left–right dividing line, but in the end all the 'centre' parties competing outside the two main left and right alliances have been heavily under-represented and have been unable to maintain their position. The subsequent elections would show in fact a rather clear shrinking of the electoral strength of the centre pole and also its changing composition (it was made up of the PPI and Patto Segni in 1994, of the Lega in 1996, of European Democracy in 2001) until its virtual disappearance in 2006. The central pole has thus become a sort of 'parking place' for political groups that have not yet decided their position or are in the process of changing it and want to capitalize on the fact that, if they cannot win a significant parliamentary representation, they can at least negatively affect the chances of victory of one or the other pole. They are, so to speak, 'on the market' with a view to the next election. This game was particularly clear in case of the Lega which, having left the centre-right alliance at the end of 1994, wanted to show that without its contribution the alliance could not win.

In the new party system the disappearance of the DC on the one hand, and the success of the Lega and Forza Italia on the other, are probably the most striking novelties. The collapse of the DC is one of the rare cases, in European politics, of the sudden and complete crisis of a major party. We have already seen some of the reasons for this collapse; the question is also why attempts to face the crisis through a profound renewal of the party failed. A plausible explanation lies in the deeply factionalized structure that this party had developed over the years. With this structure it was extremely difficult for the party to produce a sufficiently strong and accepted leader to face the challenges of the time, and it was easy for it to become fissured and eventually to split along faction lines. In fact during these years a whole series of new parties appeared that traced their identity back to the old DC, and substantial components of its national leadership and of its local elite transmigrated to almost all the parties of the political spectrum, from the AN to the DS. It was as though the diverse political identities which in the past had been unified under the roof of the old party could now free themselves from previous constraints.

The success of the Lega in northern Italy, and particularly in some of the areas where the diffuse network of small and medium-sized enterprises has been the main engine of economic growth in recent decades, showed how dissatisfied this social milieu was with the working of national politics and of central bureaucracy. The Lega, with its often extreme anti-centralistic rhetoric and the loudly proclaimed rejection of the traditional style of 'Roman politics', offered to this part of the country a vociferous instrument of protest. At the same time, however, this party, because of its specific nature, could not find a significant following in those parts of Italy—especially in the south—which have remained much more dependent on state aid. This situation produced, for the first time in Italian politics, the birth of a large party with a clearly circumscribed territorial basis, which was not linked to a real ethnic minority. With this party the issue of territorial autonomy vis-à-vis central government gained new prominence in the political debate. If the Lega oscillated between more moderate proposals of a federal transformation of the Italian state and the extremist request of the secession for northern regions from Italy and the construction of a Padanian state,[3] in the end all the parties had to take, in one way or the other, a position on this issue. Quite suddenly the problem of federalism, which had been absent from the Italian debate since the years preceding Italian unification in the mid-nineteenth century, gained the centre of the stage.

In the new political landscape of the Second Republic Forza Italia can be seen as the most innovative element by virtue both of its nature and internal structure and of the dynamics it has brought to the party system. The founding and leading role of an economic entrepreneur was in itself something new and utterly shocking for the political tradition of Italy, which up to that time had seen an entrepreneurial class that was rather weak and lacking in self-confidence vis-à-vis the political professionals, and where 'capitalism' and 'market' had never been particularly popular words in political discourse. In this case a leading entrepreneur entered the political arena directly and without mediation. This fact can be seen as a symptom of the deep crisis of the *partitocrazia* and of party professionalism: even if Berlusconi, given his past relationship with the governing parties, could not be considered a complete outsider, his entry into the political arena was presented by himself and his supporters as an example of civil society reaffirming itself after a long expropriation by the *partitocrazia*. And in their propaganda Berlusconi and Forza Italia would always stress their difference from traditional party models.

The party and its organization were in many respects a completely new phenomenon for Italian politics. The dominance of the leader over the party is the most evident feature. Forza Italia is the first case in Italy of a party which is almost completely the personal creation of one leader and thus heavily dependent on his choices. Its organization is very different from that of the other parties and also its personnel is, at least in part, of a new type, with a significant proportion coming from the private sector (Poli

2001).This does not mean, however, that the party is completely new in its composition: it has in fact also inherited a significant portion of the old political personnel; at the same time, it has been able to fuse together people coming not only from the DC but also from more or less all the other parties of the old governing majority (Socialists, Liberals, Republicans). In this sense it was proved that some political divisions which had been frozen by the party system of the first republic had lost much of their meaning and could be freed by the organizational collapse of the old parties.

The party and its coalition strategies have contributed significantly to the new bipolar shape of political competition in Italy. Forza Italia, while competing with the Christian Democratic successor parties for the votes of the old DC, has defined its identity much more clearly as that of a party of the right and as an alternative to the left (even making large use of the anti-communism rhetoric which the DC had in its last years watered down). Moreover, it has stressed the image of a party much more clearly supportive of the private sector (especially small and medium-sized enterprises, independent professionals, etc.) and opposed to union influence. Such themes were not completely absent in the electoral appeal of the DC, but were significantly balanced by the strength of an internal left wing which was closer to trade unions, strongly supportive of state intervention in the economy, and often linked to the large state enterprises. Forza Italia has also displayed a less confessional profile than the DC. Even though it has become the home of many former Christian Democrats and has significant electoral support among active Catholics, religion has never been a central element of its identity as it was in the case of the DC (which on this basis would keep together left and right). Within Forza Italia and especially among its leadership the 'lay' component has been much more prominent. By defining itself consistently as a party opposed to the left, Forza Italia has undoubtedly exploited the opportunities offered by the new electoral system, but has also contributed to defining the new patterns of competition.

The party proved an astounding electoral success. And, contrary to expectations, it has shown itself to be not only a temporary phenomenon but something bound to last. The success of Berlusconi's party has had some important consequences. In particular, it made it extremely difficult to put together again the pieces of the old Christian Democratic party which were thus attracted in different directions by the bipolar competition. It has also created a particularly significant and embarrassing concentration in the media (especially when Berlusconi is in government and can exert, as typically Italian governments do, also a strong influence on public TV), a manifest conflict of interest, and produced strong tensions with the judiciary (as a result of its leader's past entrepreneurial activities which have attracted the attention of prosecutors) (see Chapter 8).

Over the years the new party system has shown some basic elements of continuity but also elements of change. Among the former, four deserve to be mentioned:

1. the persistence and predominance of the bipolar shape by which two large alliances face each other at elections, a third pole at the centre of the system cannot succeed electorally, and the more centrist parties of the two sides cannot manage to escape from the embrace of their 'poles' and cannot create the platform for a government of the centre;
2. the high level of fragmentation which, election after election, is maintained by the failure of the larger parties to expand significantly their area of influence and by the proliferation of new splinter parties which are hardly ever excluded from the inclusive game of alliance building fostered by the electoral systems of the past decade;
3. the relative weakness of the two largest parties—the DS on the left and Forza Italia on the right—which has never put them in a position where they would dare to run alone in the majoritarian competition; and
4. the greater fragmentation of the left compared with the right coalition and the greater difficulty it has in finding and sustaining a leader: from 1994 to 2006 the centre-left has been guided at elections and in government by five different leaders (Occhetto, Prodi, D'Alema, Amato, and Rutelli), the centre-right always by the same one (Berlusconi).

With regard to changes one should mention the continuing reshaping of the post-Christian Democratic parties which has led to the creation of a whole series of new parties (CCD, PPI, CDU, UDR, UDEUR, DL, DE, DC), regrouping in different combinations pieces of the old centrist political elites. Mini-splinters have occurred also on the extreme left and extreme right of the spectrum, increasing the complexities of both coalitions.

In order to understand the party system in recent years one must pay attention to its two main levels: that of parties and that of coalitions. If we consider only the first level, the fragmentation of the first republic, far from decreasing, has persisted and even increased, producing a high level of activities from the parties directed mainly at reaffirming their identities (which, after the crisis of the great ideological divisions of the past, have become much more fuzzy) and marking their territory. At the same time, however, the system has worked within the firm and constraining framework of two strongly opposed coalitions, vigorously confronting each other first on the electoral and then on the parliamentary ground. The existence of these coalitions has significantly simplified the political landscape and the choice for Italian citizens, and has produced a fairly strong coalition discipline for a substantial part of parliamentary proceedings. Because of their fragmentation the life of the two coalitions has, however, been far from easy. The internal tensions have concerned both the question of the leadership and that of the definition of the programmatic platforms. The choice of the coalition leadership has been less difficult for the centre-right, where Berlusconi has had no serious challenger to date; in this case the role of the leader in putting together and shaping the profile of the alliance, the relative weight of his party, and his full control of the latter have made any other choice unrealistic. The problems have concerned the style and exercise of the leadership, with Berlusconi leaning more in the direction of a personal and solitary leadership while the other coalition parties have kept asking for a more collegial style. On the centre-left the choice of the leader has been much more problematic. Choosing a party leader as the guide of the coalition inevitably led to a dilemma: the most natural option, that of the largest party, the post-communist PDS/DS, would give to the coalition too leftist an image for the more centrist parties to be prepared to accept. These parties (the PPI first, then the Margherita) were, however, too small to make a strong claim for the leadership. Another possible solution was the choice of a leader who could not be identified too closely with any party. Between 1994 and 2006 the coalition has in fact made different choices: with Occhetto (PDS) in 1994 and Rutelli (Margherita) in 2001 it has been guided once by the party leader of the strongest, but leftist, party and then by that of a smaller, but more central, party; with Prodi in 1996 and 2006 it has chosen a guide independent of any party. Finally, between elections it has used both a party leader (D'Alema of the DS) and a non-party leader (Amato). So far the only leader able to win elections for the left has been Prodi, a non-party leader (albeit with a past in the DC and then in the PPI). This has caused in the centre-left coalition a certain degree of tension between the existing parties and the project to create around the coalition leader a new political aggregation that would go beyond the existing parties. The discussion about the creation of a larger political movement that would unify a great part of the centre-left coalition is thus at the centre of current debates. The same topic has become a theme of discussion also in the centre-right, but with the leader of the coalition being also the leader of the largest party, an aggregation would be perceived by the other parties as a takeover.

Both coalitions have also faced significant problems in defining commonly agreed platforms. The reason is that, on both sides, parties with very different ideological traditions and voting clienteles have come together. In the centre-left as in the centre-right the coalition combines parties which had traditionally been in government and parties that had always been in the opposition, market-oriented and state-oriented parties, parties with a confessional background and parties with an anti-clerical one, centralist parties and federalist ones. Some of the cleavages that had been important in Italian politics, rather than separating the two coalitions, are thus internal to them. Dissensions on foreign policy and ethical matters (such as abortion, stem cell research, etc.) are greater and more divisive in the centre-left, while perhaps those on the preferred level of decentralization of the state are stronger in the centre-right.

As we have already mentioned, a particularly crucial role has been played in the new political system by one figure, that of Berlusconi. Italian political life has acquired in this period a degree of personalization that was previously unheard of, even if some anticipation of this phenomenon had been perceived during the 1980s with the Socialist leader Craxi. With his exceptional financial resources and the large conflicts of interest they generate, his control of a significant portion of the media system, his personality of a non-professional politician and his populist rhetoric, his ability to interpret the feelings of large sections of the population, but also to generate the repulsion of many (and in particular of the intellectuals), Berlusconi has been both the focal point of attraction and of strong allegiances and the target of fierce antagonism. In a way it can be said that he has been at the same time a crucial linchpin of the centre-right coalition, where the Lega and Alleanza Nazionale could not have lived together without his mediation, and a negative rallying point for the centre-left, for whom it has sometimes been easier to unite 'against' Berlusconi than around common goals. Even his political defeats, such as the fall of his first cabinet after just a few months and the failure to win the 2006 election after five years at the helm, have not weakened his political role too greatly. This and on the other side the resilience of Prodi have contributed to making the past ten years of Italian politics something of a duel between two leaders.

Conclusion

Almost fifteen years after the great crisis of the early 1990s it can be said that the Italian party system has acquired a significant degree of stability and that the expectations of a long period of instability, which were strong at first, have not been matched by reality. It remains to be seen whether the creation of a new encompassing force within each of the two coalitions will in the end take place and stop the process of internal fragmentation.

From the heyday of *partitocrazia*, when parties through their widely diffused organizational articulations maintained a strong control over Italian society and were the main gate-keepers in the representation of interests (Morlino 1991), things have indeed significantly changed. Not only have the sheer quantitative size of membership and the number of organizational units of parties declined dramatically (even compelling parties to give up a large part of their property), but also the qualitative importance of their activities and cultural messages for people at large has shrunk enormously. It is no accident that since the 1980s, compared with trade unions and social movements, their ability to mobilize large groups of people for political issues except during electoral campaigns has become almost nil. Another field where they have lost influence is in the economic world. Thanks to the wide-ranging privatizations of the 1990s, the direct and indirect public control of economic firms has been drastically reduced and with it the possibility for parties to nominate their affiliates on the boards of public or semi-public enterprises. To balance these transformations and the negative effects they have had on the resources they control, parties have pursued with determination the strategy of increasing state contributions which by now have become their primary source of income (Conti *et al.* 2007).

It must be said, however, to complete the picture, that at another level parties have maintained and perhaps increased their role. In a political system that has become more competitive and where alternating governmental majorities have gained a stronger weight in parliament, parties that make up these majorities now have greater opportunities to pursue their policy preferences. Parties, hitherto static defenders of identities, can thus become more dynamic policy innovators.

KEY TERMS

- first republic
- second republic
- anti-system party
- bipolar competition
- electoral coalition
- multipolar competition
- *partitocrazia* ('partycracy')
- party system fragmentation
- polarized multipartism
- semi-peripheral alternation

GUIDE TO FURTHER READING

Farneti, P. (1985) *The Italian Party System* (London, Pinter).

A study of the Italian party system from post war reconstruction to the end of the 1970s.

La Palombara, J. (1987) *Democracy Italian Style* (New Haven, Yale University Press).

A penetrating interpretation of Italian politics, written under the 'partycracy' of the so-called first republic.

Morlino, L. and Tarchi, M. (2006) *Partiti e caso italiano* (Bologna, Il Mulino).

Excellent collection of recent studies on the transformations of Italian political parties and the party system after the crisis of the mid-1990s.

Newell, J. (2002b) *Parties and Democracy in Italy* (London, Ashgate).

A study of the emergence of the new party system after 1994 and its consequences.

SARTORI, G. (1976) *Parties and Party Systems: A Framework for Analysis* (Cambridge, Cambridge University Press).

The classic book by the father of Italian political science, introducing his celebrated comparative analysis and the notion of polarized multipartism.

SARTORI, G. (1982) *Teoria dei partiti e caso italiano* (Milan, Sugarco).

Sartori's interpretation of the Italian party system.

NOTES

1 At the local level (in municipalities, provinces, and regions), where international alignments do not play a role, the alliance between the two main left parties has been much easier to decide.

2 The percentage in the 1991 referendum (with a voter turnout of 62.5 per cent) was 95.6. Similarly, in the 1993 referendum (with a turnout of 77 per cent) the 'yes' vote was 82.6 per cent.

3 The Padania is the large and fertile plain, encompassing four regions of northern Italy, traversed by the River Po. This purely geographical notion has been transformed by the Lega into a political concept.

3

Electoral Systems and Elections: Between Unfinished Reforms and a Fairly Stable Electorate

Overview

In this chapter we analyze the 'electoral regimes' in Italy throughout the republican period. We start with the debate on the electoral rules within the Constituent Assembly, and the consequent choice of a proportional representation (PR) model. We then take a closer look at the long period of stability between 1948 and the beginning of the 1990s. The two fundamental components of this period were the persistence of PR as the unquestioned method of transforming votes into seats (at all levels of the Italian polity), and the stability of the party system, shaped and consolidated during the cold war. The sudden crisis of the traditional order opened the way to the introduction (1993) of a mixed-plurality electoral system which was used at three consecutive elections between 1994 and 2001. The characteristics of this system will be analyzed in depth in the second section. Such a diachronic approach will lead us also to analyze the basic patterns of voting behaviour from the first republic to the beginning of the twenty-first century, discussing some of the explanations provided by historians, sociologists, and political scientists, in order to understand the peculiarities of the Italian electoral landscape.

The final part of the chapter focuses on the current situation. We cover the electoral reform of 2005, describing its structural elements and the results of its first application, with the general election of 2006. A basic argument lies at the core of the chapter: electoral institutions are important, not only because they govern the passage from the world of votes (and political orientations) to the world of seats (and political leadership), but also for the very simple reason that electoral systems and electoral rules mirror the 'spirit' of the democratic compromise between the elites and the political community.

The Italian case is particularly relevant for such an argument. When the electoral institutions were stable and 'untouchable', as they were for a very long period between the democratic consolidation of the early 1950s and 1992, they ensured stability in a divided and difficult democracy. When these institutions (including the rules for the local government elections that we analyze in Chapter 6) have been challenged and reformed, a delicate process of readjustment has started, influenced by a bottom-up demand for change, but also by continuous elite reactions and resistances. This has created a paradoxical mix of the rhetoric of democratic effectiveness and the strategic options of the party elites guided by their ambition to maximize their institutional presence. At the same time, some achievements have been consolidated (namely the reshaping of the party system and the crystallization of bipolar competition), and a quite remarkable stability has characterized the demand side, as one can see from survey data and other indicators of voting behaviour.

This is, however, still an unfinished story: a new series of electoral reforms are indeed very likely. But this unfinished story tells us enough about the need for the electoral institutions to be consolidated in the same way as other institutional actors and rules.

The electoral regime of the Italian republic

The original choices

Two electoral dates could be considered as symbolic milestones for the democratic reconsolidation of Italy after fascism. These dates are 2 June 1946 and 18 April 1948. The first was the date of the election of the Constituent Assembly, which was held together with the institutional referendum that abrogated monarchic rule and introduced a republican form of state. After about twenty-four years of the Fascist regime and twenty-two of electoral interruption, with the last semi-competitive elections of the lower chamber having occurred in 1924, the 1946 assembly was elected on the basis of a PR system with thirty-two large constituencies, thus confirming the fundamental choice made in 1919, at the end of the period of 'liberal Italy'. The same system was then confirmed by the Constituent Assembly, through an ordinary law, as the basic rule for the election of the lower chamber of the new republic. As for the upper house, the electoral law (no. 1058, 7 October 1947) defined an apparently rather different system, combining a majority system in single-member districts based upon an 'impossible' 65 per cent threshold, with a PR system operating in regional districts, whenever the threshold was not reached. However, even this system proved in practice to be quite proportional in its distributional effects, as the majority threshold was almost never attained. Moreover, the constitutional principle stating that the Senate had to be elected on a 'regional basis' was not implemented as an equal representation of all the regions, as in the example of the US federal Senate. On the contrary, the seats were allocated to each region in proportion to the size of the population, thus completely erasing the 'over-representation effect' of smaller territorial entities which is typically at work in the senates of federal systems, like Switzerland or Germany (Lijphart 1999).

All in all, the degree of proportionality granted by the original setting of the republican parliament did not vary much between the two parliamentary branches, which therefore had a fairly symmetrical political composition. However, the different architecture of the electoral systems (see Table 3.1) and the district magnitude determined some effects in terms of party strategies. First, the multi-preferential vote used for the elections to the lower chamber was an important tool for intra-party competition, and provided a perfect electoral environment for local patrons of factional parties (above all Christian Democrats) who were able to orientate their packages of 'clientele votes' to support this or that candidate, thus creating a network of alliances (*cordate*) between national and local leaders. Second, the absence of a list system in the Senate allowed the party elites to impose their favoured candidates, who could be comfortably placed in those districts where the party was confident of achieving a high share of votes region-wide. In this way, the affirmation of local leaders without the support of the party apparatus was quite difficult.

Finally, the reduced magnitude of the Senate constituencies (or, better, the reduced number of seats to be allocated proportionally within each regional constituency) made the life of the smaller parties a little more complicated

TABLE 3.1 The electoral systems at work in Italy, 1948–1992

Elective body	Time of application	Type of electoral system	Main features
Constituent Assembly (1946) Lower chamber (1948)	1946–48	PR list system with multi-preference vote	Thirty-three constituencies electing from one to sixty members (corrected quota system) Proportional reallocation of the residual seats to the list reaching 300,000 votes nation wide
Lower chamber	1953	PR list system with multi-preference vote and majority bonus for the coalition reaching 50 per cent + 1 of votes	The reform did not change the mechanisms of the system indicated above, but it would have corrected the proportional allocation of seats nation-wide, providing 65 per cent of the seats to the coalition reaching an absolute majority of votes
	1958–87	PR list system with multi-preference vote	After 1953 (and the missing application of the majority bonus since no coalition reached the absolute majority of votes) the previous system was reinstalled
	1992	PR list system with preference vote	The multi-preference vote was abrogated by the 1991 referendum
Senate	1948–92	Single-member districts with threshold of 65 per cent and PR in regional districts	Proportional reallocation of the seats at the regional level (d'Hondt system).
Regional elections in the special statute regions (regional councils)	1947–95	PR system	Different versions of PR, all characterized by lists and preference vote

continues

Table 3.1 continued

Elective body	Time of application	Type of electoral system	Main features
Provincial councils	1951–93	PR single-member districts based system	Proportional allocation of seats in the provincial constituency; once allocated the number of provincial seats to each party the district candidates with the higher personal quota were appointed
Municipal councils (more than 5,000 inhabitants)		PR list system with preference vote	Allocation of the residual seats with the d'Hondt system; the degree of proportionality was particularly high in the large communal town were the councils could have up to 80 councillors
Municipal councils (fewer than 5,000 inhabitants)		Limited vote, blocked list	One-quarter of the fifteen councillors allocated to the minority list(s)
Regional councils (ordinary regions)	1970–95	PR system with preference vote within lists at the provincial level	Seats allocated to party lists on pure PR basis (corrected quota system)
Italian representatives in European Parliament	1979–2004	PR list system with preference vote	Seats allocated with a pure PR (corrected quota) system in five large constituencies

than in the lower chamber, where a party achieving about 0.6 per cent of nationwide votes normally had the chance to elect at least one representative.

The failed change of 1953

An early attempt to reform the electoral system and correct its proportional logic was indeed made in the first years of the republic. It was promoted in the spring of 1953 by the centrist coalition government led by Alcide de Gasperi. After a fierce parliamentary battle the reform was actually passed, with a law that the left opposition in its propaganda dubbed a fraud (*legge truffa*). De Gasperi intended to transform the Italian political system into a more effective and 'majoritarian' one, and his reform was clearly aimed at consolidating the parliamentary majority of the moderate coalition. In a nutshell, the system would have kept the skeleton of the previous system, maintaining the PR system in both chambers. At the same time, a majority bonus would have been assured to the party (or the coalition of parties) reaching an absolute majority of the votes. De facto, this device would have been realistically helpful only to the centrist coalition, as the left and the neo-fascist minorities could hardly have coalesced to reach an absolute majority.

The historical outcome was not what the government expected: in 1953, when the new system was applied for the first time, the majority bonus could not be allocated because the governmental coalition did not reach 50 per cent of the vote.[1] The reform was then immediately abrogated and the original PR system for the lower chamber was re-established, thus regulating the renewal of the Italian parliament until the 1990s.

The establishment of a 'fully proportional' electoral regime

The choice of PR was to a large extent a result of a constitutional compromise acknowledging the 'parity norm' among the parties which had been the protagonists of the liberation war. This also explains why, since the early years of democratic reconstruction, all the electoral rules have been basically orientated to admit the maximum degree of proportional representation possible, for any type of political contest, thus favouring the establishment of a coherent 'national party system' from the most peripheral of the local assemblies to the national parliament.

We will not enter here into the details of the different electoral systems used in Italy during the first republic. Table 3.1, which reports their period of application, their basic principles, and their main institutional features, tells enough in this respect. A first relevant implication of the generalized and persistent use of pure PR systems is that this choice favoured not only the reproduction of a similar 'system of competition' but also the same institutional dynamics at the level of local government. Indeed, with municipal, provincial, and (later) regional governments adopting the principle of parliamentary democracy (see Chapter 6), the existence in each regional, provincial, and even municipal council of highly fragmented political representation was conducive to a replication at all territorial levels of the same features of instability and permanent negotiation which characterized the national political scene. The second implication is that the use of PR as the unquestioned criterion of transformation from votes to seats was proposed again without major discussions during the 1970s (a period characterized by the largest extent of consensus and convergence between governmental parties and the left opposition), when it came to deciding the rules of new elections. This was the case at the beginning of the decade for the elections to the new regional councils, and at the end of the decade for the elections of the Italian members of the European Parliament.

However, as Richard Katz points out (2003: 6), already during this period growing complaints about the excessive fragmentation of the political spectrum started to be voiced. And in the course of the following decade proposals for an electoral reform aimed at curing the problem of the Italian lack of government and at creating the conditions for a moderate bipolarism and a regular alternation in office became bolder. Nonetheless, until the early 1990s such a discussion did not involve public opinion very much, and was not strong enough to bring any concrete change in the electoral rules.

Building a 'quasi-majoritarian' electoral environment: the reforms of the 1990s

A sudden but explainable transformation

In this section we discuss the electoral reform introduced at the national-legislative level in 1993, which was then used three times between 1994 and 2001. However, the Italian electoral regime after the crisis of the mid-1990s is very much changed in many other respects besides the innovations in the mechanisms of allocation of parliamentary seats.

As we have already noted in Chapter 2, the introduction of a non-proportional method of election, together with a number of other factors, starting with the political scandals of the early nineties, led to a revolutionary change in the Italian party system. Here we deal with the nature of this transformation in terms of electoral methods and other new important technicalities, introduced during the period 1994–2006 in order to reshape the 'electoral environment'.

It can surely be said that such a transformation was sudden, and to a large extent it was forced on parliament and the political class. However, some analyses have shown elements which can be considered to have anticipated, and indeed partly explained, such a change. For instance, the aggressive and leadership-orientated campaigning style of the Socialist leader Bettino Craxi during the 1980s had already been something 'new' compared with the traditional style of political competition in Italy. Moreover, the last years of the first republic had brought a number of significant phenomena which can today be interpreted as clear hints of dissatisfaction not only with the elite in power but also with a whole system of political selection and competition. The growing rates of parliamentary turnover and the emergence of less traditional types of representatives—from the decision by the PCI to open its lists to a number of independents generally with an intellectual background to the new faces appearing in the parliamentary and ministerial elites of other parties—were probably weak attempts to prevent a foreseen crisis (Cotta and Verzichelli 1996). Even more evident signs of dissatisfaction were the erosion of the most relevant parties during the 1980s (see Chapter 2) and the strong offensives against the 'party occupation' of public television and against the public financing of political parties which had been promoted by independent observers and new challengers like the Radical Party,[2] marking the difficulties faced by the political establishment in maintaining its traditional gate-keeping role between civil society and the political system (Morlino and Tarchi 1996).

However, it was clear that, if the established parties, confident in their political entrenchment, were incapable of renewal, the new ones which had recently appeared (the new left parties, the Radicals, the Greens, and the same Lega that had reached parliament in 1992) were too narrow in their appeal to hope to change the modes of electoral competition from inside.

In the end, it was mainly the Italian voters who stimulated political change, with more than one message sent to the political elites. If the most direct of them—the decline of the two most important parties and then the significant volatility, particularly evident in the local elections of 1990—have already been discussed in the previous chapter, the issue of declining electoral participation became a critical challenge for traditional parties at the beginning of the 1990s. Indeed, from 1987 onward the rate of electoral turnout was significantly lower than that threshold of 90 per cent which in Italy used to be considered a minimal rate of participation. In fact the increasing rate of abstention in Italy was not so different from the European trend (Mannheimer and Sani 2001). However, between the end of the 1970s and the mid-1990s, Italy dropped two places on the European ranking of participation (from the fourth to the sixth place), with an average decline of about 10 percentage points (from 91 to 82 per cent). Only part of this decrease was politically relevant, as most of the new abstentions resulted from an increase in the elderly population or 'generous' registrations of non-residents. The small proportion of intermittent abstentions, however, would prove to be quite relevant, being often decisive in determining the outcome of some close bipolar elections in recent years. Even the protest vote against all the party actors, expressed by means of spoilt and blank ballots, progressively increased after 1976 (Figure 3.1).

This crisis of the relationship between voters and parties was not immediately read as a message against the incumbent political class, but it was clear that the rules of the game (and first of all the traditional PR electoral system) and their typical effects did not satisfy the Italian public anymore.

The electoral reform of 1993

The adoption of the mixed-plurality system in 1993 was largely the result of the strong pressure exerted on the political class by social movements and public opinion during the delicate crisis of the early 1990s. As already mentioned, in these years, two abrogative referenda had succeeded against the indications of the main governmental parties, recording a quite unexpected level of turnout. The referenda had the explicit goal of reforming the electoral regime in Italy, although its supporters could not 'propose' an alternative rule, because of the constitutional nature of the abrogative referendum in Italy. The first referendum (1991) abrogated the multiple

FIGURE 3.1 **Electoral turnout and valid votes, Constitutional Assembly and Chamber of Deputies, 1946–2006**

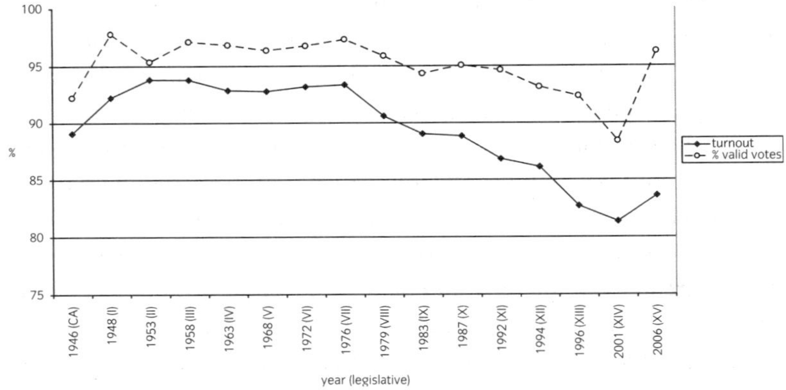

Note: Between 1994 and 2001, when two ballots were used for the elections to the lower chamber, we have considered the proportional vote (list vote) and not the vote within the single-member districts.

preference vote, a classical feature of Italian PR which had been often considered a tool for political exchange and clientelist practices. With the second referendum (1993) the so-called pro-majoritarian movement moved to destroy the foundations of PR, by abrogating the 65 per cent threshold of votes required in the Senate for assigning a seat in single-member constituencies. This threshold had de facto made the working of the plurality system impossible and opened the way to the application of the proportional method. The success of the referendum eliminated the PR system at least in the Senate, and forced the political class to provide a new electoral system, consistent with the demands for simplification and effectiveness which the referenda had manifestly showed (Katz 2003; D'Alimonte 2005).

The new rules for election to the two chambers were drafted in a hurry by a group of representatives of the majority, with the (more or less sincere) support of other political forces (namely the PDS) and under the control of a technocratic cabinet lead by the former central bank governor Carlo Azelio Ciampi. The discussion of the proposal (Katz 2003) was unusually short and the parliament, feeling the pressure of public opinion, adopted the new laws in the course of 1993 (Laws 277 and 278). According to the new rules (D'Alimonte 2005), in both chambers of parliament three-quarters of the seats were to be allocated from single-member districts by first-past-the-post, while the remaining 25 per cent was allocated following a PR principle. The technicalities of the allocation of the 'proportional seats' differed substantially between the lower chamber and the Senate (Box 3.1). Although this has not determined a too incoherent political composition of the two parliamentary branches during the three terms in which such systems have been at work, the traditional political symmetry of Italian bicameralism was slightly weakened.

BOX 3.1 Features of the mixed-plurality system adopted in 1993

For the Chamber of Deputies, each voter had two ballots: one for the vote for a candidate in the single-member constituency, and one for a list vote (with no preference) in a larger multi-member constituency. After the single-member district winners were determined on the first-past-the-post principle, the allocation of proportional seats took place. First, only party lists which reached a nationwide threshold of 4 per cent were admitted to the allocation of seats. Then, the votes the single-member district winners were required to win (i.e. one more than the number of votes received by the second-place candidates) had to be subtracted from the list totals of the parties supporting them (the *scorporo parziale*). On the basis of the figures obtained from these operations, the allocation of the proportional seats could be done at the multi-member constituency level (twenty-six constituencies with an average of six seats each).

For the Senate, there was only one vote. The single-member district seats were assigned in the same way as in the Chamber. As for the proportional seats they were in fact allocated to parties at the regional level on the basis of the vote totals of their candidates who were not elected to the single-member seats. Even here, for the calculation of the 'proportional weight' of a given party in a given region was used a system penalizing parties already receiving seats in the majoritarian competition, but this time the totality of the votes of single-member district winners was subtracted (*scorporo totale*). Not being based on a party list vote, this allocation did not consider any threshold at the national level.

Transforming the electoral environment: New styles of campaigning and the role of media

The redefinition of the electoral framework, as a consequence of the crisis of legitimacy of the political elites, was not limited to the electoral system alone but also involved other aspects of the electoral process. It can be argued that a traditional system of electoral competition, which had been somehow able to resist the innovations requested by new political actors and the evolution of technology and communication, was suddenly forced to accept these changes when the legitimacy of the most crucial actor of the old system—the political parties of the first republic—collapsed. An entirely new scenario was thus made possible.

Indeed, Italian parties had previously been a prototypical example of what some authors would call a 'stubborn persistence' in face of the innovations characterizing the campaigns' organization (Farrell and Webb 2000: 125). In 1992, for instance, the traditional volunteer-based system was still the 'normal' way of organizing the campaign. The persistence of the preference vote in elections to the lower chamber (the 1991 referendum had abolished only the multiple preference) left some room for new forms of decentralization of the campaign organization, but the rather centralized control on the recruitment system traditionally at work in Italy (Cotta 1979; Wertman 1988) was not in question. The low degree of personalization and the persistence of typical features such as the 'polarized multiparty system' (Sartori 1976) and the *conventio ad excludendum*, limiting the set of possible government coalitions to the central area of the political spectrum, meant a mix of predictability of post-electoral outcomes (in terms of coalition-building) and uncertainty about the future choice of the government leadership, which had to be left to the post-electoral phase (De Winter 1995). All these features made it almost impossible, for instance, for the instrument of the pre-electoral leaders' debate to be introduced in Italy. At the same time, there was no need to state particular rules about the use of television, other than the typical ad hoc regulation of the transmissions running during the few weeks before the vote.

However, when the traditional parties were drawn into the whirlpool of the moral crisis, and the electoral game had to be suddenly changed with the introduction of the mixed-plurality system, all the alternative modes of political competition could be employed by the bewildering array of new parties, 'anti-party' movements, and the individual political leaders populating the confused political landscape of the mid-1990s (see Chapter 2). The fact that, in the spring of 1994, a powerful TV tycoon and marketing tsar had taken the field was the quintessential sign of the space for innovation and creativity in Italian politics at that time.

Repeated attempts to give some order to this new situation came with the introduction of a set of new regulations concerning three major issues: the public financing of parties and parliamentary groups by electoral reimbursement; limits on the use of television and other media during the electoral campaign; and finally rules concerning ineligibility and incompatibility for political office. A new referendum had been successful in 1993 in abrogating the old 1974 law on public financing, and all parties—both those attached to the tradition and the new ones—were forced to replace the gap in their finances caused by this abrogation, adopting another law. The new system was mainly based on *ex-post* proportional electoral reimbursements and direct financing to the parliamentary group more than to the party organizations (Conti *et al.* 2007).

Concerning the use of media during electoral campaigns, after the first 'majoritarian' election had been held in a totally deregulated situation,[3] a number of proposals were discussed, until the decision was taken by the centre-left majority to issue a bill (Law 28/2000) strictly limiting the presence of politicians and opportunities for any form of political propaganda on TV during the campaigns. The principles of this law have divided the political spectrum for years, since Silvio Berlusconi has always defined these rules as 'liberticidal'. However, when he was in government, during the fourteenth legislature, even part of his coalition refused to revise these rules.

With regard to the third issue, the situation has been even more erratic, since the efforts of (some) centre-left politicians to regulate conflicts of interest when they were in government (1996–2001) were blocked by internal divergences and, to some extent, by simultaneous attempts to involve Berlusconi and his camp in a broader attempt to reform all the rules. We do not need to go into detail here on the regulation introduced by the Berlusconi government (Law 215/2004) and on the counter-argument of the centre-left, which always declared this law insufficient, useless, and manifestly 'servile' to the figure of the leader of the centre-right. We just stress that most of the problems related to the different conflicts of interests (of which Silvio Berlusconi concerns just an aspect, although the most complex) are still on the table (Hine 2004). In terms of new rules about accumulation of mandates and incompatibilities, the past fifteen years have brought only minor changes at the level of local government and an important achievement (the abolition of the dual mandate of member of the national parliament and member of the European

Parliament) resulted in any event from a decision by the supranational institution.

Patterns of voting behaviour in Italy: from the age of *partitocrazia* to the age of bipolarism

Voting behaviour in Italy after 1948: the structural trends

We have so far described the evolution of the electoral systems and the other rules of the electoral environment between the first republic and the long political transition following the crisis of the early 1990s. Before completing this story with the description of the 2005 electoral reform and the current electoral regime, we will briefly consider the other side of the coin, which is the evolution of the political demand side and the voting behaviour of the Italian electorate after 1945. In a sense, what we will discuss here is largely a consequence of what has already been analyzed in Chapter 2: the considerable penetration of national parties since the early years of democratization, which is the crucial phenomenon explaining the historical characteristics of voting behaviour in Italy, in particular, the high level of voters' loyalty and the predictability of their choices across the different forms of electoral competition.

Italian voters have usually reacted to all 'calls to the polls' with a very similar degree of political commitment. Average voter turnout across different types of elections is a rough estimate but there is significant evidence in this respect: with a diachronic evolution which very much resembles the series of legislative elections illustrated in Figure 3.1, both the rate of electoral participation and the percentage of valid votes were always quite high between 1951 and 1975, even if we take into consideration the series of provincial and municipal elections.

The political factors at the root of voters' expressions have also been stable over time: according to the oft-quoted analysis, three main types of voter–party relationships could be distinguished in Italy: the identity vote, the opinion vote, and the exchange vote (Parisi and Pasquino 1979). The first type is that of voters who feel themselves to be part of a particular party, even if they are not formally affiliated. Ideology plays a determining role in shaping such a political commitment, which tends to be loyal and continuous from one election to another. The second type, the opinion vote, is given after a more careful evaluation of the programmes and the quality of the political class. By definition, this vote tends to be more flexible and even volatile, but it will hardly reward the parties which are ideologically highly committed or based on patronage practice. Therefore, the flexibility of these voters either is limited to a set of (typically small) 'opinion parties', or can determine the alternation between active participation and abstention. Finally, the exchange vote is based on particularistic deals: patronage and clientelistic practices directly linking the representative to specific groups of voters and assuring the former of a pool of votes in exchange for his/her commitment to the interests of the latter.

The concrete application of this typology to the Italian vote during the period 1948–80 can be broadly summarized as follows: all three types of party–voter relations were quite well represented in the Italian scene, with the identity vote being crucial in determining the dominant orientations in the 'sub-cultural areas' of north-east and the centre (see below), the opinion vote crucial in determining minor but significant shifts in the urbanized areas, above all in the industrial triangle between Lombardy, Piedmont, and Liguria, and the exchange vote a typical feature in vast areas of the Italian south.

The persistence of this general pattern determined a high degree of predictability for all electoral events. In a sense, all elections other than parliamentary elections were second-order elections, since, whatever the nature of the vote, the main themes of national politics continued to dominate political debate. In particular, a set of general, symbolic, and systemic issues, such as the position of the country in the international community, feelings about European integration, attitudes on religion, and the defence of constitutional freedoms, played a dominant role in voters' concerns. As a result, Italian voting behaviour could never be dominated by local and 'bottom-up' forms of mobilization like the US public action committees, or suffer dramatically different patterns of voter participation and attitudes between national-legislative elections and 'secondary' ones (as for instance in the British case). The continental European variant of party government determined, among other things, the reproduction of the same pattern of competition. Accordingly, the composition of local and regional assemblies used to be very stable and dominated by the national parties, thus determining a quite structured system of political recruitment extending from the local level to the highest offices of the national institutional scene.

After 1992: the effects of the 'majoritarian' reform

The literature dedicated to the Italian case in the years following the political earthquake of 1992–94 (see for instance Gundle and Parker 1996) immediately stressed the importance of the various changes that occurred in the party strategies and the behaviour of the voters. We briefly analyze these changes starting with the mechanical effects of the electoral system used between 1994 and 2001, and moving on to the transformation of the main patterns of voting behaviour.

A first relevant effect of the mixed-plurality system is the centrality of coalition-making for winning the single-member seats. Since the capacity to build coalitions proved to be the key factor in the electoral game (Di Virgilio 2002), an evident learning process characterized the strategies of the players, although the solutions proposed by the two winning coalitions in 1994 and 1996—the double centre-right coalition with different cartels in the north and in the south, and the 'pact of desistance'[4] between the centre-left coalition and RC (see Chapter 2)—could surely not provide a solid basis for a stable government. Once the bipolar structure of the competition was consolidated (2001), the impact of the mixed-plurality system in terms of relevance to pre-electoral coalition-building was much more evident, and other indirect effects characterizing this system of competition were also emerging, including an accurate system of rating the candidates who better met the requirements of the different electoral markets, considering both the relative power of each actor within the coalition and also the overall potential of the coalition itself.[5]

Similarly, and partly as a result of the above effects, the majoritarian elections were characterized by the consolidation of a unified national campaign for each of the two coalitions, centred on the direct appeal of the leaders as candidates to the premiership. The accountability of the candidates to the leadership and the 'pre-electoral' phase of government formation was also progressively stressed (see Chapter 4), with the elaboration of a governmental programme for the whole coalition and the indication, already before the vote, of a number of possible names to be appointed and issues to be faced after the eventual electoral victory. All these elements should have thus represented the electoral face of a process of presidentialization (Calise 2005) having some similarity with other parliamentary democracies but also more than one specific Italian trait. On the other hand, one cannot say that mixed plurality has reduced the traditional fragmentation of the party system. In fact, as we have already seen in Chapter 2, fragmentation has increased, thanks to an effect of re-proportionalization among the actors within each coalition: small parties which had no chance to get seats in the proportional quota, could be generously compensated by having their own candidates in a number of safe seats (districts with very high probability of victory for their respective coalition). Of course, the extent of such compensation depended on the different blackmail potential of the smaller parties. This was particularly pronounced in the centre-right coalition, where the coalition leader's party, Forza Italia, was usually prepared to sacrifice some seats and a pivotal party territorially concentrated like the Northern League normally achieved an oversized quota of safe seats.

A natural consequence of this learning process in the supply side was the tendency of the voters to behave rationally and concentrate their consensus on the two largest coalitions: with the passing of time, the 1993 reform could therefore determine the basic condition for a logic of bipolar competition (see later, Figure 3.4). In fact, already in 1996 the space for a third coalition disappeared and only some parties with specific motivations decided to run alone (for example, the Lega in 1996, Communist Refoundation in 2001).

Other minor effects should be noted. Without doubt, the mixed-plurality system of 1993 determined a radical reduction in the number of candidates compared with the list system and the total abolition of individual preferences. Moreover, it introduced a rule of incompatibility between candidature for the Senate and for the Chamber. These innovations determined some precise constraints on the process of parliamentary selection. If one adds that the relevance of the personal profile of candidates in single-member districts could make the difference in a high number of uncertain constituencies, it is clear that the framework of political competition was significantly changed and party elites had to accept a new electoral regime which could somehow reduce their traditional omnipotence. This also explains the reforms of the financing of campaigns and the phenomenon of the personalization of the political competition.

However, several political variables have influenced the idea of strong innovation in the regulation of campaigns and political communication. The use of TV has been even more politically driven than in other countries, and the typical trend towards a permanent electoral campaign has been accompanied, in Italy, by a permanent fight about the legitimacy of the opponents.

Perhaps this peculiar situation in Italy has prevented the creation of ideal conditions for institutionalizing a new form of electoral competition, as recent events and the current uncertainty about the future rules of the games clearly show (see below). On the other hand, the experience of the 'majoritarian' electoral regime is not completely lost and, in general, this period seems to have brought some significant irreversible effects.

A controversial transformation

On the basis of what has been said above, it is clear that the constant rate of electoral participation and a high predictability of the vote distribution used to be the two main structural elements of voting behaviour in Italy until 1992. These elements have been challenged and somewhat reduced by events that have occurred in the past couple of decades, although they are far from being completely undone. To assess the effective magnitude of the recent change in the Italian patterns of voting behaviour, we can propose a diachronic analysis, centred on some simple measures of electoral volatility and electoral change. More precisely, we can look at the measures of total volatility—that is, the net change within the party system resulting from the sum of the differences in the percentages of votes achieved by a given party from one election to another—and the bloc volatility—a similar index which measures the transfer of votes from the left to the right wing of the party system (Table 3.2). Moreover, Table 3.2 provides two other measures that are correlated to the magnitude of electoral change: the overall performance of the historical parties (the protagonists of the constituent phase plus the neo-fascist party born in 1948) and parliamentary turnover, which can be the result of a striking electoral swing, of the emergence of totally new parties, but also of a significant generational change of leadership within the same old parties.

As more detailed analyses have already shown (Bardi 2006), both total volatility and bloc volatility suddenly increased with the elections of 1992

TABLE 3.2 **Measures of electoral change, elections to the lower chamber, 1953–2006**

	Total volatility	Bloc volatility	Electoral strength of historical parties	Parliamentary turnover
1953	13.3	8.7	90.3	35.9
1958	4.5	3.6	93.6	33.9
1963	7.9	6.6	97.0	34.6
1968	3.4	2.0	92.7	36.6
1972	4.9	3.8	96.0	32.5
1976	8.2	4.0	96.6	39.6
1979	5.3	2.6	92.5	26.6
1983	8.5	1.6	93.1	31.8
1987	8.4	1.3	89.9	31.3
1992	14.2	7.5	77.4	41.2
1994	36.2	8.9	58.5	66.8
1996	18.2	8.9	–	43.5
2001	22.0	2.6	–	41.9
2006	19.5	2.0	–	42.3

Source: Drawn from official electoral data (Italian Ministry of Interiors). The data on parliamentary turnover come from the CIRCaP parliamentary archive (University of Siena).

and reached a peak in 1994. After this total volatility has declined a little, but maintained until the end of the party system transition a much higher level than in the first republic. Bloc volatility, however, indicates in 2001 a stabilization of the two main electoral alternatives. Further interesting insights come from the long-term analysis of the total score of the so-called historical parties of the first republic, whose overall consensus had been relatively challenged during particular moments (the protest vote in 1968 and at the end of the 1970s), and then declined much more evidently between 1987 and 1992, before the collapse of the party system in 1994.

Once again the 'second republic' seems to start, from the point of view of electoral dynamics, with the 1992 election, when both the so-called *area di govern*, 'governmental area', or parties deemed acceptable in coalition, and the two post-communist parties lost a significant portion of voters after a long period of stability.

It can be said then that the proportional election of 1992, although still characterized by significant elements of continuity with the past, brought also some relevant elements of change, anticipating the 'earthquake' of 1994. The indicators used here clearly show that a return to a more moderate degree of electoral change could be reached only in the two most recent parliamentary elections (2001 and 2006), when the party system and (above all) the coalition dynamics have proved to be to a large extent consolidated.

Differences across types of electoral competition

Another historical element of the general pattern of voting behaviour in Italy, to be re-evaluated after the recent phase of political turmoil, is the presence of minor but not insignificant deviations in the ways in which Italian voters have approached the polls, according to the type of representative office which is at stake. It must be clear that this does not contradict the general trend of high participation in all the elections, cited above. However, the rate of popular participation has been somewhat higher at the national level. This is not very surprising, given the nature of 'civic duty' that the constitution ascribes to the vote for legislative elections. However, the gap between national elections and other types of political competition, in particular the European vote, which has always been perceived as a secondary event, has become more and more evident over the years: the popular participation at the European elections has indeed declined much more evidently than has been the case for legislative and local elections. Already in 1989 the turnout for the former was only 82 per cent and in 1994 it decreased to 75 per cent. A rate even lower than that characterized the 1999 and 2004 European elections in Italy.

A second relevant issue has to be discussed in connection with European elections: the differentiated electoral behaviour observed in the results of the European elections, in comparison with other electoral trends, between 1979 and 2004. More precisely, the European vote has always favoured the challengers of the big parties (like the Socialists in the 1980s), the small parties in search of an 'opinion vote' and, in some cases, protest and occasional lists. One can link this phenomenon to the structural explanations provided by the comparative literature: the second order nature of the European competition would lead some voters to use these 'mid-term elections' to give qualified support to parties to which they could be considered 'close', but for which they would not normally vote in the legislative elections when the going gets tough and ideological orientations prevail. At the same time, voters have also perceived the European elections simply as a less important event. This would determine a systemic increase of abstention impacting on 'normal' attitudes and, consequently, an automatic increase in the relative success of other challengers.

The combination of all these elements creates (not only in Italy) an opportunity for opposition and protest parties, which can use these factors in order to gain a good electoral result, visibility in the media, electoral reimbursement, and, last but not least, representatives in the European Parliament.[6] This 'deviant' orientation of the European vote has become more evident with the passing of time. In other words, the European elections have been used by a consistent portion of the electorate to send messages to a decreasingly trusted national political elite. The case of the success of the environmentalist candidates in 1989 and 1994 was commented upon as a new phenomenon, although it was in line with a supranational trend. Later, the largest national parties have continued to lose votes in European elections, demonstrating a rather specific attitude on the part of Italian voters. The extraordinary success of the Radical list in 1999,[7] with a shift from about 2 per cent to more than 8 per cent, was the most evident example of such a phenomenon.

Another element which emerges, when comparing different series of elections, is the better performance achieved by the left parties, and in particular by the Communist Party, during the 1950–90 period in local elections. This of course has much to do with the strong organizational structure of the mass parties, which can more easily mobilize voters, present their programmes and their candidates over the whole territory and within their own party venues, and also count on more reliable and committed candidates. One should remember here that, more than any other party, the PCI used to 'pre-structure' the ordering of the candidates, guiding heavily the preferences of the voters (which could be expressed until 1990 in all the most relevant elections), and therefore had closer control over political recruitment at all the institutional levels than other parties. Such differentiated voting behaviour between the left and the right wings of the political spectrum has partly survived the crisis of the first republic. Between 1995 and 2006, the centre-left candidates and lists performed, on the whole, much better at the municipal/provincial level in comparison with the regional and national vote. Forza Italia, in particular, seems the greatest victim of such a deviation in voter's behaviour, while the other parties of the centre-right coalition do not suffer the same risk owing to their better territorial organization.

Voting behaviour and 'political cultures': persisting differences within more blurred borders

We have mentioned already the relevance of the territorial variable in structuring the voting behaviour of the geographically and socially fragmented Italian polity. It is time now to describe more precisely, although in brief, the long-term trend of the territorial differences of the Italian vote during the republican age. Figure 3.2 provides a rough illustration of such a distribution during the age of 'partycracy'. An ecological analysis conducted at a more disaggregated territorial level (Diamanti 2003) would, of course, be more precise. However, in this description, focusing on the issue of the institutional transformation of a whole political system, it is most important to show the evidence that, for a quite considerable time, the areas of the 'white' and the 'red belt' remained unchanged, assuring to their respective dominant parties a significant relative majority. The map identifies the red belt as the four regions of the centre,[8] and the white belt as the region of the Triveneto (Friuli-Venezia Giulia, Trentino-Alto Adige, and Veneto), the province of Cuneo in Piedmont, and the eastern part of Lombardy including the area around Milan (the Brianza). The rest of the Lombard region is in fact a grey area between the white belt and the area where the opinion vote is stronger (an area which can be extended to a large part of Piedmont and Liguria). Another deeply urbanized grey area is represented by Rome and its environs, whose electorate was traditionally more orientated to the left in town but moderate in the periphery. Finally, all the regions of the *mezzogiorno* were also characterized by a relative degree of electoral uncertainty, which was, however, more the result of specific flows of individual consensus than the effect of a close electoral contest. The island of Sardinia probably represented a significant exception at the macro-level, with a clear distinction between a

FIGURE 3.2 **Sub-cultural vote areas in Italy, 1948–90**

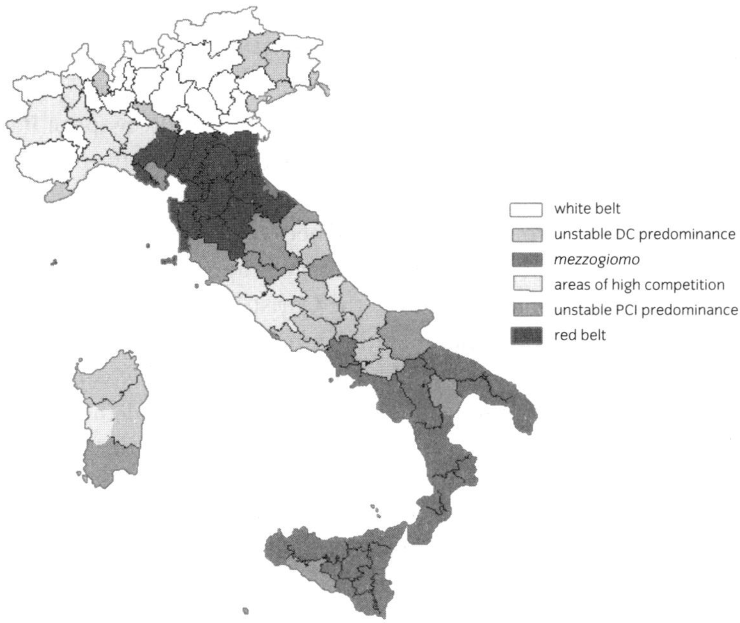

Source: Adapted from Diamanti (2003).

'red' area around Cagliari and a moderate pro-DC vote in the rest of the region.

Why, and to what extent, is this territorial diversification still relevant? Since the late 1960s, many detailed studies have stressed the importance of the cultural and territorial cleavage in explaining long-term electoral performance in Italy (Galli 1968; Cartocci 1985). Historians and sociologists, as well as some political scientists, have argued that the continuity of a clear pattern of dominance by the different party orientations in a number of territorial areas has a precise and solid cultural origin, overlapping with the territorial distribution of economic development and social capital that occurred during the second half of the twentieth century (Bagnasco 1977). Moreover, as this different distribution roughly corresponds to administrative divisions, and most of the provinces and some regions have a fairly homogeneous political colour, these sub-cultural differences have had a durable impact on the political composition of the local governments (see Chapter 6).

The relationship between territory and political behaviour is of course still an important issue today, after the emergence of the 'Northern question' and a long phase of debate on federal reform. However, the maps of Italian territorial politics seem to have significantly changed during the past fifteen years. Some scholars have in fact spoken of the dissolution of the white belt (Diamanti 2003), which is now divided between a cluster of small 'green' areas (the enclaves of militant Northern League supporters) and the urban centres where Forza Italia has received the Christian Democratic legacy.

At the same time, Forza Italia—a rather innovative model of a party with votes but no territory—has been able to gain a quite stable consensus in several 'neutral' areas, becoming the leading party in almost all the provinces outside of the red belt. However, the other two parties of the centre-right coalition have a good and stable performance in some southern areas. Namely, the National Alliance is relatively strong in Puglia, Campania, and Calabria, while the post-Christian Democratic UDC has a large consensus in Sicily and in other small provincial areas.

As regards the red belt, the legacy of the old PCI has of course been taken mainly by the DS and the party of the Communist Refoundation, with the four central regions still dominated by a high concentration of ideological and loyal-identifier support. However, the other parties of the centre-left coalition, in addition to consistent support from the traditional areas of the 'opinion vote', can also achieve a predictable quota of votes from this geographical area because of the partial erosion of 'sub-cultural' orientation of the centre-left supporters.

Overall, the political map of the second republic (Figure 3.3) looks much more complex and the borders separating the different areas are more blurred and mobile than in the past. Nevertheless, the historical subcultural explanation of the different territorial patterns of vote distribution is still a robust argument in the overall interpretation of the Italian vote, and the territorial context remains a fundamental element of the analysis of that vote, together with the 'new' phenomena which have emerged in recent years, from the electoral personalization of politics to the impact of a marketing-oriented campaign style.

FIGURE 3.3 **Political map of the second republic**

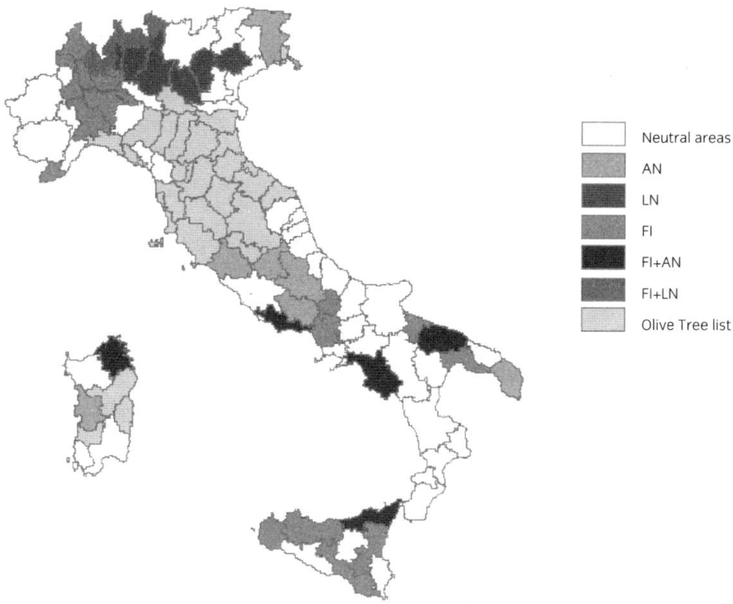

Source: LaPolis, University of Urbino.
Note: The map has been drawn on the basis of the result of the 2006 election (provincial level). In order to establish a party dominance in each province two criteria have been considered: (1) the province is included in the 25 per cent of provinces where the party (indicated by the shading) performed better; (2) in this province the coalition including that party won.

The return of PR within a bipolar environment: the 2005 reform and the 2006 election

The electoral system approved on 14 December 2005 (Box 3.2) is based on proportional representation with large regional constituencies in both chambers[9] and a blocked list vote. A series of thresholds has been introduced in order to encourage parties to form coalitions, but without forcing them to renounce their own lists and symbols. The threshold for a party which runs alone, with no links to any majoritarian 'cartel', is quite challenging

BOX 3.2 Features of the electoral system approved in 2005

The PR list system has been reintroduced for the election of all deputies (630) and elective senators (315) (Law 270, 21 December 2005).

For the lower chamber, the country is divided into twenty-six multi-member constituencies, plus one single-member constituency (Aosta Valley) and one constituency representing Italians abroad (with candidates from four broad geographical areas). Overall, the average size of the constituencies is of 22.5 seats.

The vote is expressed on the basis of a blocked list system. No preference vote is admitted. No limits are provided for the candidature of the same person in several constituencies.

The allocation of the seats is made proportionally among the lists which have exceeded the thresholds fixed by law: a threshold of 10 per cent of valid votes for the coalitions, a threshold of 2 per cent nationwide for each party included in a coalition, and a threshold of 4 per cent nationwide for those parties which run alone. For regional parties representing ethno-linguistic minorities running only locally, the threshold is 20 per cent of the vote in a given constituency.

The coalition which gains the highest number of votes, if it has not reached 340 seats on the basis of the proportional allocation, receives a majority bonus which will bring its seats to 340. The residual 277 seats from the multi-member constituencies will be allocated to the other lists on the basis of the method of the largest remainders.

Concerning the election of senators, the constituencies coincide with the twenty Italian regions, thus meeting the constitutional principle stating that the Senate is to be elected 'on a regional basis'. However, the number of senators for each region is proportional to the size of the population and the allocation of seats also follows a proportional rule, with the exception of two regions: Aosta Valley, where only one seat is to be allocated, and Trentino-Alto Adige, which is divided into six single-member districts. If one considers also the six seats to be allocated in the constituency for the Italians abroad (with candidates from four geographical areas) the overall size of constituencies is 12.1 seats.

The electoral system for the Senate prescribes similar thresholds to those for the lower chamber. However, no threshold at the regional level has been provided for ethno-linguistic minority parties.

A majority bonus is also provided but it is not designed to assure a majority of all the seats for the coalition receiving the most votes nationwide. Indeed, the bonus is allocated on a regional basis to assure to the coalition winning the most votes in each single region a regional majority of 55 per cent of seats. The allocation of seats follows the method of the largest remainders.

(4 per cent of the valid vote nationwide). On the contrary, only 2 per cent of the valid vote is enough for those parties which are linked to other lists in a cartel. These cartels are also important because they can run for a majority

bonus assuring them a minimum of 55 per cent of the seats. However, the majority bonus for the lower chamber is a unique 'prize' of seats allocated at the national level, while in the Senate the bonuses are assigned on a regional basis. In other words, in each region the largest coalition automatically gains a majority of 55 per cent of the senators, except when this limit has been reached by the 'natural' proportional allocation.

The simplest of electoral systems (pure PR) thus became an intricate game of rules about the allocation of seats, rules about the threshold of representation, and rules about the links between parties within each cartel. The new law also requires each party joining a coalition to 'subscribe to a common electoral programme' and 'indicate the leader of the coalition', thus marrying these two features typically found in other systems where the pre-electoral phase of government formation is very important (but not normally regulated by law), with a method of seat allocation which does not prevent political fragmentation and post-election bargaining.

Such a tricky and complex set of rules reflects, in the end, the very reason behind this electoral system: a deliberate design developed by the centre-right government (during a phase of declining popularity) to create obstacles to success for the centre-left coalition in the lower chamber and, above all, to create the conditions for a tie (if not a different majority) in the Senate. PR was indeed the best solution for the centre-right parties, whose overall performance in the majoritarian vote had always been poorer than the sum of the votes for their lists in the old proportional ballot. Moreover, the reform could solve some distributive problems within a coalition which, in its broader version (including the party of Silvio Berlusconi, Alleanza Nazionale, the moderate Christian Democratic party, a difficult party like the Lega, and also some minor formations of the extreme right), proved to be much more litigious than in the past. Finally, the reform aimed at weakening the position of the centre-left leader, Romano Prodi, whose peculiar status of 'leader without party' could be somehow endangered by the return of a competition between lists.

On the other hand, it is reasonable to suggest that the largest parties of the opposition (which won the majority in the 2006 election) were in the end not so unhappy at the fact that such a system would allow them, after ten years of extenuating negotiations and 'stand-down pacts', to decide the candidates in many single-member districts, to select them with no interference from their coalition allies, permitting them to offer good positions on the party list (and therefore a high chance of re-election) to all the incumbent parliamentarians, and, more importantly, to their national leadership, even when the candidature of persons with stronger roots in civil society would be more suitable for voters. It can be said then (Pasquino 2007) that, if the centre-right parties had agreed (although with different motivations) to change the mixed-plurality system for very partisan and conjunctural reasons, even some important actors of the centre-left could see in the end some benefit in the reform. This also means that any revision of the new system, even though clearly announced by Prodi and his majority during the 2006 campaign and included in the governmental programme of the centre-left, will not be without cost.

The quasi-draw of the 2006 election

The general election of April 2006 led to an incredibly close result: the final victory of the centre-left coalition led by Romano Prodi was decided in the lower chamber by a majority of only 24,000 voters nationwide (Table 3.3).[10] In the Senate, the slim majority of two senators was even more incredible: in fact, the centre-right had a higher overall number of votes (see Table 3.4) and only the good result in the constituency for Italians abroad allowed the centre-left to gain such a slim advantage in terms of seats. Given the regional nature of the bonuses, the crucial difference was ensured in the end by a number of votes even lower than that in the lower chamber: only 14,000 votes ensured the Unione an advantage of four senators in Campania and the majority in the Senate. On the other hand, the two important regions of Lazio and Piedmont, which had been conquered by the centre-left just one year before at the regional elections, gave a regional bonus to the centre-right for just a few thousands votes (Table 3.5).

Was this a real victory for Romano Prodi and his coalition, despite the attempt of the centre-right and in particular of Silvio Berlusconi to question the validity of the victory (because of a number of contested ballots) and to delay the change of power? Or was it, perhaps, a half-victory of the same Berlusconi, owing to his unquestionable recovery during the last weeks of the electoral campaign? Had the centre-right made a mistake in changing the rules of the game?

TABLE 3.3 Election results, Chamber of Deputies, 2006

Lists	Italy (excluding Aosta Valley) (majority bonus) % votes	seats	Aosta Valley seats	Italians abroad seats	Total seats
Olive Tree List (DS + DL)	31.3	220			220
Communist Refoundation (RC)	5.8	41			41
Rose in the Fist (RnP)	2.6	18			18
Party of Italian Communists (PdCI)	2.3	16			16
Italy of Values (IdV)	2.3	16		1	17
Greens	2.1	15			15
Unions of Democrats for Europe (UDEUR)	1.4	10			10
L'Unione-Prodi (Italians abroad)				6	6
Alliance for Aosta Valley			1		1
Other centre-left lists	2.0	4			4
Total: The Union	49.8	340			348
	(19,001,684 votes)				
Forza Italia (FI)	23.7	137		3	140
National Alliance (AN)	12.3	71			71
Union of Centrist Christian Democrats (UDC)	6.8	39			39
Northern League (LN) + Movement for Autonomy (MPA)	4.0	26			26
New Christian Democracy (DC) + New Socialist Party (NPSI)	0.7	4			4
Social Alternative (AS)	0.7	0			
Social Movement Tricolour Flame (MSI-FT)	0.6	0			
Others centre-right lists	0.3	0			
Italy in the World (Italians abroad)				1	1
Total: House of Freedoms	49.7	277			281
	(18,976,460 votes)				
Other lists (outside the two largest coalitions)	0.5	0		1	1
	(173,263 votes)				
Total	38,151,407 votes	617	1	12	630

Note: For a detailed description of party acronyms and names, see Table 2.2.
Source: Ministry of the Interior.

TABLE 3.4 **Election results, Senate, 2006**

Lists	Italy % votes	Italy seats	Italians abroad seats	Total seats
Democratic Left (DS)	17.5	62		
Daisy (DL)	10.7	39		
Communist Refoundation (RC)	7.4	27		
Party of Italian Communists (PdCI) + Greens	4.2	11		
Italy of Values (IdV)	2.9	4		
Rose in the Fist (RnP)	2.5	0		
Union of Democrats for Europe (UDEUR)	1.4	3		
L'Unione-Prodi (Italians abroad)			4	
Other: centre-left lists	2.4	8		
Total: The Union	49.0 (16,725,077 votes)	154	4	158
Forza Italia (FI)	24.0	78	1	
National Alliance (AN)	12.4	41		
Union of Centrist Christian Democrats (UDC)	6.8	21		
Northern League (LN) + Movement for Autonomy (MPA)	4.5	13		
Social Movement Tricolour Flame (MSI-FT)	0.6	0		
Social alternative (AS)	0.6	0		
New Christian Democracy (DC) + New Socialist Party (NPSI)	0.6	2		
Other centre-right lists	0.7	0		
Italy in the World (Italians abroad)				
Total: House of Freedoms	50.2 (17,153,256 votes)	155	1	156
Other lists (outside the two largest coalitions)	0.8 (283,271 votes)	0	1	1
Total	34,161,604 votes	309	6	315

Note: For a detailed description of party acronyms and names, see Table 2.2.
Source: Ministry of the Interior.

TABLE 3.5 **Election results by regions and coalitions, Senate, 2006**

	Votes			Seats		
	The Union	House of Freedoms	Others	The Union	House of Freedoms	Others
Piedmont	49.5	50.5	0.0	9	13	0
Aosta Valley	45.6	22.4	32.0	1	0	0
Lombardy	42.6	56.9	0.4	20	27	0
Trentino-Alto Adige	62.7	33.1	4.2	5	2	0
Veneto	39.5	57.1	3.4	10	14	0
Friuli-Venezia Giulia	44.4	54.8	0.7	3	4	0
Liguria	53.3	46.7	0.0	5	3	0
Emilia-Romagna	59.4	40.6	0.0	12	9	0
Tuscany	61.3	38.7	0.0	11	7	0
Umbria	57.2	42.8	0.0	4	3	0
Marche	54.4	45.6	0.0	5	3	0
Lazio	49.1	50.2	0.6	12	15	0
Abruzzo	53.2	46.8	0.0	4	3	0
Molise	50.5	49.5	0.0	1	1	0
Campania	49.6	49.1	1.3	17	13	0
Puglia	47.9	51.9	0.2	9	12	0
Basilicata	60.4	39.2	0.5	4	3	0
Calabria	56.8	42.6	0.7	6	4	0
Sicily	40.5	57.8	1.7	11	15	0
Sardinia	50.9	45.3	3.8	5	4	0
Foreign constituency	48.5	37.8	13.7	4	1	1
Total	49.2	49.6	1.3	158	156	1

Source: Ministry of the Interior.

It is difficult to give an answer to these questions. What can certainly be said is that the 2006 election has resulted in a curious and uncertain situation. Overall, the measures of electoral volatility (see Table 3.2) have returned to very low rates and the bipolar system has been confirmed and even strengthened by the vote: only 0.5 per cent of the valid votes supported lists not included in the two main coalitions and, for the first time since 1994, the two parliamentary branches are entirely composed of representatives from these two coalitions, with just one exception (a senator elected in the constituency of the Italians abroad). Figure 3.4 shows the path towards a 'perfect' bipolarism, whose last step has been helped by the majority bonuses included in the 2005 proportional reform. In fact, many minor lists that had run alone since 1996 could be incorporated into two extremely inclusive electoral coalitions, in some cases with the help of some tricky compromises.[11]

Another paradoxical outcome of the 2006 election concerns the degree of fragmentation and its impact in terms of decisiveness of the vote: the proportional effects of the new electoral rules were surely high but not

FIGURE 3.4 **Measures of bipolarism: elections to the lower chamber, 1994–2006**

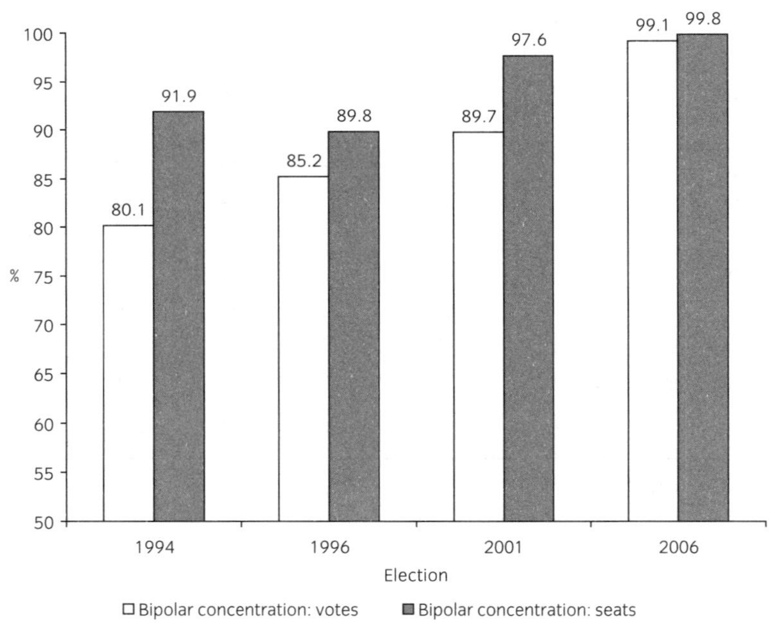

Source: Chiaramonte (2007).

higher than in the past. Actually, all the measures of fragmentation are stable or even lower than under the mixed-plurality system (Di Virgilio 2006). However, the vote has given the advantage to the more fragmented of the two coalitions, determining the formation of what promises to be a very conflictual executive (see Chapter 5). On the other hand, the electoral and political weight of Forza Italia seems quite diminished, although its parliamentary presence is unaltered, as Berlusconi's party, which under the previous system had to grant a number of safe single-member districts to its allies in order to increase its coalition potential, under the new system could keep them all for its candidates.

All in all, if the political demand seems to be rather stable and, on the other hand, the electoral supply and the parties'/coalitions' strategies seem to explain the vote transformation, with no broad changes in terms of volatility and mobility of the electorate, it seems then that, as in Tomasi di Lampedusa's novel *Gattopardo*, 'everything must change, in order that it might remain the same'.

Conclusion

At the end of a convulsive period of change, the Italian electoral regime has encouraged a bipolar electoral pattern, whereby a fragmented party system seems to be permanently 'in the making' but, in fact, is quite consolidated as regards its most relevant actors, resulting in a high rate of predictability in general elections. Of course, some critical elements of change can be expected in the near future, but it is difficult to give a complete outlook on the current prospects, or to clarify the logic and likely order of possible events. New electoral reforms, for instance, are simply difficult because of the weakness of the centre-left majority, but also because of the different interests of big and small parties coexisting in both alliances. Therefore, the conditions for a more comprehensive reform of all the rules of the electoral game, that would be accepted also by the opposition, are difficult to find.

At least three relevant developments have been announced. On the level of the electoral rules the centre-left stated officially in its programme that the PR introduced in 2005 would be abrogated. Also, several innovations concerning election-related matters—conflicts of interests, use of communication, political campaigning, and public financing—are still under discussion, with a quite broad set of different voices in both the coalitions. Finally, the two coalition leaders, Prodi and Berlusconi, have repeatedly announced their intention to form a unitary political force in their respective camps, with each of them gaining some important support but also criticism and internal opposition.

All these possible developments are therefore seriously constrained by the limited room of manoeuvre of the respective parties. But it is also true that the parties are still perceived as 'natural' destinations by a large majority of the voters. Moreover, the possibility of further change should have an impact on the other critical expectation represented by the creation of an actual 'bipartism', that it should lead to a decisive simplification of the future party system.

KEY TERMS

- bipolarization
- coalition-building
- electoral participation/turnout
- electoral volatility
- mixed-plurality electoral system
- proportional representation
- sub-cultural areas
- types of voter
- voting behaviour

GUIDE TO FURTHER READING

D'ALIMONTE, R., (2005), 'Italy: A Case of Fragmented Bipolarism', in M. GALLAGHER and P. MITCHELL (eds.), *The Politics of Electoral Systems* (Oxford, Oxford University Press), 253–76.

A well-documented account of the electoral regime in Italy, before the 2005 reform.

D'ALIMONTE R., and BARTOLINI, S. (2002) (eds.) *Maggioritario finalmente. La transizione elettorale in Italia. 1994–2001* (Bologna, Il Mulino).

CHIARAMONTE, A., and D'ALIMONTE, R. (2007) (eds.), *Proporzionale e non solo* (Bologna, Il Mulino).

Two more comprehensive books, in Italian, on recent transformations of the Italian electoral landscape.

Itanes (2006) *Dove è la vittoria? Il voto del 2006 raccontato dagli italiani* (Bologna, Il Mulino).

A comprehensive analysis of the 2006 election led by the specialists of the *Italian Election Studies* research team.

KATZ, R. S. (2003) 'Reforming the Italian Electoral Law, 1993', in M. S. SHUGART and M. P. WATTENBERG (eds.), *Mixed-Member Electoral Systems—The Best of Both Worlds?* (Oxford, Oxford University Press), 96-122.

This chapter by Richard Katz considers the 1993 reform of the electoral system for the election of the Italian legislature in a broader comparative framework.

NEWELL, J. (ed.) (2002a) *The Italian General Election of 2001: Berlusconi's Victory* (Manchester, Manchester University Press)

NEWELL, J. (ed.), (2007), *The Italian General Election of 2006* (Manchester, Manchester University Press).

Two excellent books focusing on recent Italian elections.

NOTES

1 In determining this outcome, the shift of about 250,000 votes from the centre-left governmental parties to new opposition parties, born as a result of a number of conflicts (in the Liberal party, in the Social Democratic party, and above all in the Republican party) over the adoption of the *legge truffa*, was crucial.

2 The activism of the Radicals had already led, in 1978, to a first abrogative referendum on the issue of public party financing: 33.5 million voted (roughly 81 per cent of the total electorate); among them, a significant minority of 43 per cent voted 'yes' to the abolition of the law, thus expressing a political opinion against the view of all the traditional parties represented in parliament.

3 At the end of 1993, a new law (Law 515) had adapted the regulation of the electoral campaign to the environment of the new electoral system, and had forbidden the publication of electoral surveys in the fifteen days before the day of the vote. However, all the substantive problems concerning the regulation of polls and access to TV and other forms of political communication had been ignored.

4 The desistance pact in 1996 avoided competition between the candidates of the centre-left Ulivo coalition and those of the neo-communist party (RC) in single-member districts. RC invited its voters to support the candidates of the Ulivo, while about forty safe seats were reserved for candidates of RC (in these cases there were no official candidates from the Ulivo).

5 Typically this phase of candidate selection resulted, in both the coalitions, in the inclination to select, in the single-member districts for the lower chamber and the Senate of the same areas, two candidates from different parties, as a way to incentivize the participation of all the possible supporters.

6 As is well known, the PR system adopted for the election of the Italian members of the European Parliament is applied only to five large constituencies and with no threshold of representation, thus allowing even a list with a very limited consensus to elect at least one representative.

7 On that occasion the Radical Party decided to name its list *Lista Bonino*, to stress the continuity between the support for the list and the operations of the former Commissioner Emma Bonino (one of the leading figures of the party).

8 In the accurate study by Cartocci (1985), the south of Marche and other small peripheral areas of Tuscany (i.e. Lucca) or northern Emilia-Romagna (Piacenza) were more difficult to label. Indeed, these provinces experienced some political shifts during the 1990s, when the subcultural vote was further reduced.

9 Actually the number of proportional multi-member constituencies has not changed. In 2006 therefore there were twenty-six constituencies for the election of the lower chamber, and twenty regional constituencies for the election of the Senate. However, a significant change has been determined by the approval, in the course of the fourteenth Legislature, of the constitutional law concerning the vote of Italians abroad, whose implementation has determined the birth of a new constituency and the consequent reduction of the seats reserved for the national constituencies. The seats included in the constituency of the Italians abroad are, respectively, twelve in the Chamber of Deputies and six in the Senate.

10 This is the difference in the twenty-six constituencies that determined the majority bonus. If one considers also the vote in the Aosta Valley and within the constituency for the Italians abroad, the difference between the Union and the House of Freedoms was about 130,000 votes.

11 Small parties with no chances to reach the threshold could join one of the major coalitions having as a counter-benefit the 'free election' of their most important leaders, who were hosted in a good position in the lists of one of the largest party of the same coalition. For the details of these strategies see Chiaramonte (2007).

4

The Executive: A Long Tradition of Weak and Unstable Governments Comes to an End?

Overview

Not only after the Second World War, but also during the first decades of the twentieth century, the role of the executive has been seen as one of the major problem areas of the Italian political system. The instability of cabinets, the weakness of prime ministers, the lack of coordination between ministers and ministries, the propensity to delay important decisions, the lack of cohesion of the governmental majority in parliament: all these points have been recurrently underlined by scholars and politicians when evaluating the performances of the executive. Regarding the causes, observers have directed their attention either to the original institutional design or to the features of the party system.

Proposals to reform this institution and concrete attempts to change some of its perceived weaknesses have received greater attention with the passing of time, as this has been increasingly seen as a serious problem for the satisfactory working of Italian democracy. In the 1980s some significant organizational changes took place and in the 1990s, with the deep transformation of the party system, the political bases of the executive have undergone a major reshaping. In this chapter we will demonstrate the original institutional design, how this has interacted with the changing political conditions, and the transformations that have taken place in recent years.

The original institutional design

Only with the second Italian constitution, that of 1948, did the institution of government receive detailed regulation. In the previous constitution, the Piedmontese *Statuto Albertino* of 1848, the cabinet was not clearly mentioned, as the text still reflected the model of constitutional monarchy. The cabinet, a typical product of the parliamentary form of government, came into existence as a de facto result of the new political situation and of the new constellation of political forces triggered by the implementation of the *Statuto*, rather than as a clear and direct *de jure* consequence of this constitution granted by the king (Merlini 1995).[1] As in many other European countries, the practice of parliamentary government developed in Italy within a constitutional framework that had been conceived with another model of political regime in mind.

The Constituent Assembly of 1946 attempted to define with greater stringency the position of the executive vis-à-vis the other central political institutions in order to prevent the great swings it had experienced under the *Statuto Albertino*.[2] Yet the attempt to prescribe through the constitutional text the position and functioning of the government within the political system and to predetermine its relative strength (or weakness) was achieved only in part. Reality to a significant extent followed its own course. There are two major explanations for why this happened. First, as is often the case, the Italian constitution makers were haunted by past experiences and preoccupations, but could not clearly foresee the problems of the future. In particular they could not foresee the impact that the new party system would have upon the structure and functioning of the central democratic institutions they had devised. Second, on this, as on most crucial points, a compromise had to be found between widely different constitutional models shared by the parties represented in the Constituent Assembly. This inevitably led to formulations of the constitutional text that were not very cogent.

In a democratic polity, in order for the nature and role of government to be defined, a number of questions have to be answered. We will see what answers the Italian constitution has provided and to what extent the practice of political life has followed the guidelines provided by them.

The first questions to be answered concern the relationship between the head of state and the head of government, the political legitimation of government itself, and the process through which government is formed. The second group of questions have to do with the internal structure of the governmental institution, and in particular the relationship between the individual components (the ministers) and the government as a collective unit, as well as the relationship between the Prime Minister and the other ministers (the degree to which hierarchy prevails over equality in status or vice versa). The third group of questions concerns the role of the government in the policy-making process and particularly its relations with parliament in the law-making process.

Most of the answers the constitution of 1948 offered to these questions were somewhat ambiguous and vague. The constitution, being the result of a compromise between conflicting constitutional projects, rather than a clear-cut solution, provided middle-of the-road arrangements open to different interpretations (Merlini 1995).

The head of state

As regards head of state, the choice was not too difficult. A majority of the population having decided in the referendum of 1946 for a republic and against the monarchy, the constitution provided for the head of state to be elected by parliament (Table 4.1). The proposal of an American-style, directly elected, presidency received only limited support in the constitutional debate. The Italian institutional tradition was a parliamentary one, and the legal and political culture was much more imbued with continental rather than American influences. Moreover, after twenty years under the Duce, a directly elected chief of the executive was seen by most parties as too risky a solution and discarded without too many discussions.

The President of the Republic was defined as the symbol of national unity and, in profile, preferably a non-partisan umpire. The president is, therefore, elected by secret vote in a joint session of the two parliamentary chambers to which three representatives for each regional council (but only one for the small Aosta Valley) have been added. A majority of two-thirds of the members is required for the first three votes, after which an absolute majority is sufficient. The length of the mandate—seven years—was conceived in order to avoid, as a rule, the coincidence between parliamentary elections and presidential vote.

TABLE 4.1 Presidential elections 1948–2006

President	Date of election	Number of ballots	Number (and percentage) of votes in the final ballot
Luigi Einaudi	11 May 1948	4	451 (51.7)
Giovanni Gronchi	29 April 1955	4	658 (78.9)
Antonio Segni	6 May 1962	9	443 (52.6)
Giuseppe Saragat	28 December 1964	21	646 (68.9)
Giovanni Leone	24 December 1971	23	518 (52.6)
Alessandro Pertini	8 July 1978	16	832 (83.6)
Francesco Cossiga	24 June 1985	1	752 (76.8)
Oscar Luigi Scalfaro	25 May 1992	16	672 (67.0)
Carlo Azelio Ciampi	13 May 1999	1	707 (71.4)
Giorgio Napoletano	10 May 2006	4	543 (54.3)

Source: Archives of the Chamber of Deputies.

The powers allocated to the president (Article 87 of the constitution) put him or her in the position to play a crucial role in ensuring the regular working of democratic institutions and respect of the constitution. In this perspective particularly relevant are the powers to:

- nominate the head of the government and the ministers,
- dissolve the parliament,
- call elections,
- authorize the presentation by the government of bills to parliament,
- send back bills to parliament for a new approval,
- promulgate laws,
- send messages to parliament,
- nominate one-third of the members of the Constitutional Court, and
- chair the Supreme Council of the Judiciary.

With regard to the government, the President of the Republic is assigned the role of guiding and assisting its formation through the power to nominate the new prime minister and, on the proposal of the latter, the other ministers. It is also to the president that the Prime Minister will communicate any decision to resign. The president also has powers designed to enable the exercise of some control over the legislative activities of the government and of the parliament, as he or she authorizes the presentation of bills by the cabinet to parliament and, with a written motivation, can send back to the parliament for further deliberation a bill that has been approved by the two chambers.

The role of 'protector of the constitution' is also shown by the president's power to nominate some members of the Constitutional Court and to chair the Supreme Council of the Judiciary (see Chapter 8).

The government

With regard to the government the constitution has stated that it must enjoy the explicit support of parliament (Article 94). Therefore, once the cabinet has been nominated and sworn in by the head of state, it will have to obtain a collective confidence vote from each of the two chambers of parliament (with an open nominal vote). Equally the cabinet will have to resign in the event of a no-confidence vote by either of the two chambers. As a rule the government must, therefore, command a majority in both chambers. These provisions point in the direction of a strong dependence of government on parliament (or more exactly on a parliamentary majority) and leave little space for experiments in minority government.

In order to balance the power of parliament and to reduce governmental instability, the constitution has introduced some limitations to the presentation and discussion of motions of no confidence: they must be signed by at least one-tenth of the members of a chamber and, after they are tabled, three days must elapse before they are put to a vote (Article 94). This provision, however, has proved of little effect in preventing governmental instability. This article assumed that government instability would arise from the unpredictable behaviour of individual parliamentarians and tried to reduce its effects. After the Second World War, however, instability had its origins in the behaviour of organized parties and party factions, against which such constitutional rules could do very little. As we will see governments have tended to resign as soon as the coalition agreement has broken down and without waiting for a parliamentary vote of no confidence.

As for the internal structure of government, the constitution did not opt clearly between a collegial, a prime ministerial model, or a model of ministerial autonomy. It introduced instead elements of each. On the one hand, it assigns a special status to the Prime Minister (both in the process leading to the formation of a cabinet and in the daily life of the cabinet). It is up to the Prime Minister to propose the names of ministers to the head of state (Article 92) and it is also stated that the Prime Minister should coordinate the action of ministers and lead the policy initiatives of the cabinet (Article 95). In practice, however, this special position does not make the Prime Minister more than *a primus inter pares* and does not contradict the collegial character of the cabinet (Articles 94 and 95). It is the cabinet as a whole, and not the Prime Minister only, that receives the vote of confidence (Article 94). This is in contrast to the solution, adopted in other constitutions (for instance, in the German *Grundgesetz*), which strengthens the role of the government leader. It may be worth mentioning that some recent proposals for constitutional reform have suggested the adoption of the German solution in order to increase the authority of the Prime Minister vis-à-vis the ministers and the cabinet.

On the question of cabinet collegiality versus ministerial individualism, the constitution seems at first to opt in favour of a collegial system coordinated and led by the Prime Minister (Article 95). The principle of the collective responsibility of ministers is explicitly stated. At the same time, however, the constitution introduces a somewhat vaguely defined individual responsibility of ministers with respect to matters concerning their department. More importantly, the constitution does not provide clear instruments for disciplining individual ministers (in particular, there is no mention of a prime ministerial power to dismiss them). In fact the first clear case of formal dismissal of a minister took place in 1995 under the special conditions of that crisis year, and it was done through a very peculiar procedure: the parliamentary majority supporting the 'government of technocrats' voted an individual motion of no confidence against the Minister of Justice, the government accepted the motion, and the Prime Minister provisionally took over the vacant position. But the whole procedure was extremely controversial and had to be validated by the Constitutional Court.

With regard to the power to dissolve parliament, it has been placed in the hands of the head of state. The government has at best the power to ask for it, but no special role in this procedure. The fact that the President of the Republic can proceed only after having consulted the presidents of the two chambers indicates the desire to provide a guarantee for the parliament, rather than to empower the government.

Finally, with respect to the law-making process, the constitution allocates, on the one hand, some privileges to the government, the most relevant of which is its power to enact decrees that have the same status as acts of parliament (though these decrees have to be approved within the next sixty days by parliament lest they lose their validity and effects). On the other hand, with respect to normal bills, government and individual members of parliament have the same power to initiate them. As in most countries, the details of the legislative process are regulated not by the constitution but by parliamentary standing orders. Even in this respect, the government has not received (for a long time) particularly favourable treatment compared with ordinary members (see Chapter 5). It is not its de jure but its de facto position, resulting from its majority following among members of parliament, which explains the greater success of its bills compared with that of private members' bills (Di Palma 1977).

The analysis of constitutional norms offers thus only a preliminary basis for understanding the peculiarities of the structure and functioning of the executive in the Italian political system. If we want to go beyond the level of generalities we must therefore look elsewhere. In fact, most of the peculiar traits of the Italian government find their roots not in the articles of the constitution but rather in a number of political factors which, in the absence of sufficiently compelling constitutional provisions, have been able to play a large part in directing governmental practices. The Italian constitutional framework can in fact be said to be 'permissive' rather than 'channelling' or 'supportive' with respect to the political factors (and actors). The strength and authority of the Prime Minister and of the cabinet, the internal relationship between the components of the latter, and the success of the government in carrying through its policies have been significantly affected by the changing characteristics of the party system and also by the features of the parties that have been in office for extended periods of time. As we will see significant changes have taken place in this domain even though the relevant constitutional provisions have not been altered.

The development of the executive: composition and structure

From the re-establishment of democracy until the early 1990s, four main features characterized the Italian executive:

1. coalition cabinets (all of them including the DC as the largest party) dominated the field;
2. only a very limited alternation took place among the parties involved in government;
3. the duration of cabinets was typically short; and
4. the Prime Minister was a rather weak figure.

Some changes obviously took place during this long period, but these features were not fundamentally altered. Table 4.2 summarizes some basic data concerning the Italian coalition governance in diachronic perspective (for a broader description, see Verzichelli and Cotta 2000).

After 1994 a new political phase opened and important transformations affected the executive even though the constitutional provisions remained the same. The three most significant features of the new period are that alternation in government of different coalitions has become rather evident in the system, that the Prime Minister has gained significantly in importance, and that the duration of cabinets has increased. The change of the electoral system (see Chapter 3) and the deep restructuring of the party system (see Chapter 2) were the main factors behind this transformation; but the importance of some external factors should also not be underestimated.

We can now analyze in more detail how the basic features of the party system have affected the making of governments, their demise, and their internal composition, while in the following section we will look at the main changes in their policy-making role, and in their interactions with the political system.

The making of governments

As we have seen, the power to nominate the Prime Minister was vested by the constitution in the President of the Republic (Article 92). Therefore, after

TABLE 4.2 Coalition governance and governments in Italy, 1948–2006

Legislative term	Types/phases of coalition	Number of governments	Average duration of governments (days)	Prime Ministers
I (1948–53)	*Centrism (golden age)*	3	613	De Gasperi
II (1953–58)	*Centrism (crisis, new stabilization)*	6	278	De Gasperi, Pella, Fanfani, Scelba, Segni, Zoli
III (1958–63)	*Centrism (new crisis): preparation of centre-left*	5	341	Fanfani, Segni, Tambroni, Fanfani
IV (1963–68)	*Centre-left (golden age)*	4	431	Leone, Moro
V (1968–72)	*Centre-left (crisis and new stabilisation)*	6	204	Leone, Rumor, Colombo, Andreotti
VI (1972–76)	*Centre-left (final crisis)*	5	256	Andreotti, Rumor, Moro
VII (1976–79)	*National solidarity*	3	308	Andreotti
VIII (1979–83)	*Preparation of five-party formula*	6	203	Cossiga, Forlani, Spadolini, Fanfani
IX (1983–87)	*Five-party formula (golden age)*	3	429	Craxi, Fanfani

continues

Table 4.2 continued

Legislative term	Types/phases of coalition	Number of governments	Average duration of governments (days)	Prime Ministers
X (1987–92)	*Five-party (renegotiation, new stabilisation and new crisis)*	4	405	Goria, De Mita, Andreotti
XI (1992–94)	*End of five-party formula and technocratic government*	2	280	Amato, Ciampi
XII (1994–96)	*Centre-right attempt and technocratic government*	2	311	Berlusconi, Dini
XIII (1996–2001)	*Centre-left*	4	450	Prodi, D'Alema, Amato
XIV (2001–6)	*Centre-right*	2	910	Berlusconi
XV (2006–)	*Centre-left*			Prodi

Source: CIRCaP archives on Italian political institutions, University of Siena

a new parliamentary election, or the fall or resignation of the incumbent government, the head of state must find a politician capable of winning a majority in parliament. Given the nature of the party system and the fact that no party (except for a very brief period between 1948 and 1953 and only in the lower chamber) has ever commanded alone a majority able to sustain a single-party government, the making of governments has always entailed the building of coalitions. The way this process works followed a rather stable pattern until 1992, but after 1994 it has taken quite a different turn.

In the former period the coalition-making process took place after the elections. Governmental coalitions were basically formed by adding other parties to the 'relative majority party' (Marradi 1982)—that is, Christian Democracy. No alternative coalition without that party could ever come into being, or even be realistically envisaged at the national level (while at regional or lower levels of government such experiments were more common). To use the Sartorian terminology, 'peripheral turnover' rather than full alternation characterized the government-building process in Italy (Sartori 1976). Only relatively small parties of the centre-left or the centre-right moved in and out of governmental coalitions. The main reason for this situation was the fact that the other parties of the left and centre were never ready to consider the Communist Party as a suitable government partner, which, being the largest opposition party, would have been necessary (and since 1976 could in fact have provided the required parliamentary numbers for a new majority) to build an alternative government to those led by the Christian Democrats.

In this perspective, elections, rather than deciding which would be the winning side and would thus be authorized to form the government, were an instrument in the competition between the already defined 'governmental parties' for deciding their relative weight in the coalition game. At the same time they signalled the greater or lesser parliamentary bargaining power of the opposition.

Choosing the person in charge of trying to form a government was in the hands of the President of the Republic, who conducted consultations with the leaders of all the parties with the purpose of ascertaining which coalition was at that moment possible and which politician could best lead it. For a long period, in view of the central role of the DC in the coalition-making game, it was normal for the head of state to designate a politician of this party as the government *formateur* (*presidente incaricato*). However, given the factional nature of this party, there was never only one person in a position to fill this role. The first choice was thus the result of an internal competition within the DC, but was also affected by the preferences of the other potential coalition partners. Not only the more left- or right-leaning position of Christian Democratic leaders, but also their greater or lesser weight, their personality, and their relationship with the leaders of the other parties, had a role in this often complicated selection. From the 1980s the choice of the Prime Minister was no longer confined to the DC. A 'rule of alternation' between the largest party of the coalition and the other ones was introduced, albeit not without discussions and tensions. Thus Spadolini (Republican Party), and Craxi and Amato (Socialist Party) alternated with Forlani, Fanfani, Goria, De Mita, and Andreotti (DC).

Despite the predominant role of parties and of their leaders in the choice of the Prime Minister, the head of state was, on occasion, able to exert a certain degree of influence over this process. This happened with greater facility whenever the coalition-making process was particularly difficult and relations between parties strained. When the parties faced difficulties in finding a solution, the President of the Republic could promote his own choice (Tebaldi 2005).

Once the Prime Minister was designated, it was then his turn to conduct formal negotiations with potential coalition partners in order to define the policy platform and the ministerial composition of the government. If the negotiation process failed, as happened from time to time, the president would conduct one or more new rounds of consultations and designate a new *formateur*. The role of the designated Prime Minister in the formation of the government was seriously limited, in practice, by the participation in the process of the chairmen of the coalition parties. To a great extent the choice of ministers and under-secretaries and the allocation of ministries was their preserve, rather than that of the Prime Minister, who acted more as a mediator than as the leader. Even where it concerned ministers from his own party, rather than belonging to the cabinet leader, the choice was the result of negotiations between the party factions.

With regard to the composition and political support of governments, the main alternatives were:

1. full coalition government with all the parties of the parliamentary majority holding posts in the cabinet;
2. single-party or coalition governments with the external support of other parties ensuring a clear majority in parliament;
3. minority governments, that is, single-party or coalition governments without a real majority in parliament but able to count on the abstention of other parties; and
4. caretaker governments which failed to receive a confidence vote in parliament.

All these possibilities were adopted more than once, but their relative frequency varied over time together with changes in the relations between the parties of the so-called *area di governo* (governmental area), that is the parties deemed acceptable for the purpose of building government coalitions (Pasquino 1987; Verzichelli and Cotta 2000). The first solution was more frequent when a relatively solid and stable alliance between government parties could be built. The second and third solutions were adopted as transitional devices whenever a full and public agreement could not be reached between traditional and/or new alliance partners, and one or more of them preferred to give less visible support to the government, without engaging in full participation. The last situation was the result of the lack of even this limited agreement.

The four situations provided a 'scale of declining agreement' between parties with a governmental potential. It must be added that the last solution (caretaker governments) was always adopted at election times, either when a regular election was due or in order to produce an anticipated election. The constitutional legitimacy of this solution was repeatedly questioned, and such situations in fact coincided with serious strains in the relations between political forces and between constitutional organs (in particular between parties and the head of state).

The making of governments after 1992

Things changed significantly after 1992. In a first phase the collapse of the traditional governing parties and, at the same time, the lack of a viable alternative proposal by the opposition parties, which were not able to put together a parliamentary majority, gave the then President,

Oscar Luigi Scalfaro, unprecedented freedom of action in the formation of governments. This led to the formation of a 'government of technocrats', guided by the former governor of the Bank of Italy, Ciampi, composed to a significant extent of non-politicians and with a programme defined under the close supervision of the President of the Republic. Another such government guided by Dini (again a former high-ranking officer of the Bank of Italy) was formed in 1995, immediately after the fall of the first Berlusconi government.

This phase, however, was only temporary. The renewal of the party system, combined with the new predominantly majoritarian electoral system (see Chapters 2 and 3), stimulated a new pattern of government formation which was significantly different from the past. Contrary to previous experience, parties have since been induced to form electoral coalitions, which, in a progressively more formalized manner, designate prior to election day a common programme and a common leader. The formation of the government has thus come to be determined in a much more direct way by electoral results. The consultations of the head of state have become a less relevant exercise as the choice of the Prime Minister can hardly contradict the electoral result. Thus Berlusconi and Prodi, having been the leaders of the winning electoral coalitions, respectively, of the right (in 1994 and 2001) and of the left (in 1996 and 2006), were able to form the new government immediately after the election.

The persisting coalitional nature of the majorities—the number of parties involved has in fact increased rather than decreased—has, however, continued to produce significant and rather heated consultations among the coalition parties for deciding the allocation of ministries. But the Prime Minister has played a much stronger role in this process than in the past. From being a simple mediator, he has become the leading actor. In the case of the centre-right this role has been enhanced by the fact that Berlusconi was also the indisputable leader of his party and therefore able to decide on all the ministerial posts assigned to it. Prodi, on the contrary, being a coalition leader without a party, has had the freedom to choose only a smaller part of the cabinet. Another point to be mentioned is that the leaders of the parties supporting the government have, more frequently than in the past, joined the cabinet. The increased importance and durability of cabinets has made ministerial positions more attractive.

The downfall of cabinets

No government in Italy has ever lasted for an entire parliamentary term of five years. Only De Gasperi (in the first legislature) and Berlusconi (in the fourteenth) have retained the office of Prime Minister for an entire parliamentary term, but as the heads of more than one cabinet. The fall of government, however, has never happened because of a parliamentary vote of no confidence moved by the opposition, but only because of internal problems within the coalition. Prime ministers have typically resigned, without waiting for a formal vote, as soon as they have reached a clear perception that their majority was not holding together. This has often happened after one or more negative votes in legislative proceedings (which per se do not entail a formal obligation to resign) have shown the cohesion of the majority to be seriously endangered. In one case (the Prodi I cabinet in 1998) the government itself had provoked a confidence vote in order to reconsolidate the coalition and had failed to win it. The premature fall of cabinets has meant that governments have been formed not only immediately after elections, but also in the middle of a legislature.

Before 1994 the fall of government and one or more new cabinet formations during a legislative term was part of the normal landscape and was not seen as a serious problem. New cabinets with the same or a different Prime Minister and the same or a partially different majority were formed after new negotiations between the parties of the 'governing area'. In fact governmental crises were one of the instruments for the internal regulation of coalitions. Through this process parties renegotiated their policy agreements and redefined their relative influence in the cabinet (Vassallo 1994). After 1994 the situation changed somewhat. Since, as a result of the electoral system and the new political arrangements, the coalition and the Prime Minister receive de facto a popular investiture, the (political) legitimacy of a governmental change during a legislative term has become the object of a lively political debate. The debate was particularly heated after the fall of the first Berlusconi government in 1994 when, six months after the elections, a party (the Lega) withheld its support from the cabinet and a technical government was subsequently formed with a different parliamentary majority. A similar situation arose with the fall of the first Prodi cabinet in 1998. The question raised is whether it is acceptable to have a new majority formed in parliament, which might differ from the one produced by the electoral results, or whether new elections should be called. As the constitutional text says nothing on this point, but simply requires that a government have a majority in both chambers, this is more a question of political opportunity than of legal legitimacy. So far, the two Presidents of the Republic in office at the time of such events have been reluctant to choose elections. Thus, after the crises of the Berlusconi I and II, Prodi I, and D'Alema cabinets, new governments have been formed following the pattern of the past, that is negotiations between parties. Apart from the Dini cabinet coming after the fall of Berlusconi I, all these new cabinets have been formed basically from the same coalition of parties as their predecessors. The constitutional reform, promoted by the second and third Berlusconi cabinets and approved in 2005 by parliament, introduced a rule that would have required new elections whenever a cabinet crisis was produced by a parliamentary majority different from the electoral one. As the referendum of June 2006 has rejected this reform, the question is not yet solved.

Political composition of the cabinets

Before 1994 all the coalition governments and of course the other minority or caretaker governments were always formed around a dominant party: the DC. Coalitions were thus composed of a fairly large party plus two or more rather smaller parties. Changes in the composition of coalitions concerned only the latter parties, with one or the other of them dropping out or joining in, thus defining the orientation of the government in a more centre-left or centre-right direction.

The parliamentary strength of the governmental coalitions was frequently larger than the strict majority required. One or more small parties were added even if they were not absolutely necessary. During the first republic this choice answered the need to take into account the existence of more than one dimension of conflict in the party system (see Chapter 2), but also the more practical necessity of the DC playing one against another of its coalition partners. The choice of a grand coalition, bringing together almost all the parties, which was adopted during the transition years from fascism to democracy was renewed for a short period between 1976 and 1979 when, following a dramatic electoral leap of the Communist Party in the vote of 1976 (an increase of 7 per cent), and in view of a difficult economic situation and of the threat of internal leftist and rightist terrorism, an alliance between the DC and PCI, together with the other traditional government parties, became acceptable to both sides. However, even then the Communist Party could not achieve full governmental status (that is, participation in the cabinet), but only gave parliamentary support to a cabinet composed of just Christian Democratic ministers. This 'national solidarity' (*solidarietà nazionale*) broke down before the Communist Party succeeded in passing the threshold for full participation in the cabinet.

After 1994, and apart from the technocratic *intermezzo* of the Dini government (1995–96), alternative coalitions of the right or of the left have prevailed. Exclusions (or self-exclusions) of parties of the extreme left or the extreme right have been progressively dropped, as these parties have gradually moderated their positions. The left coalition has had greater problems in incorporating the extreme left (Communist Refoundation), from which it could at first obtain only external support. In fact this party played a crucial role in the downfall of the first centre-left government of Prodi. With the successful electoral coalition of 2006 and the second Prodi cabinet this problem has apparently been overcome. As for the right, after the transformation of the MSI into the moderate right party AN, only minuscule extreme right parties have appeared, and in 2006 they have been attracted into the coalition in a subordinate role. In the end all significant parties of the political spectrum have come to be involved in the governmental game.

The ministerial structure

From the institutional point of view, the government has been typically composed of the Prime Minister, occasionally one or more deputy prime ministers, and a variable number of ministers and under-secretaries. Ministers are typically at the head of one ministry; in a few cases they may oversee two departments that, from a bureaucratic point of view, maintain their autonomy. There is always a number of ministers without portfolio, who are in charge of a specific policy area (sometimes newly created), but do not have an autonomous department at their disposal; administrative support is provided for them by the presidency of the Council of Ministers. Unlike ministers without portfolio, under-secretaries do not participate in cabinet meetings. They can substitute for their respective ministers in a number of ways, particularly in parliament, with the outside world (interest groups and so on), or within the ministry itself, but their authority depends upon an explicit act of delegation from their minister sanctioned by the cabinet. Among under-secretaries a special position is occupied by one of the under-secretaries attached to the Prime Minister, who has the role of secretary of the Council of Ministers. Alone among under-secretaries he or she takes part (but without formal voting powers) in cabinet meetings. Furthermore, as the closest collaborator of the premier, this under-secretary has a crucial role in preparing the agenda of the Council of Ministers, and very often will conduct, instead of the Prime Minister, the complex negotiations between ministers and with party representatives, which precede cabinet discussions (Cassese 1981).

The structure of the cabinet has been the object of growing concern since the 1980s and especially after the crisis of the mid-1990s, as the number of reforms related to this matter shows (Box 4.1). Some of these reforms will be analyzed later, in the discussion about the concrete practice of government.

BOX 4.1 The reforms of the government in Italy, 1983–2006

1983 (Gov. Craxi)	Informal introduction of a Cabinet Council
L. 400 1988 (Gov. De Mita)	Creation of a staff structure at the presidency of the council.
L. 537/1993 (Gov. Ciampi)	Reform of the public administration and reshaping of the ministry for administrative reform
1993 (Gov. Ciampi)	New rules of procedure of the Council of Ministers
1997–9 (Gov. Prodi)	Bassanini Laws I, II, and III (see Chapter 7): delegation to the government to issue decrees on the new distribution of ministerial functions; reform of the budget structure; reduction in the number of ministries; simplification and reorganization of the government
L. 317/2001 (Gov. Berlusconi II)	Modification to the structure of the cabinet
L. 81/2001 (Gov. Berlusconi II)	Competences of deputy ministers
2002 (Gov. Berlusconi II)	Decree of the president of the Council of Minister on the structure of the presidency
2006 (Gov. Prodi II)	Modification to the structure of the cabinet

As regards the different types of appointment, an important change has happened with the Bassanini reforms (1997–99), which have introduced, together with a reduction in the number of ministries, the figure of deputy minister (*vice-ministro*). According to the 2001 law regulating the matter, the deputy ministers have a full delegation on specific issues and they can participate in cabinet meetings in order to report on their work, without having formal rights of vote.

We can therefore describe the government as a two-tier structure, the first tier (that of the Prime Minister and of the ministers) being responsible for the collective process of decision making and the second tier (with deputy ministers and under-secretaries) being active at the level of each department (including, as we have seen, the relations between ministries and parliament, and ministries and other political and social actors).

The structure of the cabinet has been typically affected also by coalition-building problems. The position of deputy prime minister has been allocated, from time to time, to one or two leaders of important parties of the coalition as a compensation for not having obtained the top position in the cabinet and with the purpose of ensuring governmental cohesion. The general trend has been towards an increase in the number of ministerial and under-secretarial positions, as the distribution of new posts has been a handy device for solving the difficulties of fragmented coalitions. It is not the case that single-party governments have in general had a smaller number of ministers. This trend has been occasionally interrupted by attempts to bring back the cabinet to more manageable dimensions. But efforts to keep the size of the government small have not in general lasted for very long (Figure 4.1).

The positions of minister and under-secretary have been predominantly assigned to politicians with a strong party position and with a long parliamentary career (Calise and Mannheinmer 1983; Cotta 1991). It must be noted, however, that before 1994 the leaders of the coalition parties, more often than not, preferred to remain outside the cabinet. The coalitional nature of cabinets and their limited duration combined to make a ministerial (and even a prime ministerial) position often less attractive and powerful than that of leader of the party organization. Party leaders, staying out of the government, were able to outlive the duration of cabinets and to preserve the freedom of movement of their party (and themselves) from the constraints of coalitions. It happened only rarely that leaders tried to

FIGURE 4.1 **Size of government (ministers and other members), 1948–2006**

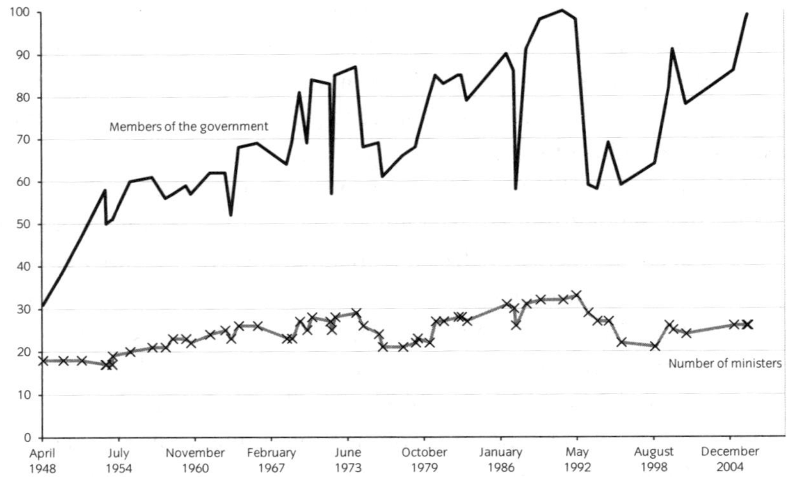

Source: CIRCaP archives on Italian political institutions, University of Siena.

combine the positions of party chief and of prime minister, with the aim of pursuing a more ambitious innovative agenda. Apart from De Gasperi at the beginning of the democratic republic, this was also the case with Fanfani, Spadolini, Craxi, and De Mita. This attempt was relatively more successful for the leaders of smaller parties (Craxi and Spadolini), while for the two Christian Democrat leaders (Fanfani and De Mita) it produced a negative reaction from within their own party where the other factional leaders joined forces to stop the hegemonic role of one person. The presence within the government of the leaders of the coalition parties became more common after 1994, as cabinets acquired greater stability. Yet some leaders have continued to prefer an external position (as D'Alema of the DS under the first Prodi government, Follini of the UDC under Berlusconi II, Fassino of the DS, Diliberto of PCDI, and Giordano of the RC under Prodi II).

In the past the recruitment of ministers without a political background was an exception. Technocrats gained a more prominent role only in two cabinets of the 1990s (Ciampi and Dini), when the crisis of the old parties was at its climax; otherwise they were offered from time to time a position in one of the more 'technical' departments, such as foreign trade, health, and higher education. After 1994 the choice of technocrats for some important ministerial positions has been a way for strong prime ministers, such as Berlusconi and Prodi, to keep these ministries under their political control and to preserve them from the influence of coalition parties. In general the allocation of ministries has followed a rule of proportionality, but in the choice of their positions parties have tried to have their specific preferences respected (Verzichelli 2001). In any case the distribution of the numerous under-secretarial positions has enabled parties to have some influence even when they have not been able to obtain the control of a ministry.

The executive at work

Governing the cabinet

The guidance and the internal working of Italian governments have been significantly affected by the features of the party system and their evolution, but also by external factors such as the development of European integration, economic globalization, and the institutional reforms introduced to cope with some of these problems.

After the first years of the republic, when De Gasperi had gained a prominent role thanks to the fact that he and his party (the DC) had won a dramatic electoral victory against the left and the weight of the external party organizations was still weak, the Prime Minister was for a long time a rather weak figure in Italy. Without a strong electoral mandate, as the Prime Minister was chosen after the elections through negotiations between party leaders, without a significant role in the selection and dismissal of ministers, and having to cope with heterogeneous and unruly coalitions, the head of the government was in the past rarely able to exert a strong guidance over the executive as a collective body and over individual ministers. His role was that of a mediator between different actors and interests rather than of a policy promoter (Cotta 1998). There have obviously been variations in the influence of prime ministers as is suggested also by the different durations of their terms of office. Apart from personality traits and differences in their party backing, the main factor for explaining these variations is that the terms of some prime ministers have coincided with the upward phase of a coalition cycle, when a greater convergence between party platforms has been reached, and others, on the contrary, have coincided with the phase of decline and crisis (Verzichelli and Cotta 2000).

The coalitional nature of cabinets, the often ambiguous and unstable nature of coalition agreements, and the fact that, typically, party leaders have not participated in the government, all meant that the Prime Minister always had to pay a tribute also to external actors. In the first republic a typical instrument for dealing with serious coalitional problems was the so-called *vertice*, a summit between Prime Minister and chairmen of the coalition parties, which, entrusted with the task of solving the problems of the day and defining the future programme of action, could become, if successful, a crucial instrument of governance of the executive (Criscitiello 1996).

The multi-party character of cabinets and the proliferation of ministries (which is partly a consequence of the former factor and partly the result of more general trends of the contemporary world) have had another important effect on cabinet life. Some of the most important policy areas (for instance, external relations and financial and economic affairs) have been fragmented into more than one ministry and allocated to the representatives of different parties. This has meant, at best, that the policy of the government in each area has been the result of long consultations between different ministers (and also their respective parties and ministerial bureaucracies) responsible for that area. In the worst case, each minister has acted independently and there has been more than one government policy in the same area.

An institutional effort to counteract the fragmentation of ministries has been the creation of inter-ministerial committees, whereby, in a given policy domain, the actions of different ministries could be coordinated. To what extent these committees are in accordance with the constitution is a matter for debate, especially for those committees whose powers are not confined to preparing cabinet decisions. A point often made against their constitutionality is the fact that they reduce the scope of collegial decisions by the cabinet as a whole and privilege some ministers (and the Prime Minister who normally chairs them) over the others. It is clear in any case that they are a deviation from the principle that the government should decide everything in its full collegiality. It is, however, not only the committees which violate that principle. A much greater breach of the principle of full collegiality comes, on the one hand, from the many decisions of individual ministers that the cabinet cannot effectively control. On the other hand, such a breach is produced by decisions taken outside the cabinet by party representatives, who may or may not be members of the cabinet, and which become cabinet policy without further discussion. As to the efficacy of ministerial committees in coordinating the policy areas for which they are responsible, the Italian experience suggests that their impact has been much less than hoped or feared (Merusi 1977). A common interpretation is that they have been an instrument more for legitimizing the independent role of certain ministries vis-à-vis the cabinet than for implementing effective coordination.

The emergence of a core-executive

During the 1980s the need to strengthen the role of the Prime Minister and its capacity to steer the executive came to be increasingly at the centre of the political debate. Among the reasons for this should be mentioned the greater frequency of European and international interactions, where Italian prime ministers have to deal with the stronger and more durable heads of government of countries such as France, Germany, and the UK, but also the need to face some of the negative consequences—such as the growth of state debt and public deficit—of an exceedingly fragmented decision-making process.

While attempts to change the existing situation through constitutional innovations—such as the proposals to have a directly elected head of state and a semi-presidential system or a directly elected Prime Minister—failed to gain enough support, other less dramatic innovations were experimented with from that period onward. A first solution, adopted to strengthen the political coordination of the executive, was the creation, within the government, of an inner cabinet composed of the party leaders, if they belonged to the government, or of the highest-ranking minister of each coalition party, together with some of the other most important ministers. This device was employed for the first time in the Craxi government of 1983, and probably played some part in its unusual longevity. The main problem with this solution was that one or more leaders of coalition parties often preferred to stay out of the government and this meant that decisions taken by an inner cabinet would not carry full party authority. Alternatively, an inner cabinet might be perceived by the Prime Minister as a sort of golden cage limiting his freedom of action. As a consequence this solution did not become fully institutionalized.

Another significant trend of change since the 1980s has been the strengthening of the prime ministerial office and of its bureaucratic apparatus. Before that time, while individual ministers could count on the resources of their departments, the Prime Minister did not have any comparable supporting bureaucracy at his disposal. His position was therefore even worse than it used to be in the pre-fascist period when the Prime Minister typically held a major ministerial position (interior, finance, or foreign affairs) and could thus use the resources of this department to support his work as leader of the government.

In 1988, under the De Mita government, a reform (Law 400) was approved with the purpose of, first, increasing the degree of collegiality through a detailed and more extensive definition of the matters which compulsorily require collective deliberation in the cabinet and cannot be decided by single ministers; second, ensuring, through an improved circulation of information among members of the cabinet and more stringent procedural rules, that cabinet decisions are really, and not only formally, collective; and third, creating an apparatus to serve the cabinet as a whole and assist the Prime Minister in particular in his or her leading and steering capacity.

The creation of a Secretariat of the Presidency of the Council of Ministers and the increment of organizational and financial resources directly allocated to the Prime Minister's office have undoubtedly provided the chief executive with significant instruments for organizing the increasing workload of the cabinet. Despite this the architecture of the Prime Minister's Office remained for a long time rather baroque, being more the result of an incremental accretion of offices and structures than of a well-defined intentional design. Moreover, during a difficult phase like that of decline of the first republic, such an innovation could hardly counterbalance the bureaucratic factors pulling towards fragmentation along departmental lines, and on the other hand; the political factors responsible for fragmentation along party lines. This does not mean that the Prime Minister had no influence. As can be expected in a situation of fragmentation, his greatest impact was not when he attempted to direct the ministers and the cabinet along the lines of a predetermined programme, but when he assumed the role of mediator (for which he was obviously in a good position) between the many actors in the governmental arena.

Among the changes that have affected the governance of the cabinet we should mention also the strengthening of the position of the Treasury and of the Finance Minister. The deterioration of the situation of public finances during the end of 1970s and the 1980s and the need to put under control, both for internal reasons and for satisfying the increasingly strict international and European obligations, the vicious circle of public deficit, growing debt, and rising interest rates, have fostered a progressive strengthening of the role of the Finance Minister (*Ministro del Tesoro*) as a check against the other ministers, typically keener to increase expenditures. The appointment as Treasury Minister of a number of expert politicians (such as the socialist professor of constitutional law Giuliano Amato) or technocrats (such as the former governor of the Bank of Italy, Guido Carli) was a first important sign in the second half of the 1980s. Later, a series of reforms of budgetary procedures (see Chapter 5), but also a significant internal reorganization of the ministry, allowed the Finance Minister to gain an important coordination role in the cabinet and to become thus the right hand of the Prime Minister in the core executive. The highest point of this development was reached in 1996 when the three ministries of Treasury, Finances (that is taxation), and Budget were unified under the roof of a supersized Ministry of the Economy.

It must be clear however that all the changes taking place during the 1980s did not dramatically alter the basic political and institutional conditions affecting the working of the executive. It was in fact with the political upheavals of the 1990s that the most important innovations were introduced. First of all is the fact that prime ministers, at least those who take office after an election, are now the heads of the governing coalition. Whether they are the leader of a party (as Berlusconi for Forza Italia) or not (as for Prodi), they are the persons who have been able to put together the electoral coalition and to lead it to victory. This has given the Prime Minister a higher degree of prominence in the cabinet: he can make an appeal to the electoral mandate he has received and remind of his role in bringing and keeping the coalition together. To steer the government the Prime Minister can now also rely on the programme with which the coalition has won the election. While in the past the coalition agreement used to be a rather weak instrument which was neither written nor made public, its role in recent years has been significantly enhanced. Albeit of a variable length and detail,[3] this text contains a list of specific pledges upon which the leader of the executive can rely when defining the agenda of the cabinet and to which he or she can appeal when dissensions between the coalition parties arise.

The changed political conditions also enable a more effective implementation of the reform of the chief executive's office: the organizational resources in the hands of the Prime Minister (with about 4,500 people working at Palazzo Chigi) are now much more considerable than in the time of the first republic. The Prime Minister's Office (Figure 4.2) is in fact organized around a limited number of units, while the private office of the Presidente del Consiglio can count on a small but significant number of staff advisers and policy experts. These transformations, reducing the scope of its direct responsibilities, but enhancing its coordinating power in the most critical domains, make the Italian Prime Minister's Office more similar to other European examples of core executives (Calise 2005).

FIGURE 4.2 The Prime Minister's Office (Prodi II government, June 2006)

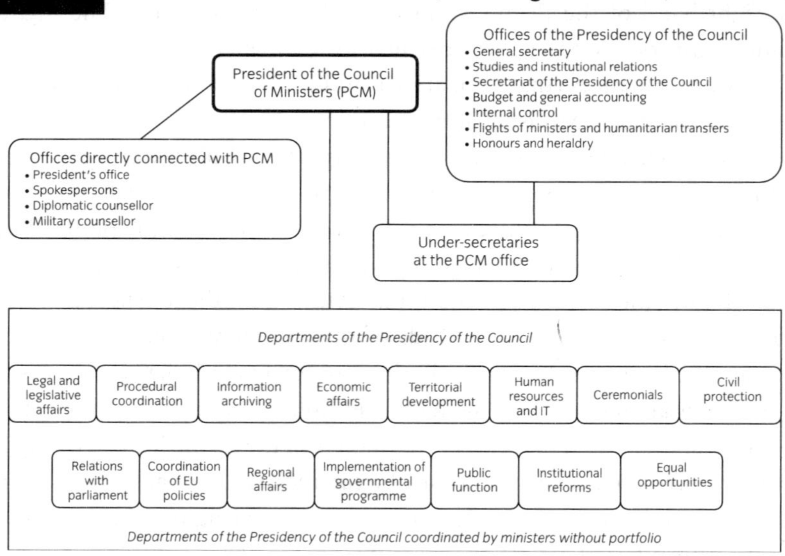

Source: Italian government.

Finally, the Prime Minister has also acquired a greater role in the selection of the ministerial team; although he cannot obviously overlook the desires of the other parties of the coalition, his position is now a central one in the process of allocation of ministries. And he has a personal say on a (variable) number of positions. Last but not least, his visibility in the media has significantly increased, thanks to the emergence of a specific set of services: a junior ministership for governmental publications, a department for the implementation of the governmental programme, and a modern internet media coverage of all the activities of the same Prime Minister.

This does not mean that in the second republic the Italian Prime Minister has overcome all its weaknesses. As both Berlusconi and Prodi have experienced, their role as coalition leaders and electoral winners cannot save them from the risk of an internal coalition crisis, which can entail their downfall (Berlusconi I and Prodi I) or require some form of renegotiation of the coalition pact (Berlusconi II). Coalitions continue to have a rather unwieldy composition. They are ideologically heterogeneous and fragmented (four parties for Berlusconi II and III and eight for Prodi II, if one does not count some other minuscule parties which, even though they do not form a parliamentary group, have nonetheless obtained at least an under-secretary); moreover, on a number of issues, the agreements reached over the formulation of the coalition programme were at best ambiguous.

The ability of the Prime Minister to engineer a reshuffle of the cabinet in order to assert authority also remains weak. He can fairly easily change the ministers that were his own choice (typically a number of technical ministers and those of his party), but with the other ministers he still depends on the agreement of coalition parties. The electoral mandate cannot thus be translated into a clear dominance over the cabinet. At the same time, however, it is now much more difficult than in the past to successfully replace one prime minister with another during a legislative term. It has happened, but the new prime ministers who have followed have felt weaker than their predecessors and somewhat more uncertain about the political legitimacy of their position, and in the end less at ease in conducting their job.

Governing with parliament (or without)

In the past the short-term perspective of every cabinet and of most of the prime ministers was undoubtedly a serious limiting factor in their ability to conduct effectively the governmental mission and this was particularly so when it was time to introduce significant reforms. It is true that the instability of cabinets, as measured by their duration in office, was to an extent balanced by the fact that the same party—the DC—was always at the centre of every cabinet and that a good many of the ministers (and also of the prime ministers[4]) would survive from one government to another. It could also be said that party leaders, who often outlasted the duration of a cabinet, were in some way in charge of pushing forward the business of government. This meant, however, that the government as an institution was in part deprived of its constitutional role and responsibilities.

The weaknesses of the Italian executives were particularly evident in their parliamentary action. The government could rarely command a very cohesive majority in parliament and traditionally lacked a strong control of the parliamentary agenda. This meant that the government has typically faced serious difficulties in pushing its legislative programme through parliament and has had to accept a large amount of parliamentary corrections to it (Di Palma 1977; De Micheli and Verzichelli 2004). Unequivocal indicators of such a structural weakness are, for instance, the high rate of failed government bills and the large proportion of bills substantially amended in parliament (see Chapter 5).

The attempt of the government to reduce the influence of parliament or even to bypass it at least partially has been an answer to this situation. For this purpose the executive has pressed to obtain preferential procedures for its legislative initiatives by which the timing of the process could become more predictable. A significant step was of course the abolition in 1988 of the use, by default, of secret voting in the law-making process (which gave many opportunities for snipers from within the majority to obtain their goals). More generally, a gradual build-up in the standing orders of the chambers (see Chapter 5) provided the government with relevant tools in order to protect its own legislation. This has facilitated a more accountable role for the cabinet in the phase of policy formulation.

But the most important instruments for the government in its day-to-day activity have come from the application of other constitutional devices. Historically, the so-called *decreti legge* (urgent legislative decrees—Article 76 of the constitution) have been an important tool. The legislative decrees are admitted as an exception for reasons of necessity and urgency, and they come into force, having the same effect as laws, as soon as they are issued by the cabinet. However, they require ratification by parliament within sixty days. Despite being unusual in nature, decrees have become since the 1980s an ordinary practice of governmental action, with an average of more than twenty decrees per month reached between 1987 and 1993. Only recently (1996) has their use been somewhat reduced by a Constitutional Court decision which banned the reiteration of decrees not ratified by the chambers within the required time (another typical practice of governments during the late first republic).

Another instrument of governmental activity has been that of the 'delegating laws' (Article 77) through which parliament, after having defined the general principles, gives power to the government to regulate a broad policy area with decrees that have the same strength as laws. This tool has recently proved particularly effective in helping the executive to overcome its traditional weakness in the law-making process (Vassallo 2001). We should mention also some 'defensive' tools which, thanks to the changed political conditions in parliament and the emergence of a more robust adversarial system, have been extensively used by the government to push forward its legislative proposals: the *questione di fiducia* (a confidence vote requested at short notice by the government on a given legislative item, which stops all the amendments to a bill and enables it to impose a disciplined behaviour on its majority), and the so-called *maxiamendments*, which work as a sort of closure.

Finally, the extension of the secondary normative power, the regulatory power enjoyed by government departments through their administrative prerogatives and resulting from the legislative simplification of recent decades, has opened another field in which the cabinet as a decisional actor can play *outside* the parliamentary arena, and introduce important rules, for instance concerning appointments, personnel recruitment, career advancements, etc.

Governing the bureaucracy

In assessing the performance of the central government, another crucial element concerns the relationship between ministers and bureaucrats and, more generally, the question of the political control over the activity of ministerial departments. From this point of view, many aspects of the permanent reform of the public administration started in 1990 (see

Chapter 7) represent evident signals of a modernization programme. This attempt has also concerned the key question of ministerial reorganization, an issue which was constantly present on the political agenda from the early 1980s. Since 1993, many reforms have been adopted, all of them inspired by two main guidelines: first, the implementation of a new public management paradigm, based on the ideas of effectiveness and transparency; second, the need to apply more rigorous principles of budgetary control, in order to avoid waste of organizational, human, and financial resources.

This was of course the theoretical approach. In practice, there have been different interpretations of both the principles. For instance, the reform of the appointments of the top administrative officers, implemented by the centre-right government between 2001 and 2006 (particularly with law 40/2002 designed by the minister for the reform of public administration, Frattini, better known as 'spoil system reform'), clashed with other rules concerning the organization of the higher civil service which had been recently decided. Furthermore, contrary to the requirements of a principle of strict budgetary control, the expansion of ministerial positions has not yet been seriously faced (Figure 4.1), and a high degree of redundancy is still present within the labyrinths of ministerial departments.

Looking at the current situation of the Italian central government (Figure 4.3), we can say that the relationship between ministers and public administration looks quite different from how it looked only fifteen years ago. The ministries are very different both in their mission and in their internal organization. Nevertheless, a number of critical points still persist of which the following are the most important:

1. the cumbersome structure of the government, determined by the multiplication of watch dog positions and the consequent policy fragmentation in many areas;
2. the creation of functional agencies (*dependent agencies*, to be distinguished from the regulatory *independent agencies* analyzed in Chapter 7) did not solve the problem of departmental elephantiasis; it sounds more like a change of terminology than a change of organizational model;
3. the overlap between ministerial distribution of portfolios and division of the administrative scrutiny among parliamentary committees is still rather imperfect; and

FIGURE 4.3 **The structure of the Prodi II cabinet, June 2006**

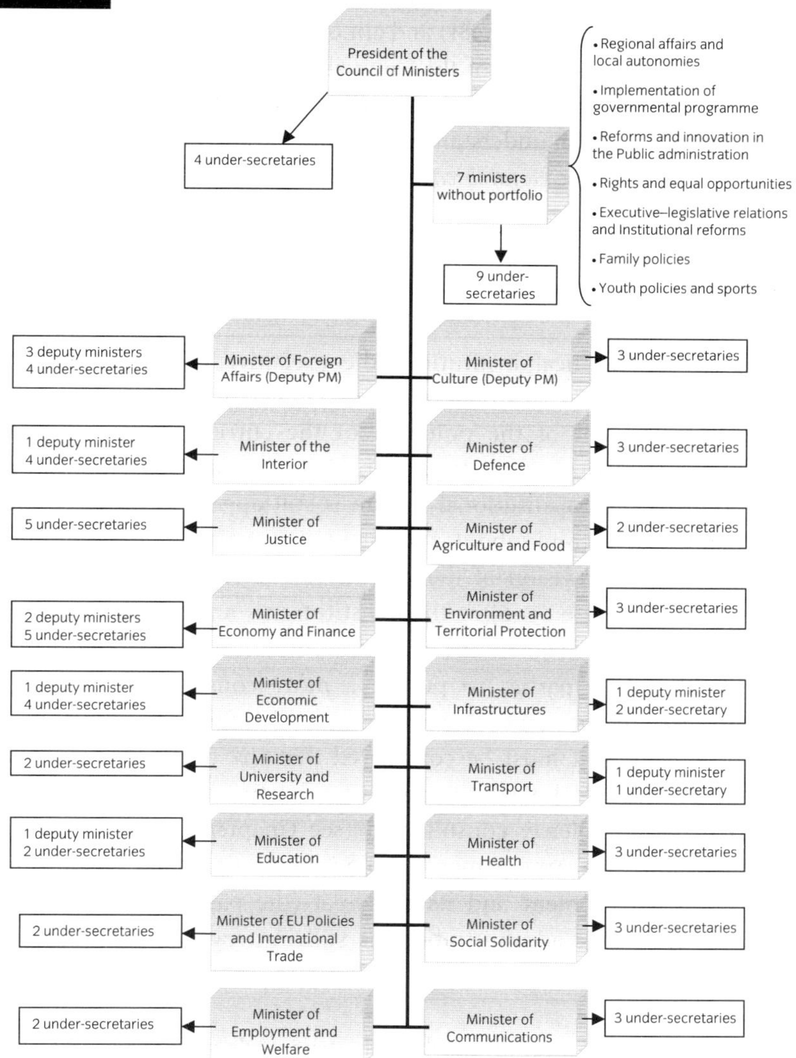

Source: Italian government.

4. the propensity of each minister to 'talk about everything' remains the same, and it grows whenever political conflict increases: twenty-five years after a famous *Decalogue* (defined by Prime Minister Spadolini in 1981) and almost fifteen years after a new set of rules of procedure for the Council of Ministers (under Prime Minister Ciampi), most of the protagonists of the Italian government still understand the notion of *collegial government* very much as a sort of *anarchical government.*

Conclusion

Among central political institutions the executive is undoubtedly the one showing the most evident signs of change. On the other hand, a careful assessment of the potential of the current Italian executive requires a longer time span. It must be kept in mind that the discussion about the big constitutional reform is still open and many political actors continue to think about a substantial constitutional amendment entailing a radical revision of the executive. The rejection, by means of a referendum in June 2006, of the constitutional amendment approved by a parliamentary majority has produced, however, a learning process that should induce parties to pursue a more consensual solution. In any case, even if the issue of a constitutional reform disappears from the future agenda, it must be considered that the future developments of the executive are linked to those of a party system which cannot be said to be completely consolidated (see Chapter 2). Finally, but no less importantly, a rearrangement of the inter-institutional relationships between the government and its principal (the parliament) as well as its agent (the public administration) is still in progress (see Chapters 5 and 6), and this is another reason for caution in assessing the present changes.

This explains the question mark in this chapter's title: the long history of weak and unstable cabinets has probably come to an end, as a number of elements reported in this chapter show. The consolidation of a more authoritative, accountable executive is grounded in the expectations and attempts which had already emerged *before* the crisis of the early 1990s, but it was surely favoured by the dramatic contingencies of that crisis entailing a deep transformation of the party system and by a number of exogenous factors such as the Europeanization of domestic politics, the greater international role of the chief executive, and the technical nature of many problems on the governmental agenda. Perhaps the main finding so far from this story is that several important changes can take place even *without* constitutional amendments. This does not mean, however, that all the problems of the Italian government have been solved by 'non-invasive' means.

KEY TERMS

- **cabinet council**
- **coalition government**
- **confidence/no-confidence votes**
- **delegating laws**
- **deputy ministers**
- **legislative decrees**
- **majority summit (*vertici di maggioranza*)**
- **ministerial career**
- **President of the Council of Ministers (Prime Minister)**
- **President of the Republic (head of state)**
- **under-secretaries**

GUIDE TO FURTHER READING

Blondel, J., and Mueller Rommel, F. (eds.) (1998) *Cabinets in Western Europe* (London, Palgrave).

A detailed analysis of cabinet formation, structure, and life in the Western European democracies, with a chapter on Italy.

Calandra, P. (1996) *Il governo della repubblica* (Bologna, Il Mulino).

A broad historical account of the Italian executive, focusing on structure, functions, and procedures.

Italian Politics (various years) (New York, Berghahn).

This series comprises the English translations of the *Istituto Cattaneo* yearbooks *Politica in Italia* dedicated to facts and interpretations of Italian politics and society. Many articles are available on the transformation of Italian government.

Müller, W. C., and Strøm, K. (eds.) (2000) *Coalition Governments in Western Europe* (Oxford, Oxford University Press)

Bergmann, T., Strøm, K., and Müller, W. C. (eds.) (2003) *Delegation and Accountability in Parliamentary Democracies* (Oxford, Oxford University Press).

These two broad volumes cover recent developments in many European democracies, including chapters on the Italian case.

NOTES

1 The organization of the cabinet was later regulated by Law 5195 of 1888.

2 One must remember that fascism deeply altered the role of the executive without bothering to change the *Statuto*.

3 So far, the electoral programmes of the centre-left coalition have been typically longer and more detailed, while those proposed by the Casa delle Libertà were shorter and more goal-orientated. Among the factors explaining such difference, the most important are probably the more fragmented nature of the centre-left coalition and the presidential style of Silvio Berlusconi. In 2001, during a pre-election programme on television, Berlusconi signed a contract with the Italians, indicating five crucial pledges and committed himself to implement these general points.

4 Of the eighteen prime ministers appointed between 1948 and 1992, eleven made a comeback as ministers in other executives, and in only three cases (Moro, Andreotti, and Cossiga) their career ended with another prime ministership.

5

The Parliament: A Case of Continuous Institutional Adaptation

Overview

By definition, the legislature is the pivotal element in the institutional framework that is commonly called parliamentary democracy. Such a statement seems particularly true if one looks to the degree of attention paid by the current Italian constitution to parliamentary structures, processes, and functions. Moreover, Italian democracy has often been depicted as a democracy 'without government' (Allum 1973; Cassese 1981), and this has made the role of the legislature even more crucial, sometimes intrusive, in the basic functioning of democracy.

In this chapter we will describe the evolution and the current institutional profile of the Italian parliament, trying to understand to what extent the transformation of parliamentary actors, processes, and functions has really changed the overall role of the legislature. This discussion is, on the one hand, connected to the complicated transition towards a system of alternation between 'majoritarian governments'. On the other hand, it is linked also to broader—and not country-specific—arguments about the 'inevitable decline' of parliaments, and hypotheses about the transformation of domestic legislatures in the context of a 'post-parliamentary democracy' (Andersen and Burns 1996), which are particularly relevant for countries belonging to the European Union. Although our assessment cannot entirely leave aside the diachronic evolution (for the very simple reason that, as we will show in the following pages, *history matters*), our analysis will focus mainly on the current situation. To what extent is the Italian parliament of today different from that of the second half of the twentieth century? And is this new institutional setting consistent with the demand for a more functional, rationalized, and accountable parliamentary government?

The parliamentary model in Italy: earliest experiences and the 1948 constitution

Notwithstanding the diffuse presence of civic assemblies and other instruments of citizen representation during the medieval era of municipal polities, and also under the Renaissance republics, the tradition of modern parliamentarism is not firmly rooted in Italy because of a long absolutist period and the late formation of a national and constitutional state. However, the experiences of the pre-unitary Piedmontese parliament (1848–61) and half a century of constitutional monarchy during the period of 'liberal Italy' (between 1861 and 1924) are relevant in explaining the evolution of legislative politics in the country.

Three original features of this parliamentary history have to be taken into consideration. The first is the complex nature of the 1848 constitutional settlement inherited by the new Italian state which, in the end, made the legislative process rather flexible and open, over time, to changes. According to the *Statuto Albertino*, legislative power was in the hands of the king and of the two parliamentary branches, with no clear hierarchy between the elective chamber (the Chamber of Deputies) and the Senate, formed by life-time members appointed by the king. Parliamentary practice, however, determined a slow process of emancipation of the elective branch vis-à-vis the Senate.

The second concerns the basic characteristics of the parliamentary elite: a solid territorial linkage between the most prominent representatives and the leading social strata of the different regions, and the absence of clear party affiliations. To a large extent, the liberal elite was indeed a coalition of notables with very fragmented backgrounds, attitudes, and values (Farneti 1989). This diversity could be balanced by their ability to find a common framework of interests and strategies: the well-known notion of *trasformismo*, which in a narrow sense referred to the political strategy of involving personalities from opposing 'parliamentary fractions' in the practice of government, in a broader sense indicated a diffuse modus operandi compensating for the lack of cultural and political homogeneity via the exchange of patronage benefits and other package deals favouring the unity of the ruling class (Ginsborg 1990). In the end, this practice had a truly parliamentary nature: it was within the parliament that the Italian 'liberal' political class could be formed, showing its ability to find compromises and to contain the role of external challengers (Democrats, Republicans, and then the first representatives of the socialist movement) and, when necessary, to integrate them. The political cost of such a practice was the evident lack of alternation in government and the neglect of the democratic principle that, from time to time, the 'outs' should replace the 'ins' (La Palombara 1987: 13).

The third feature is that the entire period before the advent of fascism was characterized by a relatively low degree of institutional development within the parliament. Procedures for selecting and drafting legislation were initially rather undefined, and left largely to the initiative of MPs. The parliamentary sub-units which had to scrutinize and select proposals (the so-called *Uffici*) were ineffective, and unable to develop as specialized groups of legislators and functionaries. The general secretariat of the lower chamber, a crucial element of parliamentary institutionalization, was created only in 1907, a few years after the introduction of a complete set of rules of procedure in the same parliamentary branch. However, the size of the technical staff remained very limited throughout the pre-republican experience.

From the slow transformation to the sudden crisis of parliamentary democracy

Despite the structural weaknesses resulting from the elements described above, the Italian parliament underwent considerable change during the sixty years between the birth of the unitary state and the political crisis which paved the way to the dictatorship. Particularly deserving of mention are the increasing stabilization of the parliamentary personnel producing a stronger degree of political professionalization and competence (Cotta *et al.* 2000), the progressive parliamentarization of the new mass parties, and—last but not least—the ascendance of the lower elective chamber to the detriment of the Senate. The formalization of the role of the Chamber of Deputies in the political investiture of cabinets also became more evident during the *età Giolittiana* (1900–15).

BOX 5.1 The development of the Italian unitary parliament

1848	King Carlo Alberto of Savoy concedes constitutional rule (*Statuto Albertino*); the constitution establishes a bicameral legislature, with an elective chamber
1861	First legislature of the unitary state (named as the Eighth Legislature of the constitutional parliament)
1882	Introduction of multi-member electoral districts
1882	First franchise extension: the electorate increases from 2.2 to 8.1 per cent of the population
1892	Return to single-member districts
1901	Definition of a set of rules of procedure for the lower chamber
1906	The practice of an inaugural vote of confidence on the government starts
1913	Universal male suffrage introduced
1919	Introduction of a system of proportional representation
1920	Inauguration of parliamentary groups; new rules of procedure

The final stage of this historical evolution (Box 5.1) was opened by the long legislature elected in 1913, the first one on the basis of universal male suffrage, which lasted until 1919. At the closing of this term, as a consequence of the difficult political situation following the end of the First World War, the by then fragmented and uncertain liberal elite could not resist any longer the pressures for accelerating the transformation of parliamentary democracy. The choice of a PR electoral system (see Chapter 3) was one of the components of this new strategy, together with a stronger organization, after the 1919 election, of the parliamentary institution, including a full rewriting of the rules of procedure within the lower chamber and the formalization of parliamentary groups along party lines. The reforms were adopted following substantial agreement between the old liberal elites and the new political forces, including the Socialist Party and the newborn Popular Party.

In spite of these reforms the social conflicts and the political stalemate of the post-First World War period soon proved that all efforts to consolidate Italian parliamentary democracy were in vain. The two general elections held under the pure PR system (1919 and 1921) confirmed the fragmentation of the political system, which after 1921 became even more radical following the emergence of small but vigorous parliamentary groups on the extreme left (the Italian Communist Party, born of a split from the Socialists) and on the extreme right (the Nationalist and Fascist parties) (Farneti 1978). The last one in particular would soon gain a crucial role, despite its limited parliamentary weight, thanks to the political skills of its leader, Benito Mussolini, and the brutality of its followers.

The rise to power of Mussolini could in fact take place 'from within', that is to say, by means of a parliamentary crisis which allowed the formation of a new cabinet led by him and approved by parliament (October 1922). The agony of parliament began, and between the second half of 1924 and the beginning of 1925 it was easy for Mussolini, with a predominant control gained over the lower chamber thanks to the application of a 'majority bonus' provided by the new electoral law, and the decision of almost all democratic MPs to abandon parliamentary work (the so-called 'secession of the Aventino'), to complete the demolition of parliamentary rule.

Twenty years later: the rebirth of parliament

Although the transition to democracy after the long authoritarian experience had begun on 25 July 1943, when the non-elective Great Council of Fascism had voted for the dismissal of Benito Mussolini from the office of *Presidente del Consiglio*, the war, German occupation in the north, and the need to write a totally new set of constitutional rules made the reconstruction of a fully fledged parliament impossible for more than four years. The first assembly of representatives of the political forces taking part in the liberation (the *Consulta Nazionale*) was appointed by the government after the liberation (April 1945), while a Constituent Assembly was elected in 1946, with the task of writing the constitution and the new electoral laws.

After a long dictatorship the emphasis on the democratic value of the representative assembly was a common concern of all the political actors taking part in the democratic transition, and the wide popular participation in the first electoral events (the Constituent Assembly election in June 1946 and the local elections held in the same year) was a clear sign of the readiness of the Italians to trust a new democratic parliament.

As a consequence of historical legacies and new political expectations, the republican parliament designed by the constituent fathers at the end of 1947 was the most celebrated body in the new institutional framework. In fact, with a change from its monarchic predecessor, it took the central position in the constitutional text and was accredited with a large number of powers, from the classic legislative function to the new crucial roles of oversight and investigation.

The structure of the 1948 parliament can be classified as an example of co-equal and symmetrical bicameralism, since the two branches perform equal functions and have always had a similar political composition, owing to the substantial uniformity between the electoral systems used (Chapter 3) but also because of their rather large size. With the constitutional amendments of 1963, these numbers have been fixed: there are 630 deputies and 315 elective senators, while former Presidents of the Republic and a few distinguished personalities appointed by the head of state (no more than five) form the small group of life senators.

The internal articulations of the chambers are also basically symmetrical. Since each chamber is in charge of its own rules of procedure, some differences can be possible. But, since the beginning of the republican experience, the lower chamber and the Senate have tended to share the same modus operandi. Three important elements have to be sketched in this respect.

1. The growth of the standing committees in the two chambers has been parallel and the distribution of policy competences among them rather equivalent: today there are fourteen committees in each chamber, having roughly the same distribution of matters. Moreover, since the earliest legislative terms the practice of forming bicameral enquiry or special committees has strengthened the perception of 'equal dignity' of the two branches.
2. The structure of the leadership of the two chambers is also very similar: one speaker and an office of presidency (a few deputy presidents and secretaries) are elected, under similar rules, from the members of each chamber, having equivalent powers and institutional roles. The same structure is multiplied in each committee of both chambers: their top leadership is composed of a chairman, two deputy chairmen, and two secretaries.
3. Finally, the administrative structure of the chambers, their organizational design, and even the prevalent profile of their functionaries are very close to each other: a general secretariat, controlling a complex system of offices and departments (*servizi*

parlamentari), is present in both parliamentary branches. The recruitment of the top officers, their typical background in constitutional law studies, and the organization of work are not very dissimilar, although the Senate, with its smaller bureaucratic structure and its emphasis on historical archives and traditional procedures, has been traditionally less interested in modern technologies. In any case, the circulation of functionaries and advisers from one chamber to another is very frequent.

BOX 5.2 Functions and prerogatives of parliament in the 1948 constitution (relevant articles)

Legislative power exercised symmetrically by the two chambers (70)
Procedures of discussion and deliberation within the standing committees (72)
Possibility of a limited legislative delegation to the government (76)
Confirmation of law decrees issued by the executive (77)
Declaration of war (78)
Ratification of international treaties (79)
Approval of the budget law (81)
Powers of investigations (82)
Examination of citizens' petitions (50)
Allowances for MPs determined by law (69)
Motions of confidence (inaugural confidence in new governments, motions of no confidence) (94)
Election of the President of the Republic (parliament in a joint sitting of the two chambers) (83)
Election of one-third of the members of the Higher Council of the Judiciary (104)
Election of one-third of the members of the Constitutional Court (parliament in a joint sitting of the two chambers) (135)
Impeachment of ministers (parliament in a joint sitting of the two chambers) (96, modified in 1989)

Coming to the powers of the republican parliament (Box 5.2), the first is obviously the legislative one which will receive special attention later on. A second group of powers has to do with the control of the executive: besides the inaugural vote of confidence in the government which is a prerogative of both chambers, the constitution, directly or indirectly, provides practically all the possible tools to sanction or otherwise control the executive (Verzichelli 2003a). The most extreme is the motion of no confidence against the whole Council of Ministers and, as it has been recently clarified, against individual ministers. To this should be added the power to examine popular petitions, to carry out investigations with the same powers as judicial authorities, and actively to review the budgetary policy of the government by means of a formal vote on the yearly budget law. As concerns the other tools of oversight, the constitution has acknowledged their role, experimented with already in the late practice of liberal Italy, mentioning the right of MPs to ask questions, even in written form, of the government.

Finally, the parliament is endowed with significant nominating powers: in addition to the election (every seven years) of the President of the Republic, the chambers in a joint sitting (*Parlamento in seduta comune*) are called to choose, according to a logic of checks and balances among different powers, one-third of the members of the Constitutional Court, and one-third of the Higher Council of the Judiciary. Ordinary legislation has also provided the parliament with other relevant powers of appointment, concerning the leadership of state holdings and, more recently, that of different regulatory authorities and executive boards of quasi-public institutions, for instance the state television company.

In a sketchy summary, it can be said that three broad principles, strictly interconnected with each other, were (and to a large extent have remained) at the basis of the constitutional image of the parliament: the *parity norm* among all the political actors of the 'constitutional front' imposed, by means of the adoption of a PR electoral systems and of very consensual internal rules of procedure, a very inclusive power-sharing logic in all parliamentary activities; the principle of a *co-equal bicameralism*, putting both chambers on an equal footing, reinforced the centrality of parliament and the rituality of its works; finally, a broader logic of *institutional polycentrism* penetrated parliament and around it, in order to set in place a system of institutional checks and balances aimed at preserving the democratic equilibrium of the whole system.

The law-making process

Special attention must now be paid to the main features of the law-making function. The preliminary point to be mentioned is that the constitution has defined a multiple set of possible procedures for producing laws which assign different roles to the parliament and its internal bodies. The three main procedures are those concerning the ordinary legislation, the 'decree laws', and the delegating laws. The so-called ordinary legislation reflects per se a complex procedure (Figure 5.1), as the extremely long average duration of the law-making processes clearly shows. In short, the constitution imposes, in both chambers, an examination by a committee, a vote article by article, and a final vote on all bills submitted either to the lower chamber or to the Senate. The *navette* process—that is the transfer of the proposal from one chamber to another—has to be repeated as many times as necessary until the same text is passed by a formal conclusive vote of both parliamentary branches.

FIGURE 5.1 A simplified scheme of ordinary law making

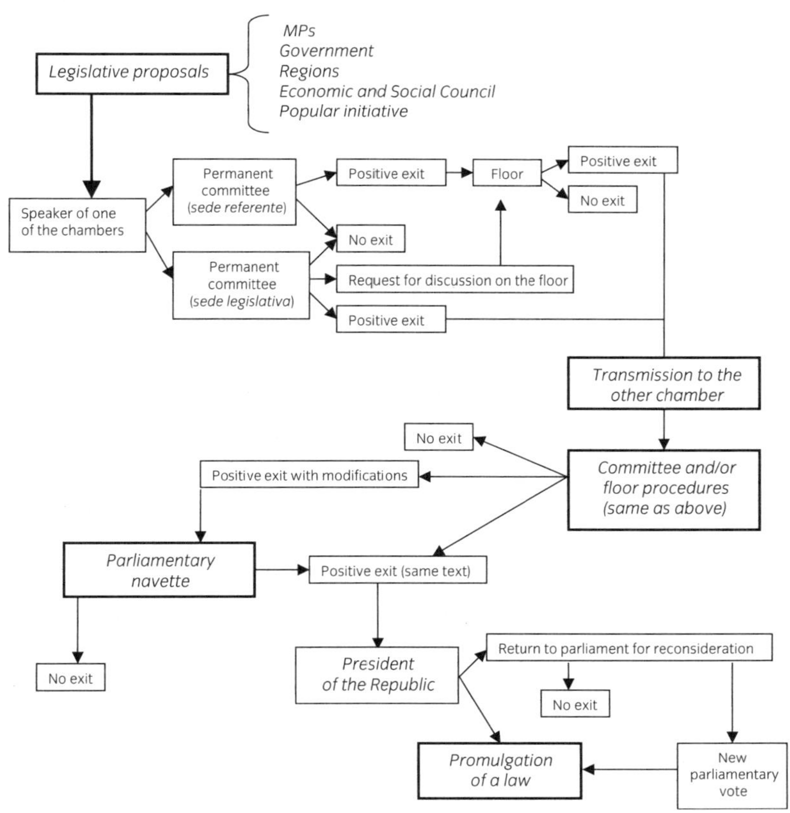

However, ordinary legislation represents just one possible law-making option. The two other legislative outputs mentioned above are extremely important as they prepare the ground for a different 'legislative game'. They give the executive autonomous powers to force decision making and its timing (decree laws) or to control its content (delegating laws), but at the same time leave strong countervailing *ex ante* or *ex post* powers to the MPs. In the first case the decree enacted by the government with temporary effects must be submitted, in order to be transformed into a permanent law, to the parliament and approved by both chambers, following in parliament the same itinerary as ordinary bills (except for the fact that it cannot be approved in the committee stage). The countervailing powers resting in the hands of MPs derive from the tight time limit (sixty days) within which such a decree must be confirmed. The government, pressed to have the decree approved, will be inclined to accept even substantial modifications proposed by MPs. In the second case the procedure is that the parliament will approve—following its normal procedures—the delegating law (but in some cases one or more delegating articles within an ordinary law) defining the principles and criteria of guidance the delegated legislation is to follow, and the time limits within which the cabinet must act. After this the government will approve the delegated decrees which will have the same legal status as ordinary legislation.

The peculiarities of the committee system have had important consequences for the working of the law-making process, enhancing its polycentric character. In particular, the full legislative autonomy of these internal parliamentary units deserves to be mentioned; it is probably unique among democratic parliaments (D'Onofrio 1979) and it determines a set of alternative routes for legislative items. The most peculiar of such routes[1] consists in the possibility of the permanent legislative committees legislating directly without the need to bring the bill to the floor (*commissioni in sede legislativa*).

The final stage of the law-making process is the promulgation of a bill by the President of the Republic, which is followed by its publication in the official journal. This step is, however, not purely formal as the constitution also states (Article 74) that before the promulgation, the president may exercise a suspensive veto and request that the parliament further discusses the bill. In such a case the bill has to go through the whole process for a second time in the two chambers. The president is, however, forced to promulgate the bill if the chambers adopt it again. This is the first of an important set of checks and balances created *around* the parliament, the others being the judicial review by the Constitutional Court (see Chapter 8) and the possibility of an abrogative referendum (see below). When discussing the overall legislative process in Italy all these elements have to be kept in mind.

On the whole, the parliament designed by the 1948 constitution was a much more complete and complex institution in comparison with the pre-Fascist legislature. Over the years it has undergone a relatively rapid process of institutionalization (Cotta 1990), fostered especially by the fact that the exclusion for a long time of the opposition from access to the government has made the parliament the crucial arena for keeping a dialogue open between opposing camps. This process has probably been helped also by another significant innovation, consistent with the 'evolutionary line' of modern Western legislatures: the introduction of a parliamentary allowance. This has helped the MPs to exercise in a more professional way their role as representatives of the nation.

As could be expected, the concrete implementation of the institutional choices made by the constitution with regard to structure and functioning of parliamentary government has been considerably influenced by a number of political variables. The party system and its evolution, but also the changes affecting the executive and its capabilities, have had an important impact on the parliament and its performance.

The consolidation of parliament in the age of full democratization: myths and realities

The alternation between majoritarian attempts and polycentric phases of parliamentarism

The virtues and the paradoxes of the Italian parliament after the return of democracy and during the first republic or the 'age of partycracy' (1948–92) have been extensively analyzed (Leonardi *et al.* 1978; Cotta 1979; Calise 1994; Newell 2002b). Despite a general agreement on the description of the Italian republican legislature as a strong 'policy influencing' parliament (Norton 1998), the implications of the different analyses diverge considerably.

A theme, extensively used in the literature, is that of the progressive development of the parliamentary centrality sketched in the constitutional text. This characterization seems satisfactory when one thinks of the formal and static elements defined by the constitutional and ordinary rules that have just been analyzed. In other words, if a 'central parliament' is, by definition, a legislature with a high degree of institutional involvement, effective autonomy in deciding its agenda (which automatically means limiting the agenda-setting power of the executive), and strong tools of oversight over governmental action, there is no doubt that the features already described (positive parliamentarism with a formal vote of inaugural confidence in both the chambers, autonomy from governmental action, extensive non-legislative powers and organizational resources), together with some characteristics of the executive (see Chapter 4), made the Italian parliament an evident case of parliamentary centrality. And this centrality was easily consolidated thanks to the stabilization of the post-war party system and to the robust social penetration of the same parties, which allowed a full legitimation of the political elite expressed by them (Cotta 1990).

However, if one looks instead at the concrete tasks of a legislature, the notion of parliamentary centrality looks rather vague, and less useful in describing the strength of parliament within a truly comparative framework. As a matter of fact, considering the years between 1948 and 1992, it is possible to distinguish quite changeable practices, and several empirical dimensions can be outlined to show the transformations in the performances of the Italian parliament (Cotta 1994) between the first and the eleventh legislatures, the latter usually indicated as the terminal point of the first republic.

For instance, after a short initial phase of executive predominance, under the prime ministership of De Gasperi, there was then a gradual sliding towards an increasingly consensus-orientated mode. The predominance of a power-sharing system of governance within the parliamentary processes was fully achieved in the second half of the 1970s, with the brief experience of a national solidarity coalition. Electoral and political events outside parliament had a crucial role in leading to this development, but parliamentary groups also made a decisive contribution by promoting a number of legislative and procedural devices aimed at favouring consensus-orientated parliamentary practices. The reform of the standing orders (1971) was a rather clear expression of the dominance of the consociational principle in both parliamentary branches. The most important innovation was the creation of the conference of parliamentary group leaders which was given the fundamental power of agenda setting. This conference, where the government representative had the same weight as any other, had to work on the basis of a unanimity rule, otherwise the decision was referred to the floor. The agenda-setting powers were particularly important in that time of big expectations of 'structural reforms', and they included decisions on the referral of bills to standing committees, on the type of involvement of these committees, and on the priorities to be followed over a three-month period. The 1971 reform of parliamentary rules also introduced wider powers of oversight, such as the right of committees to ask questions of the government and to initiate investigations into the administrative sectors of their competence.

The interpretation of these innovations was at that time mainly inspired by the rhetoric of parliamentary centrality. The change in parliamentary life and its impact upon inter-institutional relationships was assessed with a great deal of optimism. The parliament seemed 'no longer just an "arena" for ideological clashes, but an institution in which political decisions can be produced in response to demands originated in other parts of the political system' (Leonardi *et al.* 1978: 168). Several pieces of evidence seemed to sustain such an optimistic view: among them, the effective functioning of a power-sharing mode within the parliament, the start of important parliamentary investigations, the growth of the practice of oversight and the reduction in the time by which the government must reply to parliamentary questions, more collaborative attitudes among leaders of the parliamentary group, and, more importantly, a number of legislative achievements in important policy sectors. Critical reforms, such as the implementation of regionalization (see Chapter 6), the regulation paving the way to the use of the abrogative referendum, and other interventions concerning the welfare system, the budgetary system, and the national health system, were in fact adopted by large majorities. The model of 'consociational democracy' (Lijphart 1968) was often proposed in those years as an example for Italy.

In the following years, however, with the failure of the attempted grand coalition between Christian Democrats and Communists, and the end of the democratic emergency of the period of left- and right-wing terrorism, this parliamentary model rapidly proved to be less functional than expected. The ability of parliament to reach decisions on the many open problems of Italian society appeared insufficient.

The 1980s would see therefore the first attempts to turn to a more 'majoritarian' model of parliament which would assign to the government and its majority a stronger role in directing parliamentary works. Among the main sponsors of this new vision was Bettino Craxi, the leader since 1976 of a medium-sized but growing party (the PSI) and Prime Minister between 1983 and 1987. But apart from relatively minor changes, a deeper redefinition of the structure of parliament could not come about until the collapse of the party system in the early 1990s opened an entirely new political phase.

Indicators of change in parliamentary practice

In order to evaluate how the Italian parliament has changed, an analysis of law-making processes can offer significant empirical evidence. The balance between the executive and parliamentary actors in legislative work is a relevant case in point. The transition from an initial period of more 'majoritarian government' to a more consensus-orientated one is well shown by the decline of the success rate of executive initiatives (from about 80 per cent during the period of centrism, to an all-time low of 50 per cent during the 1980s) and at the same time by the incremental growth of parliamentary initiative, even though bills introduced by individual MPs continued to be only rarely successful.

A second useful piece of evidence for identifying transformations in the legislative practice is the frequency in the use of the *sede legislativa*, that is to say the approval of bills directly by parliamentary committees. The trend may here look counter-intuitive, as the frequency of this procedure was higher during the more majoritarian phase, while it tended to decrease in the era of *consociativismo*. In fact, this evidence shows the 'two faces' of Italian parliamentary democracy. The first face is that of the 'hidden compromise' between political actors taking place, within the context of a strong ideological divide between majority and opposition, in the more protected environment of the committees. The aim of this practice was to *survive* in a difficult democracy (Di Palma 1977), but in such a climate of consociational adaptation the amount of micro-sectional legislation passed by committees only (the so-called *leggine*, small laws) represented a cost in terms of poor quality, inadequacy, and patronage. The second face is that of an open agreement which aims at creating a convergence in the name of shared democratic values, and does not need a peripheral arena like the parliamentary committees to reach the compromises between the different parties. It is not by chance that the lowest rate of legislation passed in the committees (52 per cent) was to be found during the 1976–79 legislature, when, under the 'historic compromise', the entire constitutional arc of parties, including the PCI, openly supported a minority Christian Democratic government.

A third element to be considered is the evolution of the internal governance of the parliament. The power-sharing mode was significantly extended in the course of the 1970s when a number of parliamentary offices were allocated to the opposition (in fact only to the 'constitutional opposition', which included the Communist Party, but excluded other parties of the extreme left and the neo-Fascist party). This practice included the chairmanships of many important legislative committees, the appointment of a common *rapporteur* between centre and left parties for the most important laws, and, above all, the post of speaker of the lower house, given from 1976 to 1992 to a representative of the PCI.

From minimal adaptations to crisis

The mid-1980s were a new turning point in the relationship between executive and legislative. The confrontation between executive and parliamentary majority became harsh. Particularly during the prime ministership of Bettino Craxi, the government increasingly challenged parliamentary resistance in law making with an extensive use of urgent decrees and, above all, persisting in reissuing decrees when they had been rejected or simply not adopted by parliament. On the other hand, parliament responded with a similar aggressiveness: less than half of the Craxi government's decrees were converted into law (compared with an average of 90 per cent in the first republican legislature), and the government suffered a massive number of parliamentary defeats, at least one each week.

The attempts of Craxi, and of the prime ministers who came after him, even though softer and more inclined to compromise, failed because of different political and structural factors at work (Hine 1993), but particularly because the majoritarian logic, and the rhetoric of *decisionismo*, did not blend easily with the existing model of parliamentary functioning.

The whole period after 1980 was characterized by persistent calls for a reform of parliament. These calls produced some responses, the benefits of which would be fully exploited only after the storm of 1992–94. At first, calls from inside were for a broad institutional revision.[2] Successively, efforts were made in order to improve specific procedural aspects. Among their significant results were the limitation of the secret vote (1988), the introduction of the budgetary session (1985–88), and other internal rules to reduce obstructionism and legislative impasse. However, the political crisis of the early 1990s overshadowed these efforts, and claims for reform moved to the streets with the demand for a referendum to adopt a plurality electoral system (see Chapter 3), seen implicitly as a tool to produce a more effective relationship between government and legislature. The failed reform attempts of the 1980s had inevitably unveiled the naked truth of an 'old' parliament and, above all, of its old parliamentary elite. In 1992, the legislature was suddenly transformed from the theatre of possible changes to the target of a change that seemed at that time revolutionary. And, when the 'moral question' could be satisfied, at least temporarily, in 1994, with the election of a parliament formed to a great extent by fresh MPs (approximately 70 per cent), the issue of parliamentary procedural reform returned. The motif of the parliament—of a legislature which is not able to produce big changes but is always able to adapt itself—was heard again.

Parliamentary processes and functions in the twenty-first century

In the light of the evolutionary dynamics traced in the previous section, what assessment can be made of the current functioning of the Italian parliament? And what are the decisive factors behind the changes we can discern today in this institution: a systemic erosion of the traditional powers (an explanation which would be consistent with the broad argument of parliamentary decline) or perhaps some specificities of the Italian system currently in transition?

Certainly, parliamentary rules and practices have significantly changed. With the bipolar phase (from 1996 onward), important reforms have been proposed and governments have been able to establish a more intense and transparent programme of legislative proposals, without being forced to resort to the defensive tool of 'decree overflow'.[3] The parliament has reacted responsibly, acknowledging the new role of the executive: among the most relevant innovations in this direction, one should mention the more binding limitations on the timing of parliamentary debates, a substantial reduction of the opportunity to amend legislative texts, and the stronger powers of formal screening attributed to the speakers of the two chambers and to the committee chairs.

It is not irrelevant in this perspective that two consecutive legislatures have completed their natural duration (which had not happened since 1968), and have seen a full alternation of roles between two opposed coalitions, something which had happened before only in 1876, when the *Sinistra storica* took over from the *Destra storica*. This is quite significant for the political system. But, in the end, the parliamentary institution has changed only where change has been necessary. As of 2006 no major changes have been agreed on the constitutional principles regulating parliamentary government and the structure of the parliament as an institution. Incremental adaptation, in other words, is still the real pace of change of this complicated machinery.

In explaining the present (and imagining the future) of the Italian parliament, we should remember that the problems which emerged in the final phase of the first republic had in any event created expectations and at least fifteen years of debate about the need to reform the rules of the game (including the work of four bicameral committees on institutional reforms, established between 1983 and 1998). The questions on the agenda could be roughly summarized by the following key words: reduction of complexity (meaning both the abolition of symmetrical bicameralism and a significant cut in the number of MPs), increased effectiveness, search for better performance in legislative outputs, rationalization in the executive–legislative relationships, renewal of the visibility of parliament in front of voters, rediscovery of the educational function of the legislature, and so on.

In order to understand to what extent these discussions and key words have been followed by some significant institutional change, we start our discussion by looking at the legislative function, before moving to the evolution of parliamentary control and to other activities.

Legislative outputs: decreasing the flow for better quality?

There is no doubt that the whole pattern of law making has been deeply modified during the past fifteen years, although a systematic analysis of this transformation is still far from accomplished. The most recent analyses of law-making activity in Italy can be summarized in three main findings.

1. There is a recent trend to reduce the legislative overflow which in the past made the Italian legislature the most 'productive' in Europe, in terms of the number of laws passed (Table 5.1): the average production of laws is now significantly lower than during the first decades of the republic, when the significant rate of one law per day was often reached.

TABLE 5.1 Laws enacted, monthly average and origin

Legislature	Laws	Monthly average	Laws from cabinet initiative (%)	Laws from parliamentary initiative (%)
I (1948–53)	2,314	37	88.7	11.3
II (1953–8)	1,394	33	74.6	25.4
III (1958–63)	1,781	30	73.0	27.0
IV (1963–8)	1,769	30	66.9	33.1
V (1968–72)	841	17	74.5	25.5
VI (1972–6)	1,122	23	75.7	24.3
VII (1976–9)	666	19	85.1	14.9
VIII (1979–83)	1,042	23	72.4	27.6
IX (1983–7)	789	16	72.0	28.0
X (1987–92)	1,065	19	69.6	30.4
XI (1992–4)	314	14	74.8	25.2
XII (1994–6)	295	12	89.2	10.8
XIII (1996–2001)	905	15	76.8	23.2
XIV (2001–6)	685	11	78.0	22.0

Note: 'Parliamentary initiative' includes also mixed initiative and popular initiative.
Source: Chamber of Deputies.

2. Cabinets tend to keep the legislative flow under control by means of assiduous attention paid to the legislature and by more efficiently pursuing the parliamentary adoption of their proposals. Indeed, the percentage of laws which are the result of the cabinet's initiative increased significantly after 1994. It is the government's legislative success rate which tells us most about the stronger role of the executive in the control of the law making. Figures 5.2 and 5.3 show that during the two long majoritarian legislatures cabinets decided to limit the number of their legislative initiatives, concentrating instead on defending their proposals. This has allowed them to see the majority of their proposals accepted (particularly so in the case of the second Berlusconi government, which could count on a large and relatively cohesive majority), thus achieving a success rate never recorded after the first decades of republican experience. On the other hand, bills autonomously introduced by MPs continue to play an important symbolic role for purposes of constituency service and are used to signal commitment to the defence of local and sectional interests. In fact, this type of initiative has clearly increased in number, but its success rate is now close to zero.
3. The percentage of legislation approved directly by committees has been significantly reduced, representing today only about 20 per cent of the total number of laws. However, this still represents a consistent rate, confirming the coexistence of different viable options for the actors involved in law-making initiatives and strategies.

A closer and more qualitative look at the way these different options are effectively managed by MPs corroborates the idea of persistent complexity in the parliamentary institution. The Italian parliament of today seems more open than it used to be in the past in acknowledging the right of the cabinet to pursue its programme in parliament. Analyses of delegated legislation (Vassallo 2001) show the substantial use of this tool by recent governments to cover the existing legislative deficit in a number of crucial policy areas, from welfare to education to problems of the economy. Also part of this trend is the recurrent practice of including a number of matters for delegated legislation within the framework of ordinary laws. The greater readiness of parliament in accepting that the power of political direction should reside in the hands of the executive is also visible from looking at other indicators. An example is that the parliament is inclined now to grant the executive a longer time period to produce its delegated decrees and, perhaps most importantly, it tends to accept—more than in the past—the legislative strategies of the government aimed at reducing the impact of external constraints on the delegation link between the parliamentary majority and governmental action (Verzichelli 2003a). Among such instruments are to be counted the use of 'maxi-amendments', proposed by the government in order to prevent parliamentary attacks on different articles of a given bill, and the more common recourse to the 'vote of confidence on legislative items' (see Chapter 4).

Structuring parliamentary processes: institutional changes 'from below'

The improved ability of the government to use its powers of initiative and to defend its proposals on the parliamentary scene is of course a necessary condition, but not a sufficient one for achieving better results in terms of the quality of law making. Parliamentary rules of procedure are critical in this

FIGURE 5.2 **Governmental legislative activity**

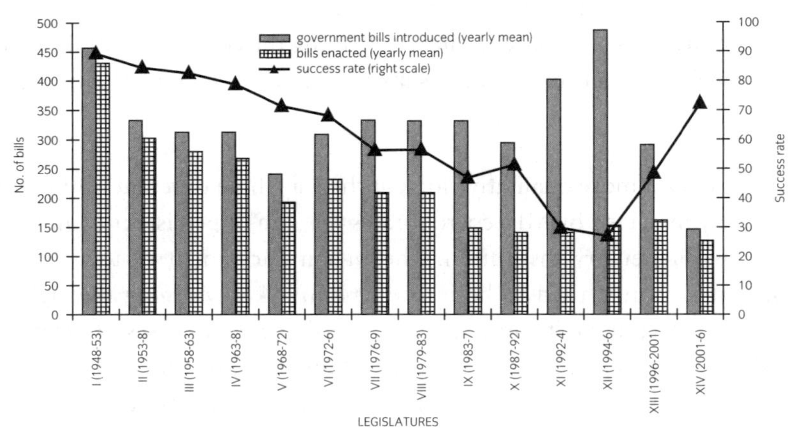

Source: Elaboration of data from the Chamber of Deputies.

FIGURE 5.3 Parliamentary legislative activity

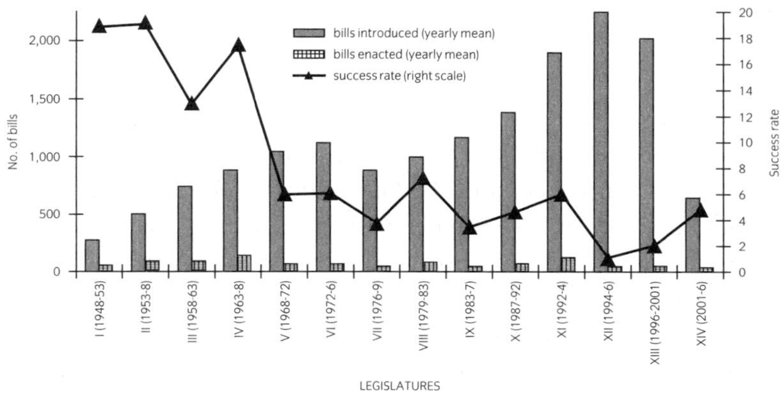

Source: Elaboration of data from the Chamber of Deputies.

respect. Their rationalization has been, in the Italian case, a long process. Both chambers have changed some rules over the years, moving further away from the consensus orientation of the 1971 regulations, but they are still far from a complete overhaul of their procedures. After the already mentioned limitations on the use of secret vote, other innovations were adopted, in order to create more binding rules governing the amendment process and curbing irresponsible initiatives of individual MPs. If the Italian Chamber of Deputies was a few years ago in an intermediate position on a comparative scale measuring the power of amendment and of individual initiative of MPs in parliamentary democracies (Mattson 1995), the corrections to the rules of procedures introduced during the past decade, with the aim of diminishing the risks of impasse and filibustering (obstruction), have changed somewhat, but not completely, this placement. The number of restrictions on the power to present bills and amendments has indeed increased, but it is also true that in Italy there is still no room for strong tools explicitly designed to protect governmental legislation, such as the French *guillotine* or the British *closure*. In the end the main tool for the regulation of parliamentary activism in the field of legislation is still the old rule, stated by Article 81 of the constitution, that all laws implying new or additional expenditures must indicate the financial means required to cover them. Past history shows that this constraint has been a weak measure for rationalizing legislative outcomes.

As a matter of fact, the decision-making power of parliament is simply more constrained now than it once was, but has certainly not been drastically reduced in scope. Clear examples of this kind of cautious rationalization are two important legislative procedures—the budgetary law and the annual law of transposition of the European Union legislation (the *legge comunitaria*)—which have been entirely reshaped and routinized during the past twenty years, and have been often seen as critical tests of the evolution of the whole system of government in Italy (Hine 1993).

In both cases the rationalization could be reached not by means of a straightforward reform but rather through a trial and error process. Several successive interventions were necessary to obtain two viable legislative tools, and the application of the reforms had to wait for the development of precise political conditions before good results could be assured. The story of the budgetary process is, in particular, rich and complicated, with three major legislative reforms between 1978 and 1999, and a number of failed attempts (especially during the early 1980s) which demonstrated parliament's ability to overrule the decisions of the executive.

Since 1993, when a dramatic financial crisis pushed the government of Giuliano Amato to issue more responsible proposals for tackling the problem of public deficits, the reformed budgetary session has allowed Italian executives to approve a series of financial bills which have been decisive in reducing the deficit and keeping public debt under control (albeit not downsizing it drastically), thereby meeting the targets set in the Maastricht Treaty, and enabling Italy to join the group of EU member states that adopted the single currency in 2001. Through these tools it has been possible to persuade MPs to reduce their claims on the 'distributive benefits' of public expenditure, and at the same time to cope with a very long economic stagnation by means of a series of difficult measures in different policy fields.

A summary of the budgetary process in Italy as it is today is given in Box 5.3. Some strong constraints on the action of parliament are now at work, and the external surveillance provided by the EU stability pact is an additional source of pressure and responsibility for the government as well as for individual MPs. However, the reiterated reforms which led to the definition of this budgetary calendar did not eliminate the original role of the parliament as a critical interlocutor of the cabinet. This makes the Italian budgetary system still quite different and more complex than the system at work, for example, in the United Kingdom. It is true that, on the one hand, the parliamentary session has been extensively regulated and MPs have now to follow severe limitations in the timing of the discussion and the possibilities of amending the text. On the other hand, however, the power of the committees and the *navette* system between the two chambers still allows significant changes in the content of an *omnibus* piece of legislation such as the financial bill.

BOX 5.3 The budgetary process in Italy (as of 2006)

January Financial year begins.
February–March Discussion within the government about the financial targets of each ministry. The Treasury defines with each administrative unit the draft of the expenditures for the next year.
March–April The government receives the estimates of the EU Council of Ministers on the previous document concerning the Stability and Growth Pact.
June The government sends the economic and financial plan (DPEF) for the next four-year period to the parliament.
July Adoption of the document by parliament and presentation of the information on the state of public finances on the basis of existent legislation.
September Discussion in the cabinet of the draft of the budget bill (the formal budget sheet for each ministry) and of the financial bill (containing all the cabinet's proposals reshaping and refinancing the existing legislation).
October Budgetary session begins. Parliament receives the budget documents; discussion in committees and then on the floor.
November Presentation in parliament of other linked legislation (policy-related bills and decrees with immediate effects on public finance).
December End of the budgetary session and approval of the financial package (budget bill & financial bill). The government reports its update of the stability programme to the European Commission.

The process determining the approval of the *legge comunitaria* is perhaps less visible for public opinion and, above all, much less intrusive in the parliamentary time schedule. Even in this case, however, it is the result of a learning process: the original procedure, shaped by two laws of 1986 and 1989, was revised significantly in the course of the following decade in order to make the decisional process faster and to provide an annual law, the content of which is really political and crucial for reducing the gap between Italy's formal enthusiasm for EU initiatives, and what in the mid-1990s was a dramatic delay in compliance with supranational regulation.

If Italy still has to fill some significant legislative gaps before achieving full compliance with EU legislation, the *legge comunitaria* has played quite an important role in improving institutional performance, while at the same time providing a good instrument of dual oversight. Similarly to the economic and financial plan in the field of budgetary policy, it provides an *ex ante* set of political statements to be implemented in the near future and to this adds also a detailed and informative *ex post* report on the state of Italian compliance with EU law.

Non-legislative functions

A similar complex evolution seems also to have characterized the dynamics of other parliamentary functions, particularly those which usually go under the label of parliamentary oversight.

Since the 1980s, such activities have increased in number as well as in their concrete impact on parliamentary life as a whole. Thousands of oversight activity items are submitted by Italian MPs in every legislature. In particular, the use of written questions increased significantly after 1979, while 'decentralized questioning'—questioning in legislative committees—became common practice during the 1990s (De Micheli and Verzichelli 2004, chapter 5).

It is correct to say that the Italian parliament is today provided with a broad set of oversight instruments (Wiberg 1995),[4] which are extensively utilized by MPs. The political potential of such instruments is, however, still on the whole unclear. For instance, a sort of 'question time', inspired by the British weekly meeting with the Prime Minister, was introduced in the 1980s (and its procedures were successively modified in the 1990s), but its impact on the political debate remains limited, largely owing to the systematic absence of the Prime Minister. Moreover, the relatively low rate of completed answers to the questions submitted and the lack of a specific form of critical scrutiny on sensitive issues (as on economic and budgetary outputs) are two indicators of the most evident structural flaws of this procedures: a generalist orientation and an inclination to produce symbolic (and often unproductive) monologues instead of a real dialogue between parliamentary and governmental actors.

In general terms, the growth in the use of the oversight tools has been interpreted as the transition from a 'silent pact of mutual non-interference' to a more active relationship between parliamentary groups and individual MPs of the opposition on one side and the governmental majority on the other side, which should improve the efficiency of the legislative process (Capano and Giuliani 2003). Some steps towards this ambitious goal have been made, thanks also to the noticeable growth in the information and technology structures supporting the scrutiny work of the permanent committees. On the other hand, countervailing forces have been at work: they include the limited ability of the government to respond as a unitary actor to parliamentary questions, and the consensus-orientated attitude of many MPs, who often prefer the more traditional practice of interest bargaining to a critical scrutiny of the government.

When evaluating the changes which have occurred in recent years, two trends look particularly interesting: a clearer division of labour between parliamentary majority and opposition MPs, and the evolution of the committee system, with a visible growth of oversight activities balancing the rationalization of decentralized law-making activities. This goes in the direction of a more effective and responsible 'delegation' between the parliament and an accountable government, implemented by means of reports by each minister to the corresponding parliamentary committee (Verzichelli 2003b).

Another interesting aspect of the recent transformation is the growing importance of different kinds of parliamentary bodies which are granted non-legislative powers. A comparative assessment some years ago had already shown the richness of the Italian parliament, with its remarkable number of special commissions, bicameral commissions and councils (Strøm 1995). Recent experience has brought further evidence of an increasing role for these institutions. Leaving aside the work of the councils (the *Giunte*), which are technical bodies dealing with internal matters of parliamentary life, the proliferation of special committees created with the aim of monitoring policy implementation in specific fields (for example, human rights or child protection) must be mentioned here. A particularly relevant role has also been played by the bicameral committee for the scrutiny of public radio and television, thanks in part to its powers of appointment to the board of the public broadcasting company.

All these phenomena can be interpreted as efforts to exploit the non-legislative functions for achieving a more productive division of labour and a more equal balance between the two sides of a more adversarial parliament. In this way, while the majority dominates the legislative process, the minority can retain and strengthen its watchdog and guarantee role.[5]

Profiles, attitudes, and careers of Italian legislators

The traditional profile and recruitment patterns of Italian legislators

If the typical MP of the monarchic age was (at least until 1919) a notable and an amateur politician, there is no doubt that the legislators of the first republic embodied a consolidated and professionalized elite. Full-time occupation within party and trade union organizations became, after the 1950s, a frequent professional background for MPs, and also parliamentarians with other occupational experiences (with lawyers, journalists, teachers, and doctors being among the most relevant categories) showed quite a long and articulate process of political socialization, whose typical steps were a series of party offices at the local and national level and some relevant experiences in local elective bodies. Empirical researches have evidenced a crucial distinction between the strong degree of centralized party control over the selection and recruitment process of Communist MPs, and the open competition among the local candidates of governmental parties, and particularly among the Christian Democrats (Cotta 1979). This difference determined two models of parliamentary career, with the Communist MPs being more bound by the decisions of the party apparatus to nominate them or not as candidates, while the Christian Democratic representatives had a greater chance of being renominated as candidates but engaged then in internal struggles with competitors from opposite factions.

Overall the parliamentary class of the first republic (including MPs from minor parties) maintained for a long time the typical outlook of a party-professionalized elite. Among the consequences of such a recruitment model was the strong external control exercised by party elites over representatives, determining an external party dominance (Helms 2000) over parliamentary groups. Of course, representatives of a factional and multifaceted party such as the DC could show occasional indiscipline in their legislative behaviour, but this did not endanger their loyalty to the basic values of the party and their support for the executives. In any case, party support both at a local and at the national level was a necessary requisite to be a candidate in the DC lists and to obtain the chance to climb to the leadership position in the executive.

Parliamentary recruitment and party linkages after 1994

What has changed after the collapse of *partitocrazia* and the rise of a new party system? The political and institutional crisis of the early 1990s has undoubtedly determined a significant discontinuity in the composition of parliament: the unprecedented rate of turnover of the 1994 parliament (71 per cent of new MPs in the Chamber of Deputies) is a clear sign of this. Less easy to determine is the extent to which this was a temporary interruption or the beginning of a different phase in the recruitment process. Among the many questions to be asked, two deserve special attention. To what extent political parties are still important in the process of parliamentary recruitment, in shaping MPs' roles and controlling their behaviours? Secondly, do MPs behave differently from the past with regard to their constituencies?

Despite the considerable use of the rhetoric of intra-party democracy and the new organizational structure of the current parties (particularly of the newest ones, such as Forza Italia and the Lega Nord), the formal criteria defined by all the parties to recruit their representatives do not look so different from those of the past: the use of a mixed-plurality electoral system in the period 1994–2001 did not lead to a significant challenge to the rather centralized processes of candidate selection. The introduction of the blocked list in the PR system of 2005 (see Chapter 3) has further increased this centralization, and the national party elites seem to be today even more able to dominate the process than the *partitocrazia* of the old days of the first republic.

If the 'selectorate' side of parliamentary recruitment still looks centralized, different considerations come into play when considering candidates' characteristics. The parliamentary elite elected by the two newest parties, Forza Italia and Lega Nord, showed indeed some innovative features: Forza Italia recruited a large number of MPs from managerial careers (and, above all, in the beginning, from within the group of managers already employed by Silvio Berlusconi in his previous economic businesses), while the Lega recruited a number of young local activists who represented well the socio-economic core of its electorate (small business people, craftsmen, farmers, and other middle-class professions which had been 'forgotten' by the traditional parties).

However, after a few years of instability resulting from the uncertainties in the new party system (Verzichelli 1998), the social and political outlook of the parliamentary elite very much resembles the profiles of the first republic. If the introduction of single-member districts in the electoral competitions had determined an increase of local candidates—personalities with visible social and political backgrounds within their own constituencies, such as professionals and higher civil servants or local government office-holders well known by the voters—the reintroduction of a PR system and of large constituencies has marked the return of more 'traditional' party candidates (Papavero and Verzichelli 2007).

All in all, the current parliamentary class is not dramatically different from that of the days of the first republic. Particularly, it seems that the non-political characteristics are quite stable: Italian MPs continue to have quite a high level of education, with about 85 per cent of MPs having a university degree (and law predominant as a disciplinary orientation), they are rather old (an average age of about 51 years across both chambers), and they still represent one of the most male-dominated political elites in Western Europe.

Nevertheless, at least three pieces of evidence indicate an interesting evolutionary trend: the first is the political background of MPs, which is definitely more orientated to local and administrative experiences than to a pure party career. This is not surprising, in part because of the decline of party organizations and, more generally, of the reduction of party-led mobilization. In perspective, we can hypothesize that patterns of pre-parliamentary career might be more flexible in the future, and a mix of 'managerial' and 'political' commitments could predominate.

The second element has to do with the occupational profiles of the MPs: if the overall figures are not so different from the past, an interesting feature emerges from the disaggregate analysis of representatives of the two competing coalitions. Since the emergence of a bipolar system after 1994, centre-right MPs have been most likely to have private-sector, managerial, or professional backgrounds, while among centre-left parliamentarians the over-representation of academics, employees, and (higher) civil servants prevails. These differences are anyway limited to the social-occupational backgrounds of MPs, since political experiences tend to be similar across the two coalitions, with inter-party differences in both camps.

The third aspect concerns the development of political careers. It is increasingly evident that Italian MPs are ready to leave parliament if they have no chance to improve their political influence in this institution and other opportunities are available. The parliamentary turnover in the course of the past fifteen years has been quite striking (see Table 3.2), and the effects of the party system change of 1992–96 and of the following electoral swings (2001–6) alone are probably not sufficient to explain it. It can be argued that this is also a result of the fact that the 'market' for good and visible positions has been significantly widened by the direct election of local chief executives (see Chapter 6) as well as by the emergence of European institutions. Other indicators of change within the parliamentary elite, still unclear in their magnitude, include the frequent occurrence of mid-term substitutions after a turn of local or European elections, and the emergence of a bi-directional political career, with a number of representatives 'moving down' to the sub-national representative offices or 'up' to the European Parliament. On the whole, it can probably be argued that the office of national MP may be less relevant today than in the past.

Parliamentary roles, territorial and social linkages

The notion of constituency service, that is an MP's commitment to the problems and the concerns of her or his constituents, is in Italy less relevant, in comparison with the tradition that is firmly institutionalized in the US Congress and also among British backbench MPs. But this does not mean that territorial issues have not played any crucial role. On the contrary, during the age of the first republic the large diffusion of the preference vote was a typical indicator of the salience of territorial consensus. However, as we have seen in Chapter 3, the use of such a tool concerned the governing parties more than the opposition ones and was particularly strong in the southern regions, where the exchange vote was a crucial tool for generating electoral support. Therefore, the degree of territorial linkage of MPs varied greatly from one party to another, from one region to another, producing a far from homogeneous framework of territorial representation. The importance of the local preference vote was a key to establishing strategic links (*cordate*) between national leaders able to deliver the required policy outputs and the local leaders who could mobilize the preferences of the voters.

The introduction of the mixed-plurality system, however, did partially change the relationship between representatives and voters, and also between national and local politicians. During the relatively short period of its application, a number of MPs tried to organize (and personalize) the relationship with voters, establishing a local office and promoting civic associations with the aim of keeping their voters united (even if their party preferences were probably diversified) (Legnante 2004). The adoption of a new PR system in 2005, with no significant hints of a 'rebellion' among centre-right MPs, is by itself the proof that these constituency-orientated representatives were, in reality, very limited in number, or in their political weight. Today individual MPs are pure party nominees and their participation in the electoral competition has significantly diminished. It can be argued, therefore, that the current PR system has 'frozen' the process of territorialization.

If one looks to the broader system of interest representation, the pluralistic model institutionalized during the years of democratic consolidation (Morlino 1991) has not been erased by the recent political changes. Rather, it has adapted to the changing social networks (Pasquino 2001) and, of course, the main interests tend today to be distributed in a different way among the contemporary party actors. The most relevant case of change is that of the multiple links of the Catholic Church, which took the place of the 'exclusive' relationship with Christian Democracy after its disappearance in 1994.

Finally, one has to consider that the role of the legislators is also changing as a result of the impact of the multi-level and inter-institutional environment: if Italian MPs say they are ready to work in a multi-level context, being quite open to the perspective of a deepening process in the European Union[6] and, more generally, confident in the process of

European integration, it is hard to say which kind of capabilities they will be able to retain in the near future when confronted with the powers of new formal and informal institutions, from the independent agencies, to local governments, from the new social movements to European Union actors. In other words, the role and the credibility of MPs face a delicate phase of transition, and even Italian public opinion seems aware of it, since its trust in the national parliament is, almost fifteen years after *tangentopoli* (the term currently used to describe the financial scandals of the early 1990s), still rather low, according to the Eurobarometer and other polls.

Conclusion: between incremental changes and a 'permanent claim for reforms'?

In this chapter we have briefly scrutinized historical legacies and current dilemmas of an institution which has always been a primary concern for political scientists and other analysts of Italian political institutions. For decades, they have debated the problem of parliamentary institutionalization, looking for the reasons for the unexpected equilibrium of a legislature which showed a low degree of public appreciation, high internal fragmentation, and quite a complex legal and political structure. When the 1992 crisis came, both observers and voters suddenly changed perspective, considering parliament as the eye of a hurricane crossing the Italian political system. Although *tangentopoli* was a phenomenon involving the whole political class (and to some extent other components of the broader ruling class), Italian public opinion was particularly struck by the number of MPs who had to renounce their ambitions for political office.

In the following years, the main theme for analysts was the new shape of parliamentary democracy (Bull 2004), taking for granted that, after such a destructive phase, the 'fresh start' should necessarily be grounded upon different institutional bases. In some cases, the definition of a new role has been explicitly indicated as the puzzle for the Italian parliament (Koff and Koff 2000; Capano and Giuliani 2003), but all these titles or subtitles have ended with a question mark.

Almost fifteen years after the first signs of what was labelled a revolution in Italian politics, the question mark still stands. Many changes have been experienced over the past twenty years (thus including the last years of the first republic) but, on the whole, they seem to represent another aspect of the same adaptive pathway started in 1948. In the end, most of the changes which seemed to suggest a clear discontinuity have turned into changes of a more incremental nature, thus confirming the resilient disposition of this legislature.

The analysis of the role of parliament in the law-making process is in this respect very illustrative. In the past, all the assessments have insisted on the powerful role of this institution, classifying the Italian parliament as a 'transformative arena' (Polsby 1975) or a 'consensual legislature' (Lijphart 1999), thus anticipating Philip Norton's definition, already mentioned in this chapter, of a 'policy influencing legislature'. These definitions are hardly in question today, but the overall impact of the Italian parliament on law making has been changing, as several indicators show, from the decrease of legislative overflow, to the changing law-making strategies, to the increasing success of governmental initiatives. If we are not concerned with ideal-typical images, but instead accept the relevance of each single step in the context of a basic continuity of a *hybrid* model of parliamentary democracy, the evolution of the Italian legislature has much to tell us, providing quite an interesting case of institutional adaptation (Capano 2005).

Speaking more broadly, the current practice of parliamentary functions seems to tell a rather chaotic story: the call for a more adversarial model of parliamentary work, highly recommended in many comments of the early 1990s, has rapidly evolved into a more complex game, and, in some cases, has been forgotten. The Italian parliament is therefore *still* a hybrid model (like most Western legislative institutions), mixing different 'consensual' and 'majoritarian' practices together.

However, this finding does not mean that the changes reported above, including more adversarial patterns of composition and behaviour within both chambers, have been insignificant. On the contrary, what happened to the budgetary system or, to a certain extent, to the practice of parliamentary oversight are clear indicators of relevant, although not revolutionary, transformations. It is impossible to assess the impact of these transformations without considering the changing role of other institutions involved in the sub-systems considered here. For instance, it is clear that, in the redefinition of the law-making responsibilities, the parliamentary resistance to the majoritarian thrust has forced the executive to look for alternative tools, such as legislative delegation and other forms of legislating outside of the ordinary process. But this is just one of the interesting aspects here. Other decision-making fora and institutions, from the European Union, through independent authorities, to the growing system of local and regional governments, have become in fact crucial actors in a number of policy areas.

KEY TERMS

- budgetary process
- co-equal and symmetrical bicameralism
- legislative process
- parliamentary government
- parliamentary oversight
- parliamentary party groups
- parliamentary recruitment
- parliamentary rules of procedure
- permanent (standing) committees
- representation
- small laws (*leggine*)

GUIDE TO FURTHER READING

Best, H., and Cotta, M. (eds.) (2000) *Parliamentary Representatives in Europe* (Oxford, Oxford University Press).

A broad, long-term comparative analysis of parliamentary recruitment in Europe, with a long chapter on the Italian case.

Capano, G., and Giuliani, M. (eds.) (2001) *Parlamento e processo legislativo in Italia* (Bologna, Il Mulino).

Recent trends in law making and patterns of legislative behaviour among Italian legislators.

Cotta, M. (1979) *Parlamento e classe politica in Italia* (Bologna, Il Mulino).

The political profile and the career circulation of the parliamentary elite in the first thirty years of republican democracy

De Micheli, C., and Verzichelli, L. (2004) *Il Parlamento* (Bologna, Il Mulino).

A textbook in Italian on structural and functional characters of the Italian legislature.

Di Palma, G. (1977) *Surviving without Governing: The Italian Parties in Parliament* (Berkeley, University of California Press).

A classic interpretation of the law-making processes during the first republic.

Leston Bandeira, C. (ed.) (2005) *Southern European Parliaments in Democracy* (London, Frank Cass).

Comprehensive analyses of the recent transformations of legislatures in Mediterranean countries, with two chapters dedicated to the Italian case.

NOTES

1 We concentrate here on the difference between the autonomous legislative power of the committees and all the other procedures, without considering the distinction between two forms of 'non-autonomous' active law-making procedures within the committees: the power of critical analysis of a text to be sent to the floor (*sede referente*) and the power to draft the article before a general vote on the whole text by the floor (*sede redigente*).

2 In 1983 a special bicameral committee for the drafting of an institutional reform was established. Three other similar initiatives would follow, with no effects, until 1998.

3 We remark once again that, since 1996, the reiteration of urgent decrees has been banned by a ruling of the Constitutional Court.

4 Namely, they are the questions (oral, written, and urgent), the interpellations, the motions, and the resolutions. The rules of procedure of both the chambers regulate all these procedures, with some minor differences in their application.

5 For instance, the chairmanship of the bicameral committee for the scrutiny of public radio and television is still allocated to a MP from the opposition.

6 According to comparative research, the national Italian parliament in 1996 was among those with a more 'open' view about the possibility of limiting their own powers in favour of the European Parliament (see Katz and Wessels 1999).

6

Local Government: The Long-Term Path towards a Federal System

Overview

The institutions of sub-national governance are the focus of this chapter. In Italy, this aspect of the political system has recurrently been a major concern of political actors, although the reasons for this concern have been very different and somewhat at odds from one period to the next. The main concern of the 'nation's fathers' during the *Risorgimento* was to limit the role of local governments, in order to facilitate the emergence of a core set of national values in a country of recent unity, which was noted for its high degree of social and cultural fragmentation. In the late 1940s, after the Fascist regime had further increased the control of central government over the periphery and incessantly stressed the rhetoric of 'national unity', the concern of the 'constituent fathers' was to find a good balance between local administrative units and national politics, without putting the unitary nature of the state into discussion. This led to the birth of a quite atypical form of asymmetric regionalism. More recently, at the end of the twentieth century, the concern of the political class has been to respond to a growing but disorderly demand for federalism. The first results of the new wave of reforms are a strong reshaping of local governments, a significant constitutional reform of the regionalist state, and the attempt at a more complex reform rejected by the referendum of June 2006 (see Chapter 1). Other adaptations are commonly perceived as necessary, and the possibilities for major reforms are still open.

For reasons of space, a fully fledged exposition of the historical transformation of the local government system in Italy is not given here. Less ambitiously, we intend to describe the basic components of this system, identify the critical junctures in their recent adaptations, and assess the current 'weight' of the different sub-national political institutions. This aim will be pursued starting with a concise picture of the local government system during the first republic, particularly stressing the watershed of the implementation of the 'regional governments' during the 1970s. After that, we will focus on the current features and perspectives of local governance and regionalism in Italy, devoting particular attention to the complex interconnection with the other tiers of modern governance, namely the central state government and the European Union politics and policies.

The traditional fragmentation of the Italian state and the constitutional compromise

Unitary but not united?

Most textbooks in comparative politics produced in the second half of the twentieth century stressed the *unitary* nature of the Italian state, and this is consistent with the standard indicators which can be used to classify political systems on the basis of their degree of centralization. Nonetheless, a certain degree of caution is needed when applying the adjective 'unitary' to the Italian polity.

A first reason has to do with the 'latecomer' nature of the Italian state and its difficult history: as a matter of fact, the process of state-building was conducted, in Italy, by regional elites who had to coalesce on the main reform issues and continuously negotiate about the allocation of political spoils at the central level (see Ginsborg 1990). Therefore, although, owing to the need of the political elite to consolidate the unitary nature of the newborn state, there was no formal recognition of any 'sub-national entity' in the original constitution of Italy (the *Statuto Albertino*), the political game was played on the basis of a delicate equilibrium between the different groups forming the ruling elite, whose regional or territorial connotations were strongly marked.

In other words, one can argue that an implicit feature of the early 'de facto constitution' of Italy was the equilibrium reached, within a very segmented predominant ruling class, by means of a quite consensual representation of the elites from different areas of the country. This is of course something different from the institutional dynamics which took place in the early days of purely 'federal' contexts, as for instance the United States of America or even the new German state after the formation of the *Kaiser Reich*. However, it is also something different from the decisional flows from the centre to the periphery which were a typical phenomenon of the crucial phases of state formation, for instance, in France and in Britain.

An interesting comparative interpretation of the Italian peculiarity can be found using the conceptual map developed by the Norwegian sociologist Stein Rokkan (1970). The rather solitary position of the Italian case in the European context is a result of the occurrence of different historical contingencies: Italy in fact shares with the German territories and also with other areas like Belgium a legacy of territorial division and strong urban networks (compared with the relative weakness of its different centres). However, differently from these other cases, territorial unification was in Italy more protracted and contentious. This difficult historical process of unification, of course related also to the presence of the political organization of the Roman Catholic Church, made this political system different from other examples of European polities formed between the seventeenth and the nineteenth centuries.

In the end, it is correct to classify the Italian experience until the end of the twentieth century as a 'unitary state', clarifying that this was possible because of the elevation of one of its peripheries (the Piedmontese constitutional monarchy) to the status of 'centre' and by means of a number of costly events and compromises, which have inspired a wide historical literature about the myth of the 'unfinished unification', of the Piedmontese 'takeover', and other conflicting issues which emerged with the Italian *Risorgimento*.

A second good reason critically to discuss the unitary nature of the Italian state lies in the fact that the local administrative units, in particular the municipal administrations, have always worked as a relevant political component of the nation-state, and they have had a significant importance, during the crucial turning points of Italian history, as a sort of catalyst of political change. This was for instance the case of the years 1920–22, the age of the penetration of mass party organizations at the local level, and the years of the debate about the 'municipalization' of the state.

As a consequence of these historical and cultural factors, one can say that the experience of the unitary state in Italy did not necessarily mean the affirmation of a united state. On the contrary, during the sixty years of the first democratization of the Italian political system, many causes of territorial division remained at work. At the same time, the political convergence of the different local elites was strong enough to preserve the centralized structure of the state and to reject the federalist claim which had been raised during the unification process (although in the two rather different versions of the *neoguelfismo*—a confederal-like perspective maintaining the temporal power of the Catholic Church and giving a role of arbiter to the Pope—and of the federal-secular state, centred on a system of strong regional devolution) (see Chapter 1).

Historical interpretations: an irregular system of territorial cleavages

The work undertaken by historians on the legacies of the processes of state and nation-building has underlined the existence in Italy of important internal differences which came to the attention of the political debate in the late nineteenth century and, to a large extent, persisted in the course of the following century. The framework resulting from all these differences can be defined as a system of territorial cleavages, a concept evoking both the salience of the different polity levels (municipalities, large towns, provincial units, regions, macro-regional areas), and also a different degree of relevance attributed to these sub-national communities, in comparison with the idea of 'nation-state', by public opinion's perceptions.

This intricate framework of Italian localism has been analyzed by many scholars, using different methods and in turn generating many interesting theories. With no pretence of producing an exhaustive overview of the studies on Italian localism, we will mention here just some of these 'schools of thought' which have been most relevant for the reflections of political scientists on the nature of the Italian state.

The first to be mentioned is the approach based on the specificities of territorial 'microcosms,' and developed from a historical and anthropological point of view, which inspired important studies like the well-known *Moral Basis of a Backward Society*, written by Edward Banfield in 1958. In this work, 'amoral familism'—that is, the egoistic maximization of personal and familiar benefits with no regard for any form of collective cooperation—was epitomized as the prevailing pattern of social and political life in southern Italy. Among the possible solutions for overcoming this condition and the poverty of the depressed south, Banfield identified a real process of decentralization, that is, the 'devolution of as many governmental functions as possible', in order to teach the people the virtues of self-government and, consequently, of a positive social attitude (Banfield 1958: 172 ff.). The extreme fragmentation and isolation of the Italian periphery should have been reduced, according to this recipe, by bringing the public sphere closer to the people and creating more efficient channels of democratic participation.

Another traditional field of studies is based on the analysis of 'macro-areas', and aims to show the different historical and cultural legacies coexisting in Italy. Southern underdevelopment has traditionally been the main concern in these analyses. The *questione meridionale* had been since 1861 one of the first crucial issues on the political agenda of the new state (together with the *questione romana*, the difficult diplomatic relationship with the Vatican, originating from the conquest of Rome and the transfer of the capital to the 'eternal city'). The economic and social development (including the diffusion of basic public education) of the south and the reduction of anti-state phenomena such as the *banditismo* (a dangerous mix of political protest of the periphery and criminality) were also the first big questions studied by parliamentary investigations in the 1860s. These problems were at the centre of a wide debate involving historians, economists, and, later, social scientists, and were dealt with by the central government by means of 'exceptional measures' which, however, for a long period never envisaged a multi-tier state.

In this perspective some contributions have stressed the connection between the different political and cultural development of the south, and the survival and adaptation to the emergence of mass politics of the traditional southern politician, the notable. This phenomenon has significantly affected the evolution of the national political elite (Farneti 1985), but also that of local governance (Ginsborg 1990).

The historical literature on the big divide between the north and the south of the country has been very relevant, even more recently, to sociologists and economists who have studied the factors of Italy's complex development in the course of the twentieth century. The well-known classification of the *tre*

Italie ('three Italies') (Bagnasco 1977) has much to do with the traditional works on social and cultural fragmentation. Also related to the above notions is the extensive research conducted, starting in the 1960s, by voting behaviour experts and sociologists on the theme of the Italian sub-cultures (see Chapter 3).

Finally, the development of the notion of 'social capital' has stimulated researches, using this conceptual lens, into the differences between various Italian political sub-systems. A seminal contribution is that of Robert Putnam (1993), based on data covering about twenty years of implementation of the Italian regional system, and focusing on the problem of regional government performance. Here, the 'big divide' between north and south, as well as the impact of other sub-national divisions, continues to be important, but the main research unit is the region, as the study proposes to explain how and why the implementation of regional government brought quite different results in different settings. With this study, Putnam and his associates[1] could stress the role of 'regionalism' in an (already) changing political system such as that of Italy in the late years of the first republic.

Overall, these phenomena can be considered the historical legacy, in terms of fragmentation and complexity, of the process of state-building in Italy: they survived (and in some cases were strengthened) during the age of 'Liberal Italy' when the political system was basically stalling, oscillating between some prudent forms of decentralization at the micro-levels (the *municipi* and the *dipartimenti*, then renamed *province)* and strong central control exercised locally by the *prefetti*, the typical figure of the French model, appointed by and responsible to the central government. It was the Fascist regime, with its emphasis on patriotic and nationalist myths, the strengthening of the powers of central administration (see Chapter 7), and the additional pervasive political controls typical of the dictatorial regime, which would complete the work of centralization and, in the end, transform the Italian political system into an effective unitary state. The consolidation of the centralistic state was, however, bound to be only temporary: although the authoritarian government was supported by quite a broad consensus for about twenty years, its strong centralism was grounded on artificial and somewhat unrealistic symbols, which could hardly be shared fully by the population. Particularly impressive, not only for its short-run impact on the regime discourse but also for its degree of anachronism, was from this point of view the frequent reference to the Roman empire. The second reason is that the protagonists of this process of centralization were typically political instruments of the regime: this was the case in particular for the regime's party organization, the Partito Nazionale Fascista, as well as for the local governmental representatives, the prefects and the directly appointed heads of municipal government *(podestà)*, who, from 1926, substituted the elective mayors. These instruments played a fundamental role in reducing the space of spontaneous political activity at the local level, celebrating in the meantime the superiority of the nation-state over any deviant expression of localism. But their fate was linked with that of the Fascist regime.

One of the by-products of Fascist centralization was the relatively more effective action of the state, during this period, against the Sicilian mafia. However, it could not erase the system of strong local identifications, the cultural differences between regions and provinces, or even the lively competition between the middle-sized towns of the same area, which remained a peculiar character of the Italian polity.

Municipalities and provinces: the local government in the 1948 constitution

We have already defined the local governance framework shaped by the 1948 constitution as an institutional compromise, still inspired by the French model of unitary state (Loughlin 2001), which had been at the core of the old constitution of liberal Italy, but also acknowledging in a clearer way the need to decentralize some power through different tiers of government. The inclusion of a formal acknowledgement of the principle of territorial autonomy in the first part of the constitution (Article 5), the one dedicated to the basic principles, is a clear sign of such a new sensibility.

The constitutional rules were to a large extent the result of a difficult bargaining process between rather different positions. The original views can be summarized as follows: a minority of left-liberals (Action Party and Republicans) were inclined to a federal perspective; the left and the far right were, although for different reasons, against the introduction of any significant decentralization; while the largest part of the centre pushed for a moderate form of it, based on a regional 'meso-level unit' between municipal authorities and the nation-state. The final compromise isolated both the most radical and innovative views based on a truly federal model, as well as those defending a fully unitary and centralized form of government.

As a result the 1948 constitution introduced a whole chapter (*Titolo V*) dealing with the different aspects of local governance (Articles 114–133).

The system of sub-national governance defined by the 1948 constitution was thus a three-tier structure of responsible sub-national governments: the municipalities (*comuni*), the provinces, and the regions. Although the constitution did not cover in detail the division of work between the two lowest levels of government, the municipality was clearly conceived as a more relevant autonomous power, thanks to the number of delegated welfare policies and services. Moreover, the dual role of the mayor, at the same time the political head of a local government and the administrative representative of the central government, gave to the municipal leadership a more visible political prestige and, more generally, provided the communal administrations with a bulk of administrative powers and resources, in order to manage important services like demographic registers, marriages, voter and military service registers, and statistical services.

The province, on the other hand, had a very limited political role, being overshadowed by the *prefettura* (the office of the prefect) in terms of central authority, and having only residual autonomous power. Indeed, according to the 1948 constitution the provinces had to take care of rather heterogeneous and somehow vague policy fields such as flora and fauna, local transport, environment, professional training, and others (see Vandelli 2005, for a broad description).

The municipality was thus confirmed as the most important administrative unit, and proved an important arena for the training of political personnel to be recruited at the higher levels. The allocation of the office of mayor in the largest cities was always considered an important political issue involving the national leaders of all the parties and the competition between Christian Democratic factions.

The vertical linkages between local and national politics (see Hine 1993:260) emerged immediately, but they were always conditioned by the specific characters of the local ruling elites in different areas of the country (La Palombara 1964). The same applied also to the provincial administrations, which, however, suffered, from the beginning of their experience, from a sort of inferiority complex. This was a result of both the lack of a clear social and cultural identity for the province, in a country dominated by towns and villages, and the weaker institutional position of such a meso-level of local governance, inspired by the model of the French *départements*, and overshadowed by the weight of the prefect as the powerful representative of central government.

Both municipalities and provincial governments adopted after 1948 a parliamentary form (see below): an elective council of between fifteen and eighty members elected among its components an executive body composed of a chief executive (mayor or president of the provincial government) and a few departmental delegates (*assessori*). This high number of elective positions at the local levels provided the entry level for most political careers, and a significant part of these mandates (namely those of the executives at least in the most important municipalities and in the provinces) constituted a relevant part-time job for political professionals (Recchi and Verzichelli 2003)

One the other hand, it should be remembered that the strong controls of the central government (and successively, of the regions) over the acts of local governments and, above all, the strict centralization of fiscal resources were considerable elements of weakness within the local political institutions in Italy until the 1990s. In a short assessment, it can be said that the powers and the autonomy of municipal and provincial governments were, during the period 1948–90, modest. However, their political role was far from irrelevant: they allowed a more diffuse participation in public life, tackled many of the day-to-day problems of the population, offered the first training ground for politicians, and sometimes opportunities for new political experiments, institutionalizing a closer relation between politics and local communities. As an acute observer wrote, 'this makes local political life important, even if the institutions of local government themselves dispose of relatively little real decisional authority' (Hine 1993: 260).

The uncertain nature of Italian regionalism

After the unification of the country and before the opening of the Constituent Assembly in the summer of 1946, the federalist position had carried little weight in Italian political culture. At that point, however, at least two good arguments could be advocated by supporters of a more strongly decentralized model of state. First, they could use the rhetoric of the 'completion' of the process of national formation, which would have reached a more advanced state through a new and innovative series of reforms. According to this vision, a fuller democracy should have been grounded upon a bottom-up mechanism determining closer linkages between centre and periphery, and a more respectful behaviour of the state towards the different cultural and social identities scattered across the territory of the Italian nation. Second, they could exploit the belief, almost universally shared among the anti-fascist parties, that the fascist experience had been somehow facilitated by the centralistic character of the Italian state.

Despite these arguments in favour of regional devolution, there was in the assembly no shared vision on the merits of regional autonomy. As already mentioned, the left parties were actually very reluctant towards a strong decentralization: they saw it as an obstacle to the sweeping reforms that, once in power, the working-class parties would have introduced from the centre. Christian Democratic politicians were, on the contrary, generally in favour of regions, as they had traditionally little sympathy for the central state and endorsed the subsidiarity principle developed by the church since the late nineteenth century. The result of negotiations within the Constituent Assembly was the introduction of a third tier of sub-national government, the regions, with limited legislative powers in a number of policy sectors (health, tourism, fishing and hunting, local transport, agriculture, and forestry).

In contrast to the quite limited number of articles concerning municipal and provincial institutions, the constitution describes in a detailed way the characters of the new regional institutions. These bodies were conceived not as merely administrative entities, but as political institutions, provided with a higher level of autonomy vis-à-vis the central state.

In order to give an immediate answer to the requests of devolution coming from the far peripheries of the country, without immediately pushing the whole system towards an effective decentralization, the constitution recognized the status of 'special region' for five border or insular regions with relevant ethno-linguistic minorities. In this way, the special statutes of these regions could be immediately drafted and their experience of decentralized government could start.

According to the constitution, the special statute regions are endowed with particular forms and conditions of autonomy. In practical terms, this brought a limited devolution of powers to these five regions, since their exclusive decision-making competences were in fact limited until 2001. However, the recognition of the special statutes as primary normative sources (as they were approved through special constitutional laws) is not merely a legal difference between the two groups of regions: this original bifurcation of regional organization determined indeed a greater political influence of the institutions of the special statute regions and, above all, their immediate implementation (with a delay only for Friuli), while, for the reasons discussed in Chapter 1, ordinary regions which were not really sustained by any significant regionalist movement were shelved for a good number of years. This led to a staggered implementation of regional governance (see Box 6.1).

BOX 6.1 **Election of regional elective bodies and political composition of the executives, 1947–90**

Regions (first election)	Composition of the regional executive
Special regions	
Sicily (since 1947)	Centre; grand coalition DC-PCI (1958–61)
Trentino-Alto Adige (since 1948)	Centre; centre-left
Aoasta Valley (since 1949)	Centre; centre-left; grand coalitions; left
Sardinia (since 1949)	Centre; centre-left; left
Friuli-Venezia Giulia (since 1964)	Centre; centre-left
Ordinary Regions	
Abruzzo (1970)	Centre; centre-left
Basilicata (1970)	Centre; centre-left
Calabria (1970)	Centre; centre-left; left
Campania (1970)	Centre; centre-left
Emilia-Romagna (1970)	Left
Lazio (1970)	Centre-left; left
Liguria (1970)	Centre-left; left
Lombardy (1970)	Centre-left
Marche (1970)	Centre-left
Molise (1970)	Centre
Piedmont (1970)	Centre-left; left
Puglia (1970)	Centre; centre-left
Tuscany (1970)	Left
Umbria (1970)	Left
Veneto (1970)	Centre; centre-left

Note: Centre includes Christian Democratic governments or coalitions with other central parties; centre-left includes different formulas with DC and PSI; left includes different formula with PCI and other left parties.

The second step of regionalism after 1970: limits and outcomes

Institutionalizing a 'weak regionalism'

As already said, the decisive step towards the implementation of the regionalist state designed by the 1948 constitution was the parliamentary approval of the rules for the election of the representative councils in the fifteen 'ordinary regions', followed by the elections of 1970. But to make these bodies viable required a long and often contentious process. During the following years a number of legal dispositions had to be taken by the national parliament and by the government effectively to transfer to them the powers and resources they were entitled to. A first law concerning the tax revenues to be reallocated to the regional governments came the same year (Law 281/1970), while in 1972 some legislative decrees granting the regions limited authority in the fields already indicated by Article 117 of the constitution were issued. The regions' normative competences were better defined by the later Law 382/1975, which clarified the scope of the different 'delegated policy areas' in the hands of the regional governments. Further regulations issued between 1975 and 1978 transferred part of the central administrative personnel to the newborn regions and created the conditions for implementing the devolution of power in policy areas such as health and transport. Finally a system of budgetary processes at the regional level was introduced, following the French model of the annual financial bill, which would have been implemented also at the central level in 1978.

However, the construction of the new decentralized system was a very slow and complicated process because of the national parliament's delay in producing the legislation which, according to the constitution, was to define the general principles within the framework of which regional legislation was then to regulate the policy sectors of its competence. Among the difficulties of this period, the limited financial autonomy of the regions clearly emerged as the most critical aspect of this step of Italian regionalization (Putnam *et al.* 1985). The 'power of the purse' of regional governments (including those of the special regions) was very constrained by the top-down conception of the centre–periphery relationship still prevailing in the constitution and even more in its implementation: Article 119 stated, indeed, that regional financial autonomy was limited by the general amount of resources fixed by the state, with only a very restricted flexibility attributed to the five regions with a special statute. This meant that until the end of the 1980s only 3 per cent of regional income resulted from the sum of two bottom-up sources such as local taxes and charges for regional services.[2] Overall, the relationship between regional and state expenditures continued to be quite unbalanced throughout the first twenty years of implementation of the regional system, and the legislative superiority of the regions vis-à-vis the other local entities was also not very well supported by political practice. This persistent situation was the basis for assessments such as the following, expressed before the new cycle of reforms which occurred during the 1990s : 'the essential problem of the Italian regions [lies in] the ambiguity in which they languish and the lack of a clear agreement on their relationship to the centre and to the local governments' (Hine 1993: 271).

A consensual parliamentary form of government

The standard institutional configuration for both the five 'special' and the fifteen 'ordinary' regions was composed, following the old text of Article 121 of the constitution, by an elective assembly (*Consiglio regionale*), an executive body (*Giunta regionale*) selected within the council, and a president. The implementation of ordinary regionalism in the 1970s, coinciding with the years of consociationalism at the national level (see Chapter 5), also meant the extension in all the regions and at all the sub-national levels of a parliamentary form of government whose main features were a strongly proportional electoral system, the dominant position of the representative assemblies, and the weakness of the executive. While the distribution of the powers between *Consiglio* and *Giunta* resembled the executive–legislative relationship typical of the first republic, the president of the *Giunta* was something between a prime minister and a sort of regional president, but without normally being able to achieve neither a strategic role in the decision-making process at the regional level or the political prestige of a national top politician.

Reflecting the constitutional idea of the centrality of the legislature, it was the council that in each region was to be in charge of the drafting and approval of regional statutes, by means of an absolute majority vote. However, since the system was rigidly top-down orientated, the statutes had to be approved by a law of the national parliament. In the end, the institutional framework of Italian regionalism looked homogeneous and very constrained by the consensual nature of the Italian constitution. The regional political systems were very similar to each other, in spite of the evident differences between regions in their political orientations.

In this context regional elections played an important role as second-order elections—a sort of anticipation of the national competitions. Not only because of the limited political impact of regional governments, but also because of the simultaneous election of the councils in all fifteen ordinary regions (the five special regions followed their own specific electoral calendars originated years before), all of them using the same 'pure' PR system, these elections offered an extraordinary opportunity to test the shape of the national coalition and the popularity of each national party.

Similar institutions, different performances

Given the homogeneity of the institutional arrangement at the regional level, the range of variations in the outputs produced by these institutions, with regions in the north and in the centre performing consistently better on most indicators than regions in the south and the islands, can be prima facie surprising. The variable capability of similar institutions to respond to the needs and meet the demands of their political communities is a classic question in political science. However, this question is usually applied to the comparison between *national* systems rather than among *sub-national* units. It took the above-mentioned work by Robert D. Putnam, *Making Democracy Work* (1993), to open the debate about the factors behind the different performances of the Italian regions during the first twenty years of regionalization.

In order to measure the dependent variable, Putnam built an index of institutional performance based on several empirical indicators (quality of legislation, development of welfare institutions, bureaucratic responsiveness, budget promptness, and others), and considered its distribution in the context of a diachronic-experimental research design and in the light of a theoretical approach based on the relationship between historical sources of social capital and democratic performance. The main findings were positive correlations between the degree of performance and the attitudes to the civic community—that is, the attitudes towards collective forms of participation and a sense of political tolerance, developed through centuries-long historical tradition.

Even if we leave the methodological and theoretical architecture of this book aside and focus only on its substantive findings, Putnam's work remains extremely illuminating, providing us with a number of insights for understanding *how* and *why* the evolution of Italian regionalism has produced such different results. According to Putnam, the practice of local democracy in Italy has developed more successfully where the positive effects of long-term attitudes to 'civicness' are evident, while other regions are still characterized by a system where 'mutual distrust and defection, vertical dependence and exploitation, isolation and disorder, criminality and backwardness have reinforced one another in interminable vicious circles' (Putnam 1993:181).

However, a second relevant finding in the book has to do with the growing capability of the new institutions to accelerate civic community and, to some extent, reverse its trend: as the changing formal institutions can change political practice, the Italian regions can virtuously use their new powers in order to increase social capital. In this respect, some relevant differences even within the macro-areas of centre–north and south were emerging, leaving space for a new interpretation of the different perspectives of the different regions (or provinces). Other research by political scientists, sociologists, and historians has followed this line and provided useful information about the developments of Italian localism. The different impact of forms of civicness, to use Putnam's term, or the effects of different economic models of development (Trigilia 1992) still make the difference in the institutional performance of Italian regions and more generally of local institutions.

Overall, a mix of several possible explanatory variables, resulting both from path dependencies and from political and economic contingencies, creates a rather interesting range of variation. A recent proof of this can be found in the ranking of regional performances with regard to the 'virtuous' use of EU cohesion funds and in the degree of Europeanization. The Italian regions have in fact recently shown an interesting and rather differentiated institutional capability both in organizing their presence at the EU level and in reshaping their internal organization in order to adapt themselves to the requirement of multi-level governance (Fargion *et al.* 2006): the north-eastern regions and the central regions of the red belt seem much more prepared to face the challenges of supranational governance, but a relevant degree of variance is also present in southern areas.

Sub-national governance after 1990: how many steps forwards?

A continuous flow of changes

The system of sub-national governance is today quite different from the one we have briefly described above. The important changes experienced between 1990 and 2006 have been, to a large extent, the outcome of a growing dissatisfaction with the performance of the earlier institutional setting and of the consequent rise of a territorial cleavage epitomized by the electoral success of the Northern League (Cento Bull and Gilbert 2001; Diamanti 2003). However, even this aspect of Italian political change can be partly linked to a wider set of explanatory factors, whose origins can be traced back up to the fundamental features of the Italian polity. To start with, the regions and the most important local institutions had significantly grown in political prestige during the 1980s, pressuring the central government in order to obtain a wider devolution of powers. Second, the series of institutional reforms that will be briefly reviewed in this section (see Table 6.1) began just before the crisis of the first republic, when the old establishment became aware of the necessity to provide the system of local government with new effective tools. An important law on local government (Law 142/1990) was in fact adopted in 1990. This reform was motivated by the need to make the local institutions more accountable and transparent, but also by the quest for a general rearrangement of the complex system of interactions between the different tiers of local governments. To the first objective were linked a number of important innovations, such as the new rules on the transparency of all local administrations, the introduction of legislative referenda at the local level, and some form of direct popular oversight over the work of local executives, such as petitions. A local ombudsman (*difensore civico*) was also

TABLE 6.1 Steps in the recent reforms of local governance in Italy

Year	Issues	Related legislation
1990	General rearrangement of local governance	L. 142/1990
1993	Direct election of the mayors and heads of provincial government	L. 81/1993
1995	Reform of the regional electoral system	
1997	Delegation/reorganization of local governments (Bassanini Law)	L. 59/1997
	Other dispositions for reorganization (Bassanini Law II)	L. 127/1997
1998	Other dispositions for reorganization (Bassanini Law III)	L. 191/1998
1999	Reform of L. 142/1990 on local governance	L.265/1999
	Little constitutional reform on regional elections	
2000	Coordination of regulations on local governments	TU 265/2000
2001	Constitutional reform of the *Titolo V*	
2003	Implementation of the 2001 reform (La Loggia Law)	L.131/2003

introduced at all sub-national levels of government. As far as the overall redefinition of the local government is concerned, this law increased the role of regions and assigned to them the function of determining general policy objectives, while delegating more consultative and executive powers to the local governments.

This reform was just the beginning: only two years later, in a totally different political conjuncture, owing to the effects of the *tangentopoli* scandal, the parliament was pushed to adopt another one (Law 81/1993), which introduced the direct election of mayors and presidents of provincial governments. This reform, adopting, for the very first time, a form of directly elected and not party-mediated mechanism for the appointment to the top political office of a government level, was a watershed for the whole Italian political scene. Public opinion and political entrepreneurs 'rediscovered' local institutions and the merits of a more direct relationship between voters and politicians. Political competition was immediately pervaded, initially only within the context of local politics, by a 'new' sense of personalization and by the increasing visibility of the figures of the chief executives (Baldini 2002). Moreover, the law substantially reshaped inter-institutional relations at the local level, introducing a neo-parliamentary system, that is, a much more balanced system of government, whereby the chief of the local government was granted a set of considerable powers, being allowed to hire and fire the members of the local executive (*assessori*) and to decide the main policy priorities. Furthermore, governmental crises, at both the communal and provincial level, would now trigger an immediate dissolution of the council, following the principle of *simul stabunt simul cadent*.

In so doing, the parliament proved (or perhaps was forced) to be much bolder than with the 1990 reform, which had introduced just a few incremental changes, such as the constructive vote of no confidence, in order to avoid the continuous recurrence of crises, reshuffles, and partial changes in the composition of the local executives.

After the 1993 reform, and thanks to some further corrections to the same law adopted in the course of the following decade, the political role, social visibility, and popularity of local governments and of their chief executives, particularly in the largest cities, have clearly increased. It is also undeniable that the reform has given greater stability to municipal executives, offered a new autonomy to their administration, and provided the actors of local governance with a more relevant political stature (Bobbio 2005: 41).

However, the reform of the system of local government could not be considered complete without touching the third and most delicate tier: the regions. This has been done by means of a number of incremental changes and, indeed, with a greater degree of uncertainty (Bobbio 2005). In fact some of the crucial demands raised by the regions, particularly from the 'special statute' and the northern ones,[3] could be considered only in the context of a broad revision of the constitutional text which, after the failures of the 1993 and 1998 bicameral committees, finally produced some results in 2001 (see below).

Similar to what happened at the national level, the change of electoral rules has come first, at the beginning of the new political cycle. In 1995 regional elections were held after a significant correction of the old PR electoral system: a majority bonus of about 20 per cent of the seats of the regional council is now allocated to the winning coalition on the basis of a shortlist of candidates, not running in the normal electoral districts but linked to the winning coalition. Together with the immediate effect of pushing also at the regional level in the direction of a bipolar competition, the reform gave a clear signal that a more hierarchical executive and the direct choice of its leader by the voters had to be the decisive steps in building a more effective government in each region. The final step in the pursuit of this goal was finally taken with a limited constitutional correction (1999) which introduced the direct election of the president of the *Giunta regionale* (although regional statutes can decide otherwise) and formally stated his powers in the government formation. Quite significantly, during this period, journalists started to use, for regional presidents, the American term of 'governor', thus stressing the visibility and the political autonomy of this figure, who had until recently been quite anonymous.

Another important step in the redefinition of local governance was the adoption by the national parliament of a number of bills concerning the fields of inter-institutional relations and administrative reorganization. From this point of view the second half of the 1990s, with a series of minor adaptations of the systemic laws mentioned above and of other relevant norms, was quite productive. In particular, the period of the adoption of the so-called Bassanini delegating laws (from the name of the then Minister for Public Administration; see Chapter 7), and of the delegated decrees deriving from them, has been called the 'busiest and most innovative period in Italian local government since the establishment of the regions' (Gilbert 2000). In a nutshell, the main outcomes of this period were:

1. the definitive and concrete assertion of the principle of decisional autonomy of local authorities, by which even the smallest units received more resources and operational responsibility, and innovations were introduced in matters such as evaluation, internal management, responsibility of administrative officers, etc;
2. the rise of the regional tier as a true political actor and legislative source, by means of a more effective application of the constitutional provisions and of some legislative reforms in the fields of public finance, budgeting, health-care system, and other welfare sub-sectors; and
3. an important step towards a system of cooperative federalism, with the institutionalization of a unified conference of all the actors involved in centre–periphery relations. This conference, chaired by the president of the Council of Ministers, is formed by all the

> ministers interested in this system of relations, the presidents of the regional executives, and representatives of municipal and provincial chief executives. This small parliament, which can then be disaggregated into two more focused conferences (the State–Regions and the State–Local autonomies conferences), has become increasingly relevant for reaching agreements concerning the different functions, for debating the allocation of resources, and in general for preventing jurisdictional conflicts between the different levels of government.

The final decade of the twentieth century was closed by two other important events, which marked a change in the speed of implementation of a new system of local governance with a 'quasi-federal' architecture: they were the approval of a consolidated law (*testo unico)* including and rationalizing all the relevant innovations of the past decade, and the decision of the centre-left majority to proceed, after the failure of the bicameral committee, with the reform of *Titolo V* of the constitution. The first act, although it did not bring any new crucial element into the already existing picture, had the effect of introducing a principle of coordination in different fields of legislation concerning administration, local forms of government, electoral laws, etc. The second decision was much more substantially relevant: it led to the rapid parliamentary adoption, in the spring of 2001, of a constitutional amendment supported only by the centre-left majority, and therefore requiring a confirmatory referendum.[4] This was held a few months after the victory of the centre-right coalition, but did, however, lead to the approval of the reform, with more than 60 per cent of votes in favour on a very low turnout (34 per cent).

The 2001 constitutional reform

The reform introduced by Constitutional Law 3/2001, better known as reform of the *Titolo V*, has defined what is still, at the end of 2006, the status quo in Italian regionalism. In a nutshell it pursued three main goals:

1. to redefine the distribution of powers between central state and local governments;
2. to modernize the overall framework of local governance in Italy; and

3. to strengthen the political role of the regions, solving conflicts of attribution and introducing a more marked element of federalism *from below.*

A thorough redrafting of Articles 117 and 118 of the 1948 constitution was the instrument for achieving the first goal: Article 117, innovating from the original version, now lists the matters on which the central state has exclusive legislative powers and those subject to a concurrent legislative power, where state and regions must cooperate, with the state defining the fundamental principles and the regions subsequently producing ordinary legislation within the framework of these principles (Table 6.2).

TABLE 6.2 Distribution of legislative powers between state and regions (effects of the 2001 revision of Article 117 of the Italian constitution)

	Before the reform	After the reform
National defence	Exclusive state	Unchanged
Justice/prisons	Exclusive state	Unchanged
Security/public order	Exclusive state	Unchanged
Local administrative police	Concurrent	Exclusive regions
International relations and EU	Exclusive state	Unchanged
Relations between regions and EU	Exclusive state	Concurrent
Monetary policy, public finance, competitiveness	Exclusive state	Unchanged
Citizenship, immigration, religious matters	Exclusive state	Unchanged
Basic principles of civil and social rights	Exclusive state	Unchanged
Agriculture and forestry	Concurrent	Exclusive regions
Handicraft	Concurrent	Exclusive regions
Industry	Exclusive state	Exclusive regions
Commerce, markets	Concurrent	Exclusive regions
International trade	Exclusive state	Concurrent
Tourism	Concurrent	Exclusive regions
Energy	Exclusive state	Concurrent
Fishing and hunting	Concurrent	Exclusive regions
Local saving banks	Exclusive state	Concurrent

continues

Table 6.2 continued

	Before the reform	After the reform
Education	Exclusive state	Concurrent
Professional training and permanent education	Concurrent	Exclusive regions
Culture	Exclusive state	Concurrent
Technology and scientific research	Exclusive state	Concurrent
Pensions	Exclusive state	Unchanged
Employment	Exclusive state	Concurrent
Social work and welfare	Concurrent	Exclusive regions
Health	Exclusive state	Concurrent
Environmental protection	Exclusive state	Unchanged
Town planning	Concurrent	Exclusive regions
Main transport networks	Exclusive state	Concurrent
Airports and seaports	Exclusive state	Concurrent
Local transports	Concurrent	Exclusive regions
Aqueducts and local infrastructures	Concurrent	Exclusive regions
Communications	Exclusive state	Concurrent
Regional political and administrative organization	Concurrent	Exclusive regions
Functions and electoral regulations of local government	Exclusive state	Unchanged
Regional and local finances	Exclusive state	Exclusive regions
Coordination public finance	Exclusive state	Concurrent
Civil protection	Exclusive state	Concurrent
Public sport organizations	Exclusive state	Concurrent

Source: Adapted from Baldi (2006).

Since there is no specific mention of the remaining policy fields, for which regions have full legislative power (as there was in the pre-2001 version of the constitution), local institutions are supposed now to have a substantial freedom of manoeuvre in quite wide sectors. These sectors are in any event not very different from those of the previous framework, the only significant exception being a wider competence in the field of economic policy and planning. Regional legislatures have exclusive legislative powers on these matters while, according to the application of the subsidiarity principle (introduced by the *new* article 118), provincial and municipal institutions can issue secondary regulations and take care of policy implementation in the different fields.

The second goal, the modernization and rationalization of the institutional setting, has led to the formal definition of the different units comprising the Italian republic (Article 114 of the constitution). The metropolitan cities (already introduced by ordinary legislation, but never implemented) now have their own constitutional place, after municipalities and provinces, and before regions and the central state. All these entities are entitled now to financial autonomy and can establish their own taxes and revenues, in accordance with the principles of coordination of public finances and within the general taxation framework (Article 119). The new formulation of Article 116, after reaffirming the peculiarity of the five 'special statute regions', allows the state to assign, if needed, further particular forms and conditions of autonomy to individual ordinary regions.

With regard to the effective development of a 'federal-like' system in Italy, a final assessment of the effective outcomes of the 2001 reform is still quite difficult. In a sense the state has been 'hollowed out' and this gives room to the regions and the other local governments to play an enhanced role in the redefinition of the political system. An important innovation, from this point of view, has been the suppression of the system of central control exercised by the government through its commissioners, which used to be the ordinary way to protect the state and its competences from regional legislative initiatives. Within the current framework, the central government can only refer a regional act to the Constitutional Court, without being able to suspend its application.

On the other hand, the 2001 reform presents many aspects of uncertainty. The same notion of federalism has been used with excessive easiness and a great deal of ambiguity. The lack of uniformity and the failure to reach the goal of a drastic simplification of the procedures have been noted in the literature (Cento Bull 2002). Furthermore, its implementation has been characterized by a sort of stop and start, since the regulating law of 2003 was considered by the centre-right government at that time in charge a purely transitional passage, while the big reform was announced and then introduced, before the referendum rejection of 2006. Many questions are therefore still open; among them, those about the adoption of fiscal federalism and a new structure of opportunities for the regional legislative institutions. But it is a clear and shared view that, with regard to federalism, the situation must still be considered transitional (Cento Bull 2002: 199) and that an effort to complete and/or clarify some of the aspects introduced by the 2001 reform in the broader framework of a more comprehensive and coherent institutional rearrangement is necessary.

Conclusion

Multi-level devolution at work? Realities and perspectives

As mentioned in Chapter 1, during the fourteenth legislature, the centre-right government of Silvio Berlusconi committed itself to revise the 2001 reform with the purpose of achieving a deeper and more organic 'devolution'. A very ambiguous Italian transposition of this term (*devoluzione*) was included among the official tasks of the Minister (without portfolio) for Institutional Reforms, the historical leader of the Lega Nord, Umberto Bossi, who was called upon to take this role, indicating the priority of a new reform of the *Titolo V*. After a long period of consultations and negotiations within the coalition, the 'devolution' was included in the broad constitutional reform approved between the spring of 2004 and the autumn of 2005. In reality, the proposals of the Berlusconi government would not have changed dramatically the system of multi-level government created by the 2001 reform since the centre-left had to a great extent anticipated the reforms that the centre-right (and in particular the League) wanted. It can even be argued that in many respects the authors of the new reform have been even more cautious than the previous centre-left government, creating in fact the conditions for a reduction of the actual powers of regional institutions (Vassallo 2006). The new version of Article 117 of the constitution, providing the regions with exclusive legislative competence in matters like health care, school organization and programmes, and local police appeared mainly as a symbolic benefit to reward the Lega for its loyalty to the coalition. In other fields the reform gave back some controls to central government and introduced the principle of national interest as a general limit to regional legislation. The ambivalences of *Titolo V* of the constitution, which had been increased by the 2001 reform, as some leaders of the centre-left admitted, were not fully tackled by this proposal, which was also unclear about the implementation of a 'fiscal federalism' and about the new distribution of resources between the state and local governments.

Criticisms of the 'devolution' promoted by the centre-right reform were directed also to the rather chaotic system of legislative competences and procedures, according to which the central parliament would have worked, depending on the type of legislative competence, along one of at least three alternative institutional levels: through the 'federal senate', whenever matters of exclusive regional competence were concerned, through the lower chamber, for matters of exclusive state competence, and through a third procedure involving an eventual 'reconciliation committee' in cases of disagreement between the chambers. The first and more obvious objection raised by many observers was that the high flow of referrals to the Constitutional Court on grounds of conflict of competence, already produced by the 2001 reform, would have been further increased.

After the failure of the reform, it is doubtful whether the window of opportunity for the completion of 'Italian federalism' is still open. While the centre-left coalition in government after the general elections of 2006 may count on the support of many regional executives having the same political colour (Figure 6.1), the weakness of its parliamentary base and its extreme internal fragmentation may herald a new pause in the reform process. In the end, it seems more realistic to expect the implementation of the norms achieved in 2001 rather than new sweeping reforms. Ordinary legislative innovations can be proposed in order to adjust some of the less successful aspects of the current framework. In particular, it seems that new steps are necessary towards the simplification of the excessive number of local entities and in order to reach a functioning collaboration between them. Second, a less ambiguous definition of the principle of subsidiarity would help the concrete application of the principles of the new *Titolo V*. Finally, a consolidation of the 'fiscal federalism' along the lines of the already achieved 'administrative federalism' could be a decisive step in setting an acceptable model of reallocation of the resources between the central state and the multifaceted entities of local governance.

FIGURE 6.1 **Regional governments and political competition in the Italian regions, 2006**

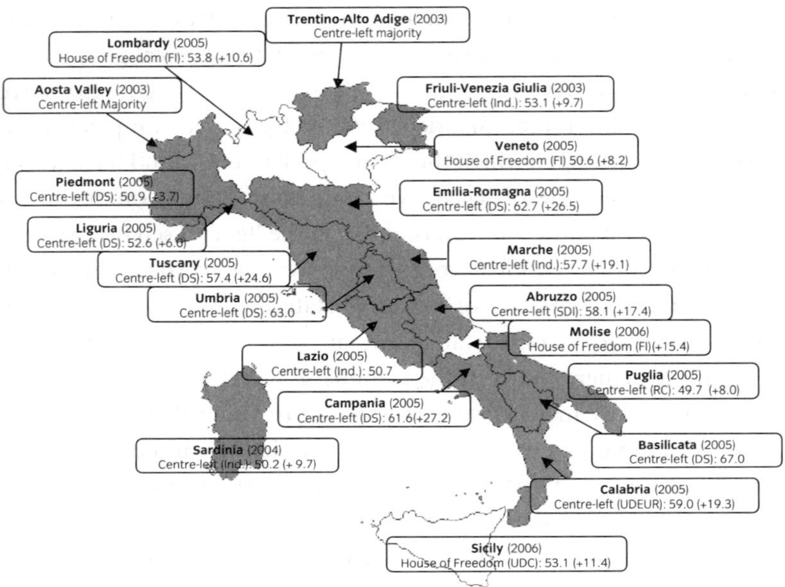

Note: The darker shading refers to centre-left governments. The lighter refers to centre-right governments. The figures refer to percentage of votes achieved by the winning candidate to the presidency of the regional government (the party affiliation of the candidate within brackets). We also report the difference (in percentage of votes) between the votes for the winning candidate and the candidate from the opposite coalition. The year refers to the last regional elections. Aosta Valley (last election 2003) has a different party system. In Trentino-Alto Adige (last legislature formed in 2003, with a centre-left majority) the regional council is formed by the provincial deputies elected in the two autonomous provinces of Trento and Bolzano. The candidate of the centre-left coalition in Tuscany in 2005 was not supported by the party of Communist Refoundation.

The current map of local governments in Italy

Although the system of sub-national institutions is still in a transitional phase, we can attempt an assessment of what is the situation now at work and what can be the future developments of local governance in Italy. Two basic statements can be offered which reflect the unquestionable achievements of the past thirty years and indicate a trend which can hardly be reversed in the near future.

The first statement underlines the success of a model which can be broadly defined as a process of progressive devolution: Italian public opinion has been shown to like the idea of a government 'closer to the people', more accountable, and working on the basis of the principle of subsidiarity. The reforms introducing a variety of neo-parliamentary systems from the local to the regional level have been generally perceived as positive, quite differently from proposed reforms at the level of the central state. These feelings are not limited to the rich and 'globalized' areas of the north but are also found in the southern periphery.

The second statement indicates the ascendance of a multi-level model of the political system. This model looks today inescapable for a number of reasons: the constitutional reform, even in the limited version adopted in 2001; the bottom-up pressures for a more flexible and accountable delegation of power, exercised by the regional and local governments; and, last but not least, the external constraints determined by the European Union, which subordinates important policies, in particular cohesion policy, to the effective implementation of a multi-level institutional system.

This is enough to suggest that the Italian system of local governance will continue to evolve in the near future along the lines of an even more pronounced, although temperate, devolution.

Today, the overall network of sub-national units can be summarized as follows: at the end of 2006, Italian territory is distributed in a rather irregular way between 20 regions, 109 provinces (3 of them still to be implemented), and more than 8,100 municipalities (Table 6.3). With the introduction of the metropolitan cities, another tier will be added, even if this change should only give more organizational resources and more visibility to a kind of special province coinciding with the territory of a particularly large city.

The last link of the chain, the one to which important regulatory and implementation powers are delegated, is the one with the highest degree of internal variability. The family of Italian municipalities encompasses a truly wide range of communities (Table 6.4): more than half of them are towns and villages with fewer than 3,000 inhabitants. If we take 10,000 inhabitants as a threshold, municipalities below this threshold represent more than 86 per cent of local authorities, but their overall population is only 32 per cent of the nationwide population. Moreover, the pattern of distribution of the different sizes of municipalities is quite varied from one region

TABLE 6.3 **Distribution of local authorities among the Italian regions, 2006**

Regions	Population (thousands)	Population density	Metropolitan cities	Provinces	Municipalities
Special statute					
Aosta Valley	120	37		—	74
Trentino-Alto Adige	924	68		2	339
Friuli-Venezia Giulia	1, 185	151	(Trieste)	4	219
Sicily	5, 108	199	(Palermo)	9	390
Sardinia	1, 661	69	(Cagliari)	8	377
Ordinary statute					
Piedmont	4, 291	169	Turin	8	1, 206
Lombardy	8, 989	377	Milan	12	1, 546
Veneto	4, 469	243	Venice	7	581
Liguria	1, 642	303	Genoa	4	235
Emilia-Romagna	3, 947	179	Bologna	9	341
Tuscany	3, 527	153	Florence	10	287
Umbria	832	98		2	92
Marche	1, 451	150		5	246
Lazio	5, 243	304	Rome	5	378
Abruzzo	1, 276	118		4	305
Molise	330	74		2	136
Campania	5, 797	427	Naples	5	551
Puglia	4, 090	211	Bari	6	258
Basilicata	610	61		2	131
Calabria	2, 070	137		5	409
Italy	*57,564*	*191*	*9/12*	*109*	*8,101*

Note: Three provinces included in our figures (Monza/Brianza, Fermo, and Barletta/Andria/Trani) were established in 2004 but their institutions will not be elected until at least 2009. The definition of some metropolitan cities is also to be decided (those in brackets are uncertain).

to another: in the Alpine Aosta Valley more than 90 per cent of the local administrations (68 of 74) are villages with fewer than 3,000 inhabitants, while, especially in the centre–south, there is a predominance of larger

TABLE 6.4 **Italian municipal administrations in 2002, by classes of resident population**

	N	%	Population	%
Up to 5,000	5,826	71.9	10,593,226	18.5
Between 5,001 and 10,000	1,154	14.2	8,088,910	14.1
Between 10,001 and 50,000	983	12.1	19,004,839	33.2
Between 50,001 and 100,000	95	1.2	6,317,517	11.0
More than 100,000	43	0.5	13,316,578	23.2
Total	8,101	100.0	57,321,070	100.0

units. In Tuscany, Emilia-Romagna, Puglia, and Campania the impact of the large cities is remarkable, these regions having 59 of the 138 municipalities with more than 50,000 inhabitants. The recent reforms have tried to face the problem of this excessive fragmentation, extending and strengthening forms of cooperation, such as the inter-municipal unions and the consortia for mountain areas, and introducing coordination measures to be assigned to provincial administrations. However, the costs of fragmentation are still high, and the need for a further simplification of this framework remains on the agenda.

A growing competition for local power

If we consider now the political value of these institutions, there is no doubt that the significance of local government is much greater today in Italy compared with the first decades of the republican experience. The different rounds of local elections and the renewal of the regional councils are *still* a test for the popularity of national policies and national leaders. But it would be wrong to consider them only as second-order elections. On the contrary, above all in the regions where the erosion of the traditional sub-cultural vote has favoured the alternation in power of the two coalitions and the emergence of a closer bipolar competition, the relevance of 'local stakes' is increasingly evident. The regional governors and the mayors of the largest towns have assumed a quite significant authority, which can only partly be explained by the growth of their *de jure* powers. Since the mid-1990s, it has been a recurrent pattern to recruit mayoral or gubernatorial ('governor') candidates from the most visible and prestigious positions in civil society, or, on the other hand, to select, as possible contenders, experienced national party leaders. This has led to some changes in the structure of political careers and has increased the role of the local executive offices in comparison with other political appointments at the national or supranational level (Fabbrini 2001; Di Virgilio 2005).

Since 1993, many close elections for the leadership of the most important Italian towns or provinces have become crucial tests for adjusting the marketing and electoral strategies of national parties. In some cases, the experience and the support achieved as a mayor of a large city has been decisive in building credibility for a role as a national political leader.

As regards the regional level, the competitiveness between the two coalitions clearly increased between 1995 and 2005: Figure 6.1 shows that, although the set of regional executives is at the end of 2006 clearly dominated by the centre-left coalition, the number of 'close calls' where alternation in government seems a realistic prospect is growing, as well as the number of candidatures for the position of governor offered to minor 'pivotal' parties or to independent candidates in order to maximize the chances of victory. Roughly speaking, we can say that 'sub-cultural' dominance seems still a decisive feature in explaining the political continuity in Lombardy, Veneto, and Sicily (in the hands of the centre-right) and in Emilia-Romagna, Tuscany, Umbria, and Marche (under centre-left rule). But in the other regions the competition is much more open.

KEY TERMS

- civic community
- concurrent legislative power (between state and regions)
- federalism
- governor (president of regional government)
- mayor
- meso-level government
- municipalities
- provinces
- regionalism
- special (regional) statutes
- subsidiarity principle

GUIDE TO FURTHER READING

CENTO BULL, A., and GILBERT, M. (2001) *The Lega Nord and the Northern Question in Italian Politics* (London: Palgrave).

Research into the emergence of the Northern League and the transformations of the regions of the North.

DIAMANTI, I. (2003) *Bianco, rosso, verde e azzurro. Mappe e colori dell'Italia politica* (Bologna, Il Mulino).

A detailed analysis of the current patterns of electoral behaviour, in the light of the geo-political approach.

LEVY, C. (ed.) (1996) *Italian Regionalism: History, Identity and Politics* (Oxford, Berg).

An interesting collection of essays on the fragmentation of the Italian polity.

PUTNAM, R. D. (1993) *Making Democracy Work: Civic Traditions in Modern Italy* (Princeton, Princeton University Press).

Oft-quoted research on democratic performance and civic community in the Italian regions.

VANDELLI, L. (2005) *Il sistema delle autonomie locali* (Bologna, Il Mulino).

A recent comprehensive textbook on the institutions of local governance in Italy.

NOTES

1 Other works from this long research project stressing the different evolution of the regional systems in Italy are Nanetti (1988) and Putnam *et al.* (1985).

2 The data about the financial resources of the regions in comparison with the central administration can be found in the historical series of the *Annuario Statistico* of the ISTAT (National Statistical Institute). See also, for some elaborations, Bull and Newell 2005: 159.

3 Already in the course of 1990, the regional council of Friuli-Venezia Giulia had approved a resolution for a federalist reform of the Italian state. Similar requests were approved by the councils of Trentino-Alto Adige and Aosta Valley (1991), but even in 'ordinary regions' like Emilia-Romagna and Veneto, the proposal to reform the constitution and to introduce a strong principle of devolution, was passed.

4 Article 138 states indeed that laws concerning constitutional amendments should be submitted to popular referendum when, within three months of their publication, a request is made by one-fifth of the members of either chamber, by 500,000 electors, or by five regional councils. No referendum may be held if the law has been approved by each chamber in a second vote with a majority of two-thirds of its members.

7

Bureaucracy and Regulatory Bodies: From Immobility to Permanent Reforms

Overview

Slowness, heaviness, disorganization, and patronage have no doubt been long-established problems for Italian public administration, and they still represent some of the most common stereotypes of Italy abroad. It is easy to find evidence for justifying these stereotypes, from the country's poor historical record in transposing EU directives, to the low ranking in the Transparency International index of corruption perception (where only Greece, among the EU15 member states, has been classified in a worse position). Above all, it is easy to enumerate very concrete examples from the day-to-day performances of public services in Italy, from the postal service to trains, to health care. To a significant extent, these examples still represent a challenge for the political system, with bureaucratic performance being the other side of a coin—the overall effectiveness of the political system—which people tend to remember only when the *res publica* proves to be particularly ineffective towards individual citizens. As a matter of fact, the functioning of public administration is inexorably linked with the evolution of the state and with the performance of the other political institutions.

Several factors are behind the traditionally poor performance of the administrative system in Italy. Following an eminent expert (Cassese 1993), they can be summarized as follows:

1. an ambiguous perception of the state among citizens and public employees as well as a perception dominated by a high degree of

legalism but by low respect for the public sphere and state authority;

2. an excessive stress on *ex ante* formal control over administrative acts, but insufficient powers of *ex post* control over real performance;
3. an organization traditionally centralized but also very fragmented and with poor internal connections;
4. an evident inconsistency between the centralized collection of financial resources and highly decentralized powers of expenditure;
5. an excessive emphasis on equality within the civil service and too little attention paid to merit;
6. the tendency to consider the level of importance of a public administrator by the size of her or his office, rather than by responsibility;
7. a poor and not very transparent relationship with the public.

To these factors should be added also the frequent use of public resources as a 'social buffer' in order to compensate economic, social, and geographical differences, more than for effectively achieving administrative goals and the limited ability of important sectors of the public administration to eradicate corruption.

Just like the other institutions, Italian public administration has faced in the past fifteen years a massive wave of reforms, with the purpose of overcoming its contradictions. However, as for the other pillars of the political system, these reforms have had a complicated story. In some cases they originated in previous failed attempts at reform, while in others they could be implemented using the window of opportunity of a sudden political change at the domestic or at the European level. Resistance to change, both openly voiced and silent, has always been strong and able to mobilize large and transversal parliamentary supports. In the end, just like many other developments, this cycle of reform seems far from complete, making Italian public administration a sort of experimental, 'hybrid' model of public management.

In this chapter we will move from a short historical overview of the traditional features of Italian public administration, to a more systematic assessment of recent changes, both in the traditional central state sector, namely that of the ministries, and in the growing network of 'independent' authorities which compose the current administrative landscape. We will focus mainly on the changes which have occurred in the organizational setting, in the patterns of personnel recruitment and career progression, and in the relationship between bureaucrats and politicians. A final section will be devoted to the future challenges and to the prospects for reforms that are still in progress or even in the phase of policy formulation.

The historical model and its legacies

The foundations of the Italian public administration model can be traced back to the 1853 reform which took the name of the Piedmontese (and later Italian) Prime Minister, Camillo Cavour. This reform, refurbished a few years later after the proclamation of the unitary state, introduced a small number of crucial elements of the state machinery which lasted for about a century and a half, surviving full democratization, the long and disruptive authoritarian break, and even the return of democracy and the new 1948 constitution.

These original characteristics can be reduced to two: a highly structured bureaucratic model of the ministries, instead of a more flexible government based on a plurality of agencies, and a strictly 'vertical' relationship between the political head of each unit (the minister) and its administrative summit, based on a key organizational institution, the general secretariat, present in each ministry.

A few other innovations marked the development of the early model of Italian administration during the historical phase of liberal Italy: the birth of a Treasury department (1877), the introduction of ministerial undersecretaries (1888), and a first extension in the number of ministries (see Box 7.1).

The expansion of public administration followed during this period a linear curve of growth, similar to the pattern of the other European nation-states (Rose 1985). From a more qualitative point of view, its structure was not characterized by major changes until the second half of the 1930s, that is to say, after the full consolidation of the authoritarian regime. At that time, the Fascist government felt confident enough to give a more definitive form to the structure of the 'totalitarian state', to use the expression coined by

BOX 7.1 The structure of the Italian government from 1861 to 1920

1861	President of the Council of Minister and nine ministries (Foreign Affairs; Internal Affairs; War; Justice; Finance; Education; Navy; Public Works; Agriculture, Industry, and Trade)
1877	Establishment of the Treasury Ministry
1889	Establishment of the Post and Communications Ministry
1887	First appointment of ten under-secretaries
1911	Establishment of the Ministry for Colonies
1916	Establishment of the Ministries for Weapons and for Sea and Rail Transportations
1917	Creation of two separate Ministries for Agriculture and for Industry, Trade, and Employment

Mussolini. These reforms soon received a further stimulus from the need to respond to the challenges that had arisen in Europe following the Great Depression.

In fact the Fascist government had since its early years displayed the willingness to centralize and strengthen the administrative structure of the state, but had not dared initially to change too much in the existing state apparatus. The main innovation was the unification in 1923 of the decentralized accounting offices in a general accounting office (Ragioneria generale dello stato). Later on, when the Fascist government felt ready to create a truly Fascist state, a more comprehensive reform of the public administration took place (1930–6). Its foundations can be summarized in three terms: dirigisme, state intervention in the economy, and social assistance. The first term refers to the realization of a strict logic of political planning and control over the numerous departmental and territorial units of state administration, with the ultimate goal of realizing a wide programme of economic and social interventions. The completion of existing public structures, that is the public school system, the security services, the national postal service, and the public transport system, was pursued by way of important reforms[1] and determined quite an interventionist mode of policy making. As a consequence of this new orientation, the second important innovation, the creation of large state holdings (*partecipazioni statali* in the Italian administrative jargon) in the field of economic life, was pursued. This entailed the establishment of public enterprises having as their specific mission to pursue public objectives in different fields of industry, infrastructure, and communication. The first giants of this 'holding state participations system' were two bodies—the Italian Credit Institute (*Istituto Mobiliare Italiano*, IMI) and the Institute for Industrial Reconstruction (*Istituto per la Riconversione Industriale*, IRI)—established in the 1930s to rescue private banking and industrial firms which had gone bankrupt after the great crisis.

The third term refers to the development of the limited welfare system existing then in Italy. By the late 1930s the state was becoming a machine orientated to a very peculiar form of totalitarian welfare, combining the pro-state orientation of the fascist ideology (and some of its original socialist catchwords) with the need to consolidate the autocratic nature of the new regime. The creation of a system of social assistance and the introduction of different pension and social insurance schemes, drastically changing the structure of the original welfare system introduced by Crispi in the 1880s and developed by Giolitti between 1900 and 1915, were, during the second decade of the Fascist regime, the best means of achieving those goals.

The republican model of public administration

Between continuity and adaptation

Evaluating the public administration model born after the return of democratic rule and the 1948 constitution has stimulated a wide debate. Commentators have stressed the welfare orientation or, alternatively, the liberal conceptions that can be found in the general principles of the constitutional text, thus generating different interpretations of the basic features of the administrative system in Italy. Similarly, a variety of explanations have been provided about the subsequent expansion of the wider public sector (*settore pubblico allargato*), an expression which includes beside the ordinary bureaucracy also the so-called parallel administrations (*amministrazioni parallele*), that is, the autonomous entities which enable state intervention in a variety of economic sectors. However, most of the analyses agree on the simple assertion that the rebirth of a democratic system did not erase the basic foundations of the administrative model which had developed with the unitary state and later under the Fascist regime. It produced a form of *adaptation* rather than a significant *transformation* of the previous model.

Signs of the continuity with the Fascist public administration can be seen by looking at the ministerial structure and at the persistence of the top bureaucratic elite (Melis 1993). After a short phase of interdiction, a large part of the previous administrative elite could be reinstated in office, and the same organizational culture continued to permeate the state machinery. However, it was also necessary to introduce some innovations, both in order to democratize the procedures of recruitment and accountability of the public administration, and to facilitate the modernization of a centralized system of 'parallel branches' that, in the aftermath of Fascism, had suddenly appeared anachronistic and ineffective.

In line with this combination of a significant degree of continuity and the necessity of adaptation, the 1948 constitution formulated a very general notion of public administration (Articles 97–8), confirming the Weberian notions of neutrality and rationality of the bureaucratic mission. It avoided, however, any binding definition of the 'borders' of public administration. In this way, the republican model could be characterized, from the very beginning, by a strong dualism: while the central body of the ministerial bureaucracy, having a structured and relatively stable organization, could be easily identified and measured, the 'wider public sector' included a plethora of different bodies and subsidiaries, making the Italian administration quite heavy, and surely one of the most complex state machineries of the Western European administrative landscape.

The growth of the public sector after 1945: proliferation of new structures and new organizational aims

The process of adaptation of the public administration was, at the beginning of the republican age, limited to the redefinition of a few ministries (Box 7.2) and to the consequent redistribution of the responsibilities among departmental structures. Later on, the new needs of political life, but also the logic of distribution of political spoils, favoured an incremental proliferation of full ministerial posts—in the mid-1950s, they reached the considerable number of nineteen—as well as of ministers without portfolio and of under-secretaries (see Chapter 4). Such an incremental development would continue until the beginning of the 1990s, fuelling within the public administration the vicious circle of political clienteles, a phenomenon often referred to as 'under-government' (*sottogoverno*).

BOX 7.2 The structure of the Italian government: ministries between 1945 and 1990

Ministries already existing in 1945 Interior, Internal Affairs, Foreign Affairs; Justice; Finance; Treasury; War; Navy; Aviation; Education; Public Works; Post and Communications; Transport; Agriculture; Industry and Commerce; Employment and Social Pensions; Italian Africa (until 1953)

Ministries established after 1945 and then abolished Ministry for the Constituent Assembly (1946–7); Ministry for Reconstruction (1945–7); Ministry for Post-War Assistance (1946–7)

Newly established ministries Defence (1947) (unification of the ministries of War, Navy, and Aviation); Commercial Navy (1946); Budget (1947); State Participations (1956); Health (1958); Tourism and Leisure (1959); Culture (1974); Environment (1986); Higher Education (1989)

The structural adaptation of Italian central administration followed a political logic, much more than a paradigmatic project of change orientated to its modernization. The story of the Office for Administrative Reform created in 1950 within the presidency of the Council of Ministers, and then transformed into a department led by a minister without portfolio, is rather significant in this respect: in spite of the abundance of reports and data it produced, the department was unable to promote a substantial reform of the central administration for at least twenty-five years.

Probably the most significant elements of bureaucratic innovation, during the early republican age, were those affecting the broad family of autonomous administrative entities, which was constantly expanded and progressively transformed, according to many commentators, into a real second bureaucracy. A particularly important role was played by the system of state holdings which was strengthened and extended to cover a new set of sectors. From the early 1950s public enterprises rapidly increased in number, with a striking expansion of state entrepreneurship in the industrial sector, most notably in fields such as those of steel, chemistry, communication, and gas. These activities were motivated in theory by the need to pursue a more harmonious and territorially balanced socio-economic development in a country where the entrepreneurial culture was rather weak and concentrated in limited areas. In practice, state intervention was often dictated also by more practical needs: the failure of a private enterprise and the political need to avoid the consequent risk of massive workforce cuts, or by the possibility it offered to influence the opening of new plants (and the creation of new jobs) in critical electoral areas. This does not mean that public enterprises were predominantly run according to political criteria. In fact, the state holdings system could work thanks to the presence of a significant number of able and often enlightened public managers, such as Enrico Mattei or Oscar Sinigaglia, who saw the opportunity to use old or new public entities to fill an entrepreneurial deficit and to cope with some of the structural problems of the Italian economy, especially in the southern regions.

The history of Mattei's most significant creation, ENI (the largest Italian oil and gas corporation), founded in 1953, shows very well the paradoxical mix of benefits and costs of state holdings. Thanks to this state company, Italian industry was able to convert itself rapidly to modern energy technologies based on gas and oil. In the meantime, ENI rapidly transformed itself into an unusual multi-sectoral holding with diffuse economic interests, increasing the competition between public and private economy, and, in the long run, contributing to some serious obstacles to the process of modernization of Italian society. In particular mention should be made of the extensive use of corruption by its leadership and the political influence exercised through its ownership of important newspapers.

Other stories, certainly less successful than that of ENI, can be told about other well-known autonomous bodies, such as the National Institute for Popular Housing (*INA-Casa* 1949) and, above all, the Fund for the Promotion of Southern Italy (*Cassa per il mezzogiorno* 1950). The latter, originally conceived as a sort of governmental think tank to cope with the *questione meridionale*, the problem of the social and economic underdevelopment of the south, rapidly evolved into another heavy bureaucratic entity dispensing large amounts of financial and human resources, which were confirmed and refinanced for years, without a serious evaluation of their policy impact.

In 1956, a new ministry explicitly in charge of state holdings was created, with the clear intent of ensuring a more rational direction of the activities of the state holdings and to limit the excessive power of their managers. But these goals were never reached: the same ministry saw an irrational growth of its structure and personnel in only a few years, and the state holdings system maintained its chaotic and pluralistic institutional setting. If one also counts the state-owned banks, the number of employees of this second bureaucracy reached the considerable level of 700,000 at the end of the 1970s. With passing years an increasing politicization of the top ranks of these enterprises, which became part of a spoil system among parties in government, and a greater political interference in their economic choices took place.

Outside the state holdings system, the so-called 'autonomous administrations' also grew during the post-war reconstruction. Several large entities with a certain degree of managerial autonomy were established (or reshaped): among them, the State Monopolies Board (including salt, tobaccos, etc.), the National Postal Service, the National Forestry Company, the National Road-Building Agency, and the National Railway Company, the last of which had more than 200,000 workers on its books already during the 1950s. With the nationalization policies of the first centre-left coalition cycle (see Chapter 4) important new units were added to this group: the most significant were the electricity giant ENEL and the national telephone company, SIP.

In the mid-1960s, when the reconstruction of the Italian state could be said to have been completed, an important peculiarity of the Italian administrative system—its internal heterogeneity—was emerging in full. The decade of the economic boom and of the centre-left coalition is thus also to be considered as the decade of the maturity of the Italian administrative heterogeneity. A plethora of bodies and functions now composed a multi-faceted public sector, covering a wide range of public services and economic activities. The sustainability of this complex public administration was not immediately perceived as a problem, both because of the benefits of the positive economic cycle and also thanks to the far-sightedness of the protagonists of the early centre-left (Amato 1976), who were able to control the whole politics of policy making with modern planning and programme management. However, the changing economic and political conditions of the following years put the structural problems of the Italian administration in a clearer light, and brought new questions and new problems to the surface.

The personnel of the Italian public sector until the early 1990s

Long before the 1990s, several commentators were signalling that the Italian public sector was too complex and overstaffed. As a matter of fact, a precise estimate of the size and distribution of the labour force involved in Italian public administration has always been difficult, owing to both the late consolidation of an appropriate statistical record, and also the multifaceted and complicated reality of the wider public sector itself. We know, however, from documented studies (Cassese 1981; Melis 1993) that the overall number of public employees multiplied several times from the age of unification to the final years of the twentieth century: after the proclamation of the Kingdom of Italy (1861), this overall figure was slightly lower than 70,000 individuals, reaching the level of 250,000 at the end of the nineteenth century, when the traditional core departments—the army, the bureaucracy of the Interior Ministry, and the public primary schools—provided the largest sectors of the civil service. Only twenty years later, with Mussolini about to reach power and to build the authoritarian state, the civil service already included more than half a million people, a number that the reforms under Fascism increased in absolute and relative terms. Indeed, at the end of the authoritarian regime, the wider public sector numbered around 1.5 million employees, or about 20 per cent of the total working population.

After the Second World War, the relative weight of the civil service's workforce remained fairly stable, but the absolute number of people included in the public sector continued to increase, at least until the mid-1980s. Recent assessments considering different historical series (Capano and Gualmini 2006) assert that the overall number of 'ministerial' employees, that is those of the proper state administration, was in 1986 close to 2 million, but the number rose to more than 3 million if one considers also the other categories of the wider public sector (employees of regional administrations, of state companies, and of the independent authorities). The quantitative increase observed during the second half of the twentieth century entailed also a changed distribution among the different departments: looking at the figures for 1991, the largest slice of the bureaucratic 'cake' was represented by the personnel of the Ministry of Education (which was by then close to one million people), followed by the employees of the national health system, the regional bureaucrats, and the personnel of the Interior Ministry (police, etc.).

In general terms, such a historical evolution does not deviate from the trends seen in all the advanced democracies between 1945 and 1980 (Rose 1985), but at a closer glance reveals some interesting features of the Italian model. These peculiarities can be briefly summarized in five points.

1. The career patterns of Italian bureaucrats (above all those within the ministerial departments) looked very structured and rather predictable, since length of service used to be the most important requisite for career progression, and mobility from one branch to another was a very unusual practice.
2. With the passing of time, southernization (that is, the predominant presence of employees and functionaries coming from southern regions) had become an evident phenomenon determining, among other things, different rates of turnover and geographical mobility from the regions of the centre–north to those of the Italian *mezzogiorno*.
3. Higher civil servants, and particularly the ministerial general directors, typically had a generalist-legal background, while those with a technical and social-science expertise remained a small minority.
4. The average productivity of the Italian bureaucracy progressively decreased during the late 1970s. This phenomenon was to some extent a consequence of some of the above features (particularly the lack of mobility and the low degree of technical expertise), but also resulted from the increased influence of trade unions and the standardization of working times (reduced to about six hours per day during the seventies) across different branches.
5. The pronounced gender gap, which had been evident since the age of democratic reconstruction, persisted, particularly in the top-level bureaucratic elite, even after the years of social revolution and of the feminist movement at the end of the 1960s. Only some

specific administrations (namely, schools and the Ministry for Culture) showed a significant degree of 'feminization'.

Signs of crisis, signs of change

The continuing growth of the normal state bureaucracy, the expanding pluralism of 'parallel bureaucracies,' and the consolidation of a quite heavy system of state holdings were thus the pillars of the Italian model of public administration during the second half of the twentieth century. Undoubtedly, together with the swift economic and social reconstruction of the post-war years and the consolidation of democratic institutions, the public administration with its different faces also contributed to the impressive growth of the Italian economy in that period. At the same time, however, the performance of this model of bureaucracy was recurrently the object of criticism from the population and in particular from the private economic sector. The slowness and rigidity of its procedures, the limited attention paid by bureaucrats to the rights and the needs of the public, the lack of innovation, the frequent disclosures of episodes of corruption, and a generalized use of patronage in significant administrative sectors, have been at the centre of innumerable debates. These complaints tended to increase with time as the needs of the population at large and of economic enterprises became more sophisticated, while the transformations of the public sector generally lagged behind.

The relationship with politics has obviously been a central problem. If on one side the constitution prescribed the neutrality of the administrative system, the consolidation in the Italian political system of a very dense partycracy and the uninterrupted governmental role of the same parties for approximately forty years led almost inevitably to very close relations of patronage between political and administrative actors. The Christian Democratic party played a particularly relevant role, with the two models of *clientela* and *parentela*, described in a book by Joseph La Palombara (1964) that soon became famous. More precisely, the *clientela* relationship indicates a practice of closely knit contacts between specific interest groups and bureaucratic actors (using La Palombara's example, the historical link between the main farmers' association and the Ministry of Agriculture), while the *parentela* relationship occurs when, in a given policy sector, a broad range of activities is conducted, with the participation of social and administrative actors who share with their political counterparts a set of similar values and common backgrounds. A typical example, in this respect, was the policy making in the field of public education, where for a long time ministers and a large number of higher civil servants and policy experts had a common experience in Catholic organizations.

It must be said, however, that because of its nature the ordinary bureaucracy was far from completely open to party influence and penetration, and on the other side, politicians often complained about its (passive) resistance to the innovations they wanted to introduce. It is for these reasons also that parties often promoted the development of alternative bureaucracies as a means to exert a more effective influence on the administration. In fact the penetration of parties at the top levels of state holdings and other extraordinary bureaucratic entities was always larger than in the top ranks of the ordinary administration. When the power of Christian Democracy began slowly to decline during the 1970s, and the weight of other parties, in particular the Socialist but also the Communist party from the opposition, rose, the system kept working under the same rules, and the fragmented Italian bureaucracy gradually adapted to a more plural relationship with political elites. This meant, for instance, that within the field of state holdings, alongside the more traditional Christian democratic fiefdoms, Socialist fiefdoms developed and, albeit on a more limited scale (for instance in public television or in the regional bureaucracies), also Communist ones.

The relationships between bureaucratic personnel and political elites were able to remain in equilibrium, during a period in which the growth of local governments and other important innovations such as the founding of a national health service (1977) created the conditions for a further fragmentation of the administrative system. On the other hand, the new demands and expectations voiced by the public were mounting, at the same time as budgetary and financial constraints recurrently pressed the government leaders with the need to reduce the elephantiasis of the state holdings system (and its increasing debts), and to introduce a greater flexibility in several sectors of the central administration. Studies inspired by the theory of public organizations and some pioneering sociological surveys on bureaucratic personnel conducted between the 1960s and 1970s documented the peculiarities and the problems that were progressively emerging in the management of the Italian state. Among these problems were the already mentioned questions concerning the profile of the personnel, namely the process of

Southernization and the lack of new technocratic skills, as well as the insufficient orientation among higher civil servants to develop more synergetic forms of circulation and mobility. Furthermore, the economic crisis of the 1970s exposed to growing criticism the unsatisfactory relationship between the constant expansion of the administration and its very poor performance.

The process of regionalization, begun in 1970 (see Chapter 6), could have been a first element paving the way to a bureaucratic reform, since it provided a good opportunity to rationalize the organization of public offices, according to a more synergetic and functional division of work. Unfortunately, both the resistance of ministerial civil servants and the political difficulties between the parties in government and those controlling specific regions (namely the Communist party in the regions of central Italy) proved serious obstacles to an effective and rational reduction of the central bureaucracy. Therefore not much was done until the 1980s, when the need to reform the government from within became a priority, to a large extent linked to the new urgent goal, which had emerged after the fiscal crisis of the late 1970s, to reduce state expenditures through strong policies of austerity. It was not by chance that a well-known professor of administrative law and a supporter of bureaucratic innovation, Massimo Severo Giannini, started a new wave of discussion when, in 1979, he was appointed Minister for the Reform of Public Administration. His white paper, however, orientated to a rigorous sense of efficacy, persuaded neither the bureaucrats, nor the political actors, and the big reforms had to remain on the waiting list for about fifteen years. Three improvements were in any event achieved during the 1980s, although by means of measures which only partially affected the bureaucratic organization. The overall departmental structure was corrected, with the creation of important ministries like those for the environment and for higher education (Box 7.2); the reform of the Prime Minister's Office in 1988 (see Chapter 4) allowed a wide revision of the core of government and, particularly, of the old department for public administration which was equipped with new organizational resources and a more precise mission. And finally, the long discussion about the responsibilities of different bureaucracies brought about a first crucial regulation of the governmental structure of local governments (Law 142/1990) which can be considered (see Chapter 6) the dawn of the new era of political and institutional reforms in Italy.

The new administrative system amid innovation and resistance

An ongoing process of reform

The signs of crisis and the limited changes which had occurred during the period 1980–92 were followed by an abundance of proposals and concrete reforms that occupied the legislative agenda for at least ten years, between 1993 and 2003, and the ultimate effects of which still have to be evaluated with precision. Together with important modifications of the administrative system, the recent period has also been marked by an enduring academic debate about the nature of Italian bureaucracy. Impressive amounts of data have been produced in order to support such a discussion and to find adequate solutions to the traditional problems of public administration.

It is also important to remember that during the past two decades the Italian academic and cultural environment has seen the growth of a modern science of public administration, developed with the contributions of political scientists, sociologists, and lawyers. A community of experts emerged indeed, the most eminent personalities of which have been often directly involved in the concrete reforms, being appointed as technocratic ministers or as members of ad hoc ministerial committees. It is not by chance that, fifteen years after the ill-fated attempt at reform by Professor Giannini, the office of Minister for Administrative Reform, in the technocratic cabinet led by Carlo Azelio Ciampi in 1993, was offered to another well-reputed expert on Italian administration, Professor Sabino Cassese. For the same reason, the political cabinets of subsequent years have chosen for the same role distinguished personalities such as the political scientist Giuliano Urbani (centre-right government, 1994), the constitutional lawyer Franco Bassanini (centre-left, 1996), and the experienced public manager Franco Frattini (centre-right, 2001). These personalities have linked their names to relevant reforms. Together with other eminent politicians, they have produced in less than fifteen years a number of legislative and regulatory decisions concerning the public administration which is perhaps higher and more consequential than the total number of decisions produced in the previous 130 years of the unitary state. Some have spoken of a period of permanent reform (Capano 2000). Other scholars have stressed the inevitable resistance and the difficulties of a process which seems still quite far from its destination. In any case, it is interesting, before any attempt at interpretation, to have a closer look at the substantive contents of these changes. We will therefore briefly report the most important steps of this process, paying special attention to some peculiar aspects of the bureaucratic transformation in Italy, namely the refurbishing and optimization of the traditional central bureaucracy, the emergence of new regulatory bodies, and the changing characteristics of the bureaucratic elite.

A paradigmatic change: the hollowing out of the state and the reshaping of its machinery

The impressive transformations which have occurred in the Italian administration since 1992 can be summarized around five major themes. The first theme is the structural change of the central administration, including the new organization of ministries, public bodies, and agencies. The second is the reforms of the administrative functions and procedures. A third major point is the introduction of a new system of administrative controls focusing on efficiency and quality, and assigning priority to the results of administrative activity rather than conformity to the rules. The reform of the budgetary system, in different branches of public administration, is a technical but not irrelevant fourth element of change, while the fifth theme is the reform of public employment and, within this context, of the top administrative elites.

As far as the organization is concerned, a decisive and appropriately oft-mentioned change has been the one promoted in 1999 by two legislative decrees, included in the so-called Bassanini reform, that have drastically reduced the number of ministries. The innovative twist of the reform was, however, largely diminished during the years following its introduction, as politicians of both centre-right (in 2001) and centre-left (2006) sought to expand again the number of ministerial posts available in order to solve intra-coalition squabbles about the distribution of portfolios, and positions of deputy minister and under-secretary (see Chapter 4). The current situation, described in Table 7.1, can be summarized as a still complex central administration, formed by eighteen ministries and with a remarkable number of departments and offices within each ministry. As for organizational adaptation, it is also important to remember another

TABLE 7.1 Ministerial structures in 2006 (government Prodi II)

Ministry	General structure	Main organizational bodies	Size (full-time personnel)
Presidency of the Council of Ministers	Mixed	general secretariat of the presidency	about 5,000
		8 departments under the PdCM	
		7 departments under ministers without portfolio	
Foreign Affairs	Hierarchical	general secretariat	about 7,000
		13 general directorates	
Interior	Departmental	5 departments	about 22,000
Justice	Departmental	4 departments	about 55,000
Economy	Departmental	5 departments	about 20,000
		fiscal agencies	about 50,000
Economic Growth	Mixed	11 directorates	about 2,000
		1 department (cohesion and growth policies)	
University and Research	Mixed	1 department	about 1,500
		5 directorates	
Education	Departmental	2 departments	about 7,000
International Trade	Mixed	3 general directorates	about 1,000
		1 department (European Union policies)	
Employment and Welfare	Hierarchical	13 directorates	about 8,000
Social Solidarity	Hierarchical		
Defence	Hierarchical	11 directorates	about 55,000
Agriculture and Food	Departmental	2 departments	about 2,000
Environment	Hierarchical	6 directorates	about 1,000
Infrastructure	Departmental	4 departments	about 9,000
Transport	Departmental		
Health	Departmental	4 departments	about 2,000
Culture	Departmental	4 departments	about 22,000
Communication	Hierarchical	5 directorates	about 2,000

Note: The Ministry of Employment and Welfare and that of Social Solidarity, created in 2006 from the old Ministry of Welfare, have still to be reorganized with separate structures. The same applies to the Ministries of Infrastructure and Transport. The data about the personnel are updated to 2005.
Source: Minister of Economy, General Accounting Office.

compromise between the spirit of the reform and successive practice: many crucial ministries have in fact continued to be structured according to the traditional vertical model, based on a strong general secretariat coordinating a variable number of directorates. Other ministries have adopted the departmental staff system, which assumes a less vertical organization and a full administrative delegation to the officials appointed at the top of 'goal-orientated' divisions. However, the concrete organization of many ministries seems very often to follow a sort of mixed model (Gualmini 2006), including elements from both organizational systems. As a consequence, the structure of the current central administration shows a peculiar example of 'variable geometry' (Pajno and Torchia 2000) with a high degree of internal fragmentation and a quite variable organizational logic.

Overall, the personnel of the central administration, as summarized in Table 7.1, represents today only 8 per cent of the public sector (Figure 7.1). The absolute numbers (for the year 2005) are about 260,000 full-time employees within the ministerial structures out of 3,350,000 people receiving a state salary. We have to say that the distribution among the different

FIGURE 7.1 **Distribution of full-time personnel in the Italian public sector, 2005**

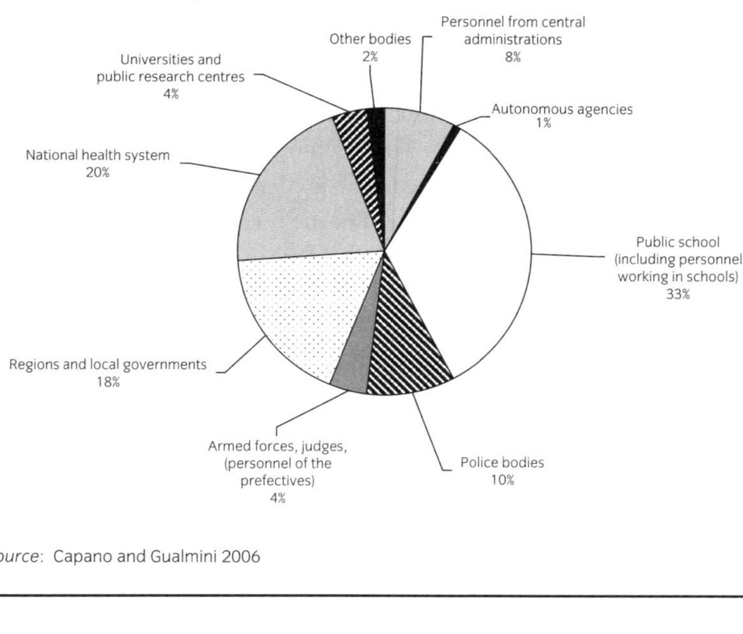

Source: Capano and Gualmini 2006

categories has not changed very much in comparison with ten or twenty years ago (Cassese and Franchini 1994; Capano and Gualmini 2006). However, two significant exceptions have to be noted. First of all, the figures hide the growing role of the regional governments, which now have more or less direct control over the personnel employed in the national health system. Second, the magnitude of the autonomous agencies and of the other non-economic bodies has been almost halved in the past fifteen years, thus showing that a more functional distribution is prevailing over the traditional logic of the 'parallel bureaucracies'.

Besides the reform of the ministerial structures, the reduction of autonomous bodies and state holdings, through processes of privatization and simplification of the state machinery, have probably been the most revolutionary changes occurring since 1992. In this framework, it is important to remember that two crucial events—the start of the process of privatization of public banks and the abolition, via a referendum, of the Ministry of State holdings—took place more or less in the same period (between the fall of 1992 and the spring of 1993) and they were somehow facilitated by the political crisis that had followed the inauguration of the Eleventh Legislature (April 1992). At the same time, these events were a sort of catalyst for further changes, since they demonstrated that the philosophy of the new public management, centred on a reduction of the state's direct control over industries and public utilities, could finally work even in Italy, after at least ten years of failed starts (Cassese 1994).

The discussion on privatization policies is not closed, also because in many cases the government has delayed the programme or maintained a significant degree of control by means of 'golden shares' in the hands of the treasury ministry. However, the extent of the policy change, in comparison with previous attempts, is remarkable. To give just a sketchy picture of the changes of the 1990s, it is enough to list the main state companies which have become part of the private sphere, such as Italian Telecom, the largest oil company (ENI), the National Insurance Institute (INA), the National Electricity Company (ENEL), and all the important national banks, or have acquired a more pronounced market orientation, such as the National Post and the railway company (see Bull and Newell 2005: 181 ff.).

Less invasive in terms of institutional configuration, but surely not in terms of institutional functioning, are the innovations of the past decade concerning administrative procedures and administrative controls. The timing of these reforms is even broader in this respect, since their starting point can be found in the very innovative principles of Law 241/1990, commonly referred to as the first structural reform of the administrative procedure in recent Italian history. These principles were inspired by some typical key concepts of the new public management paradigm: transparency of public activities, effectiveness of governmental action, expenditure control, and flexibility of the administrative structures. Not unexpectedly these principles have had a difficult transposition into effective norms, and the 'spirit' of the reform has been often betrayed by its concrete day-to-day management. Regarding administrative controls, the 1990s saw an intensive application of the notion of 'management by objectives' at all levels of public administration. Already in 1994, a reform of the financial audit office (*Corte dei conti*) had deeply modified the work of this institution, reducing the *ex ante* tools of formal control in favour of new procedures evaluating the effectiveness of expenditure. In 1999, a comprehensive set of control activities was mandated by law and linked to a new operative notion of 'administrative evaluation', which has to be implemented in all sectors of the civil service. As regards procedural innovations, two fundamental steps forwards have been, respectively, the attempts to modernize the internal procedures (recently revisited by Law 15/2005) and the introduction of an annual law of administrative simplification, a recurrent legislative tool aimed at abolishing useless regulations and increasing the effectiveness of current procedures.

Finally, there are other recent critical innovations with a potential for change but which, in the short run at least, have not yet delivered all their anticipated effects. In particular we should mention the reform of the public budget (1997) and the so-called privatization of public employment. The former act introduced zero-based budgeting, changing from the incremental budgeting which had characterized the long period of the republican cycle. Besides the goal of adapting the logic of budgetary policy making to a more project-orientated method dominated by the core executive, the reform provided the opportunity to reduce the chaotic structure of the formal budgetary sheet, which had reached the limit of 4,000 items.

The privatization of public employment refers to the complex redefinition of the whole system of labour relations within the public administration, which began with a fundamental legislative decree (29/1993) changing the legal basis of public employment contracts. This reform has allowed a number of further changes in the Italian public-sector personnel system:

for instance, a reform of the career system implemented in 1998 with the aim of simplifying the professional pathway.[2] Moreover, decree 29/1993 has better defined the accountability of the body of top administrative officers (*dirigenza amministrativa*) whose new prerogatives and characteristics are analyzed in greater depth in the following pages.

The role of the new public managers

One of the traditional problems of the Italian administrative system has always been the inadequate accountability of its top bureaucrats, linked to the persistence of an archaic system of legalistic rules which reproduced at the top elite level some of the traditional characters of the old bureaucratic model, namely: limited mobility, since their career path usually developed within the same branch, with very rare transfers between different administrative branches; a high average age; almost insignificant numbers of women; and a predominantly legal background, implying little technical expertise (D'Orta and Talamo 1996).

Among the innovations introduced by legislative decree 29 is the attempt to transform the top-ranking administrative officers into managers and, at the same time, to abandon the traditional bureaucratic model. This transformation should have gone together with the incremental diffusion of the concrete tools of management by objectives and a more flexible salary system, characterized by significant rewards dependent on internal and external evaluations of the productivity of offices and of the achievement of the objectives pursued by each administrator.

Significant changes can indeed be observed: for instance, the emergence of a plurality of career patterns among high administrative officers, with the traditional 'climber' coming from the lower steps of the same branch now flanked by some 'high fliers' directly recruited within the inner circle. Moreover, a minor but already significant quota of external managers has emerged in different sectors of the administrative system, especially the national health system, but also some ministries and regional administrations. Finally, all the salaries of the higher officers, recruited both internally and externally, now include a flexible quota linked to the annual evaluation of the objectives achieved.

At the same time it must be said that the concrete outcomes deriving from the recent reforms have been at least in part watered down by resistance from the bureaucratic body and by the choices of the politicians who often delay the innovations in order to preserve their special relations with the old bureaucratic elite. Similarly, attempts to develop a younger, gender-balanced, and expertise-orientated bureaucratic elite have been remarkable but not always effective: recent studies (Capano and Vassallo 2003) report a noticeable increase within the administrative elite of 'technicians' and a small reduction of 'lawyers'; however, the age and gender of top public administrators still reveal the resistances and inertia that confront all the efforts for change.[3]

The increasing role of regulatory bodies

The emergence of autonomous regulatory bodies which operate at the national level without any direct subordination to political institutions is another important point for an evaluation of the current changes in the institutional setting of Italian public administration. The development of a regulatory state is undoubtedly a distinctive feature of the late twentieth century in all democracies, even those of continental Europe, where the institutional and legal constraints of the parliamentary form of government on the one hand and of the civil law system on the other hand had in the past discouraged the emergence of strong independent authorities.

From this point of view, the very fact that the notion of independent authority could find fertile ground even in Italy was a relevant innovation in itself, as it happened in a country where not many years ago the rhetoric of the centrality of parliamentary government and the reality of a strong partycracy presented formidable obstacles to this development. However, once again, a degree of caution is recommended when assessing the emergence of these authorities as a revolutionary change. Some of them are in fact the natural evolution of 'old' institutions, as the story of the Bank of Italy clearly shows. Moreover, the use of the terms 'authority' and 'agency' is very ambiguous in the context of the new Italian administrative system, which is certainly different but not less heterogeneous than the old one.

The 'real' new independent authorities are to be distinguished from a broader set of formally autonomous bodies which have some regulatory functions in specific fields, but which are more or less directly subordinated to the budgetary and political choices of a ministerial department (Cavatorto 2006). The institutional framework is even more confused after a law of 1999 introducing a number of bodies called 'autonomous agencies' which have a certain degree of organizational autonomy, but are in fact organic components of the central executive. In the end, the institutions that can be labelled as true independent authorities (Table 7.2) are only a handful of entities, but operating in very important policy fields.

They include first of all the Bank of Italy, an example of a rather independent central bank which never reached the reputation of the German Bundesbank, but became sufficiently autonomous in exercising its monetary policy functions and other supervisory tasks, especially after the so-called 'divorce' from the Ministry of Treasury (1981). With its personnel of about 8,000 people, distributed among fourteen large centres and about a hundred provincial offices, the central bank has a traditional administrative organization, completely different from the slim and manageable structure of the modern regulatory agencies. However, the peculiar tasks of this institution, the supervision over monetary policy, important regulative powers over economic transactions, and a constant advisory function on macro-economic and welfare policies, have always provided its leadership with a prestigious 'external actor' role, somehow able to impact on the chain of delegation linking the purely political institutions. Even after the reduction of 'hard powers' in the field of monetary policy—with the introduction of the euro and the creation of the European Central Bank—the role of the Banca d'Italia as intellectual macro-economic think tank has not disappeared, also because of the prestige of a particularly developed research unit (*Servizio studi*).

A second relatively old independent authority is the CONSOB, a regulatory body created during the 1970s with the aim of controlling the requirements of companies admitted to the national stock market and the transparent functioning of the latter. However, the real political and normative innovation was the recent introduction of some small (in terms of size) authorities whose regulatory faculties have been growing together with the transformation (and often privatization) of public utilities, and with the emergence of new regulatory issues such as in the fields of privacy and communications (see Table 7.2). In particular, it was the establishment in 1990 of the Authority for Competitiveness and the Market (which in Italy is better known by the English expression Anti-Trust Authority) that marked the emergence of an independent regulatory power in such an important and increasingly delicate matter. For the first time, the law established that a narrow executive board (in the case of the Anti-Trust Authority it is a

TABLE 7.2 Fully independent authorities in Italy, 2006

Name/translation	Year	Main functions	Personnel (2004)
Banca d'Italia (Bank of Italy)	1861	Control over monetary policy within the EMU system Control over the bank system Regulative power on economic transaction Research	About 8,000
Commissione nazionale per le società e la borsa (CONSOB) (National Commission for Companies and Stock Market)	1974	Monitoring of the companies: admitted to the stock market Regulative powers concerning the actors of the stock market Moral suasion towards business actors	About 400
Autorità per la competizione e il mercato (Authority for Competitiveness and the Market)	1990	Regulative powers concerning competition Resolution of conflicts concerning cartels Sanctioning powers	About 200
Autorità per l'energia elettrica e il gas (AEEG) (Authority for Electricity and Gas)	1995	Regulative powers concerning the sectors of competence Conflict resolution Control of the correct management of the public utilities Sanctioning powers	About 100
Garante della privacy (The Privacy Authority)	1996	Regulative powers concerning the sector of competence Conflict resolution Sanctioning powers	About 100
Autorità per la garanzia delle comunicazioni (AGCOM) (The Communications Authority)	1997	Regulative powers concerning the sector of competence Conflict resolution Sanctioning powers	About 250

body of five people including the chairman, all of them appointed by the chairmen of the two parliamentary branches) had to be elected on the basis of specific requisites of competence and independence from any possible political and economic constraint.

Other minor authorities must be considered somewhere in the middle between this category and the 'ministerial agency', but their political impact is less relevant, even if the increase of this kind of institutional device in the past couple of decades is noticeable.[4]

As can be seen, the independent authorities, with the obvious exception of the central bank, have a quite limited set of technical and personnel resources. From this point of view they have not dramatically changed the overall configuration of the administrative system. Nonetheless, it is important to stress that these 'light' institutions have provided quite a relevant set of alternative powers which do not fit in the traditional model of political accountability typical of parliamentary government and of traditional public administration. Moreover, their personnel are highly specialized and recruited using methods, such as specific selection procedures, contracting-out, and part-time contracts, that are totally different from those of the public administration.

The Bank of Italy is still a relevant independent power, even if its institutional role has of course been reduced by the creation of the European Central Bank. The reputation of its economists and the reliability of its studies and reports were among the few credible elements of the state machinery during the dark months of the political scandals (1992–94) and, as a result, a whole generation of its top officers, from Carlo Azelio Ciampi to Lamberto Dini and Tommaso Padoa Schioppa, were called to the most important political responsibilities both in Italy and within the EU context.

The effects of a recent scandal involving the governor of the central bank, Antonio Fazio, during 2005, have exposed some of the problems of the current institutional role of the bank and signalled the need for a rethinking of its place in the new political system. With the adoption of a new law concerning the protection of savings (2005) and the decision to set a term limit to the office of governor, starting with the mandate of the recently nominated Mario Draghi, these problems have received a first solution but probably not yet a final one.

The new regulatory bodies illustrated in Table 7.2 are provided with two basic types of powers: 'softer' powers to regulate specific technical matters and, in some cases, to solve conflicts of competences, and 'harder' powers to sanction actors who have been proved to have disregarded the existing regulations. The institutionalization and increasing self-assuredness of some of these bodies is evidenced by their increasing readiness to make use also of the second category of powers and by the attention these sanctions receive in the media.

Conclusion: the condition of the Italian state at the beginning of the twenty-first century

It is certainly difficult and rather risky to assess the real impact of the plethora of innovations described in the final part of this chapter. Overall, it is justified to say that the Italian administrative system has changed a great deal. But the final destination of such a change seems to be both distant and, to a large extent, uncertain. Some of the original contradictions mentioned in the introduction are still present, and the dualism of the perception of a poor and not very effective public sector vis-à-vis what is seen, at least potentially, as a thriving and dynamic private economy, is still very evident, especially in the richest areas of the country.

These persistent problems have to do with several factors of inertia. First of all, many critical innovations bump against resistance from different actors, both bureaucrats and politicians, and the real improvements one can measure are much more the effects of processes of adaptation than of revolutionary changes. The implementation of administrative reforms seems particularly difficult in a country where the public sector has always been used to secure political support for the ruling elites by means of the classic relationships of *clientela* and *parentela*. The end of the first republic has removed some of the traditional political reasons for the lack of an adequate administration and has strengthened the claims for a change in the Italian state. On the other hand, other social, economic, and historical reasons (Cassese 1993) continue to represent serious obstacles to a transformation of Italian administration. A valuable description of the difficulties for the reformer has been provided by a distinguished expert of public administration in Italy, who asserted that 'in front of the impetuous voluntarism animating the reforms, there is the impenetrable thickness of a bureaucracy that does not seem to be able to change: this because it is afraid to lose its few but consolidated privileges, or simply because it is scared of any innovation, and it sometimes prefers to step back instead of moving ahead' (Melis 1998:99). The innovators are therefore the *protagonists* of these times, but they are not necessarily the *winners*: on the contrary, they are often isolated and neutralized by the hostility of important components of the political and administrative establishment. In the end, this is not very surprising: as with all institutional processes, public administration reform is path-dependent, and this entails, at least in a context of strong historical constraints, a long and tortuous path for such a reform.

Finally, a very important intervening political factor must be borne in mind: the reforms of recent years have been promoted, in a relatively short time, by different types of government, from the semi-technical and fully technical governments at work during the transition of 1992–4, to the political cabinets which have alternated in the following years, when the centre-right and centre-left coalitions have been in power twice each, with different majority formulas and majority size (see Chapters 2 and 4). The formulation of the reforms promoted by all these governments has generally been in the hands of technocratic and expertise-orientated ministers whose basic ideas were probably not very different, but the negotiation phases and above all the policy implementation have been affected by the changing positions of myriad political actors, whose strategic needs are not always consistent with these reform programmes.

To give just some examples of this complexity: it is unquestionable that the centre-right governments led by Silvio Berlusconi have generally shared, in principle, the managerial orientation that one can find, for instance, in the Frattini reform of 2002 (see Chapter 4), while centre-left executives have been more interested in preserving the welfare state machinery. At the same time, while many relevant attempts to modernize and simplify the obsolete administrative system came under the centre-left governments in the years leading to the introduction of the euro, evidence of acquiescence towards traditional clienteles and resistance to new management principles have been frequent under the centre-right governments.

However, the period of permanent reform has been not in vain. The massive policies of privatization, the termination of large state holdings, the transition from the *owner state* to the *regulatory state* are real phenomena which have very much changed the Italian state and its administration.

Additionally, the introduction of new procedures concerning the accountability of top public-sector officers and administrative evaluation, as well as a more transparent relationship between the state and the citizens, have significantly changed the style of administrative action. All this is reflected in the diffusion in Italy of a new public discourse centred on the themes of administrative evaluation, effectiveness of the administrative action, procedural simplification, and consumer satisfaction. In sum, if the pathway of modernization of the Italian administrative system is still long and tortuous, some important steps have been made and not least among them is a significant change in administrative culture. Following D'Orta and Talamo (1996) we can assert that the principle of guarantee today no longer overshadows another modern principle of the administrative system, namely the principle of effectiveness and efficiency, since the Italian bureaucracy is not exclusively concerned with the procedures of its activity, but rather increasingly takes care of its own objectives. However, the recent reforms have been somewhat ambiguous in their attempt to achieve a working balance between the two principles.

En passant, we have mentioned in this chapter two fundamental constraints which have aided the transformation of the Italian administrative system: the first is the process of devolution to regional and local governments that, rather timidly in the 1970s but more strongly after 1990, has offered a different mode of public organization, bringing the administrative system closer to the citizens. The second constraint is of course represented by the challenges coming from the European model(s) of public administration and by the concrete requirements imposed by the EU, especially those connected to the budgetary rules governing monetary union since the Maastricht Treaty onwards.

Taken together, these constraints are the engines of a process of 'hollowing out' of the state (Della Sala 1997) which in the long run can have very deep and fruitful consequences for Italian bureaucracy. If one takes as a very general indicator of this phenomenon the overall level of public expenditures (see Figure 7.2), it is rather evident that in recent years there has already been a strong impact in terms of alignment of the Italian model with the average among European countries, after decades of eccentricity. This is consistent with the thesis of a virtuous use of the external constraints (*vincoli esterni*) in producing a series of crucial policy changes in different economic and welfare policy fields (Ferrera and Gualmini 2004). More complicated

FIGURE 7.2 Public expenditure, public debt, and deficit, as a percentage of gross domestic product, 1980–2005

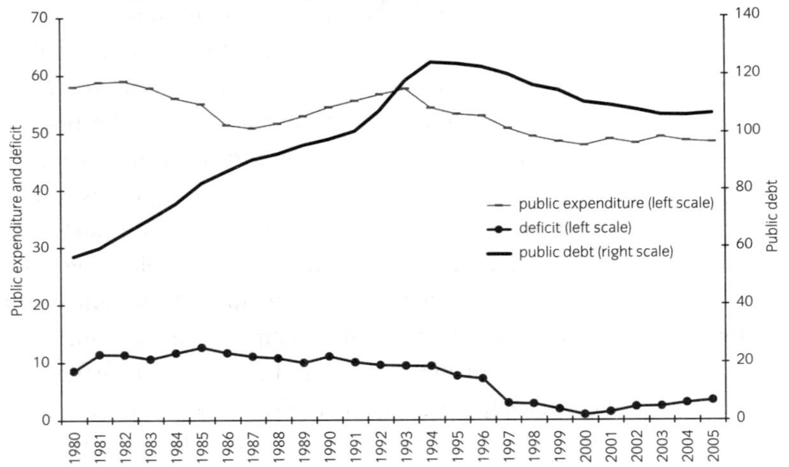

Source: OCSE.

is a precise assessment of bureaucratic performance as a whole, since the new institutional settings are too new and changes are in some cases still in progress. Although the relationship between citizens and state seems today to be stronger than in the past, the overall indicators of satisfaction are still quite frustrating. This is in itself a confirmation of the difficult challenges that have still to be faced by the Italian administrative system.

KEY TERMS

- administrative system
- bureaucratic elite
- central bank (Banca d'Italia)
- dirigisme
- effectiveness and efficiency
- ministerial organization
- new public management
- privatization
- public debt
- public expenditure
- regulatory agencies
- social assistance
- state holdings

GUIDE TO FURTHER READING

Capano, G., and Gualmini, E. (eds.) (2006) *La pubblica amministrazione italiana* (Bologna Il Mulino).

An excellent up-to-date textbook on Italian public administration.

Cassese, S., and Franchini, C. (1994) *Il sistema amministrativo in Italia*, (Bologna, Il Mulino).

A detailed portrait of the Italian bureaucratic system before the big changes.

Melis, G. (1993) *Storia dell'amministrazione Italiana* (Bologna, Il Mulino).

An accurate historical account of the Italian bureaucratic system.

Rugge, F. (2003) 'Administrative Traditions in Western Europe', in G. Peters and J. Pierre (eds.), *Handbook of Public Administration*, (London, Sage) 177–91.

An interesting reconstruction of the different bureaucratic traditions in Europe, including the Italian case.

NOTES

1 To be noted, in particular, is Gentile's reform of the public school system, developed in the mid-1930s. This reform rationalized the educational system from the pre-elementary school to the university, centralized the management of the school system, and standardized the educational programmes, in particularly at the elementary level.

2 The new system reduces the number of professional classes in the public-sector career path, from eight to ten in the past to no more than five, and introduces a flexible tool for the management of human resources, in that each administrative office can be reshaped according to its requirements.

3 The most recent figure (2003) concerning the percentage of women among top administrative officers is 15.8 per cent, compared with a female presence in the overall public sector which is now approaching 50 per cent. As regards career progression, more than 50 per cent of the top elite officers have more than twenty years' experience within the public administration, while only 26 per cent of them reach leadership positions with five years of external professional experience. For a broader discussion, see Capano and Gualmini (2006).

4 These authorities deal, for instance, with increasingly important regulatory sectors like use of e-government in public administration, control over public works, scrutiny of the activities of insurance, or private pension funds. For an up-to-date description see Cavatorto (2006).

8

Judicial Power: An Unresolved Conflict with Politics

Overview

Judicial institutions are predominantly considered non-political institutions, neutral powers. This is correct in the sense that they are normally not expected to take part in the basic political processes which concern the allocation of the power to decide for the whole political community, and which in a democracy are fundamentally regulated by competitive elections, with parties taking a predominant role. It is not uncommon indeed that members of judicial institutions are required to abstain from participating in political activities and from being members of parties. At the same time, however, these institutions have a crucial role in guaranteeing the proper working, not just of social and economic life, but also of political institutions and processes. They are an essential instrument to ensure that holders of political and administrative power do not exceed their responsibilities and that citizens' rights are respected. In this sense they play a political role, albeit of a different nature from that of cabinets, parliaments, parties, etc. At the same time, all the rules notwithstanding, they are never completely immune from political influences of different types. In some cases, however, this politicization becomes more conspicuous. This may be seen in two opposite ways: it may mean either that they have become subservient to political powers (in particular the executive) and do not fully accomplish their role of watchdogs, or on the contrary, that they have acquired a political militancy of a more oppositional type. The conflict with the executive power may in this case become significant and raise questions about the proper place of the judiciary within the institutional system of democracy.

In this chapter we will describe synthetically the organization of judicial institutions in Italy and how they have evolved over the years. We will also analyze their changing political role and in particular the long-term transformation which has led them from a rather strong identification with the executive power and the political establishment to a much more independent position, and finally also to a rather conflictual relationship with parliamentary politics, or at least with some of its components.

We will start with a consideration of the main innovations introduced in the constitution of 1948; we will then describe the organization of the judiciary with its internal articulations (civil, penal, administrative, etc.), analyze the recruitment of the judicial class, and discuss the nature of and reasons for the persistent conflict with political power in recent years. We will then examine the Constitutional Court and its role both in the field of legislative review and as arbiter in the conflicts between branches of government and between state and regions.

Historical background

The judiciary of unified Italy developed under a political regime which had only a recent tradition of liberalism and division of powers, and on the contrary quite substantial absolutist roots. Given this background it was, rather understandably, a not particularly independent body. In the age of the *Statuto Albertino* the judiciary was fundamentally seen as another, albeit special, administrative branch. Of its two main components—prosecuting and adjudicating magistrates—the first was strongly dependent from the executive. But also for the other component, that of the judges, there were no special guarantees of independence. In fact, as it has been underlined, the judiciary was to a large extent quite an integrated part of the political and social establishment of the country (Guarnieri 2001). In the first phase it was also significantly influenced by a large component of judicial personnel of political nomination and of Piedmontese origin, as part of an effort to create a body loyal to the new state. Only slowly did it acquire a stronger professional identity and a somewhat greater independence from the executive. It is perhaps a sign of this transformation that, when the liberal regime at the end of the nineteenth century had to repress popular protest movements in Milan, it preferred to use military rather than civil justice. The process of professionalization and bureaucratization of the judiciary continued until the advent of Fascism. In fact, in the last years before the instauration of the authoritarian regime, there developed the first institution, the Higher Council of the Judiciary (*Consiglio superiore della magistratura*), that was supposed to acquire some of the functions of internal governance of the judiciary, which had previously been in the hands of the Minister of Justice, and to guarantee a greater independence from the executive. All this, however, was only produced through ordinary legislation while the *Statuto Albertino* said very little about the judiciary and its independence.

The Fascist period interrupted this incremental development and marked a return to greater interference of political power in judicial activities. In this as in other crucial administrative branches of the state, the regime promoted an active policy of political penetration. In the end, however, a true 'fascistization' of the judiciary did not succeed and the regime preferred to use for its purposes of political repression special bodies as the *Tribunale speciale per la difesa dello stato* which were composed not of ordinary judges but of political personnel. It was this tribunal which issued the death penalty for political cases (in fact only a handful during the whole period).

The constitution of 1948

The new democratic constitution marked a significant change in the development of the judicial system. A number of important innovations were introduced which in the course of time would produce a substantial transformation of this component of the Italian political system.

As a first innovation there was in the new constitutional text a detailed bill of rights which would become the basis for a jurisdictional defence of citizens against the encroachment of political, economic, and social powers. As a second the judiciary became the object of a more elaborate system of constitutional provisions aimed at upgrading its status within the institutional system and guaranteeing its independence. As a third a Constitutional Court was for the first time introduced in the Italian political system, thus adding a new element in the balance between institutions.

These three elements, taken together and especially thanks to the development potential of each and the synergy in their interactions, would determine in the long run an important shift in the equilibrium between the judicial/technical elements of the institutional system and the political-representative ones.

The bill of rights

In the *Statuto Albertino* the protection of rights had received very little prominence: the list had been extremely parsimonious and full of limitations. Only a few articles, in a not very eminent position, had decreed habeas corpus, freedom of the press, freedom of meetings, and little else. In the new constitution, on the contrary, the first (and quite a long) part of the text was devoted to a detailed enumeration of citizens' rights. Not only the whole series of the classical civil and political rights of the liberal tradition (speech, press, association, movement, meeting, vote, etc.) was listed, but under the influence both of the left and of Christian Democracy, the constitutional text now emphasized the principle of equality and added a list of social rights (from the right to education to that of employment, from the right to health to those of the family). In the economic field, although it mentioned the right of economic enterprise (Article 41), it was particularly keen also to acknowledge the rights of the workers and the role of the state in guaranteeing social justice.

Obviously, as always happens with rights, their enunciation is important, but that is not enough unless the conditions for their practical implementation are in place. The role, on the one hand, of the state and its bureaucracy, and on the other hand, of the judiciary are crucial in this. The history of Italy in the second half of the twentieth century provides abundant illustrations of this point. The protection and implementation of the rights enumerated in the constitution was characterized by important variations over time. In the first period, as a result of both the greater chronological proximity with the authoritarian period and its legacies and the harsher character of political competition with all its international connections, the protection of personal political and social rights was undoubtedly more subject to limitations, which administrative and police authorities justified with reference to the need to preserve social and political order. It must be added also that, for some time, an important amount of the legislation adopted under Fascism remained untouched in spite of its being clearly at odds with the spirit and the text of the constitution. Only with the passing of time would the Constitutional Court dismantle this legacy of the past. At the same time, since the late 1960s and 1970s, magistrates, or at least a proportion of them, became much keener to implement the new constitutional rights and less ready to accept the point of view of governmental authorities or economic potentates.

The organization of the judiciary

The basic principles of the organization of the judicial system in its different components and a new definition of its overall position within the institutional system comprised the second important innovation of the constitution of 1948. As with other aspects of the constitution, the implementation of this part was initially not complete.

The new and strong attention paid by the constitution to the judiciary meant not that everything changed in this field, but that the crucial elements of this institutional sector were enshrined in the fundamental law of the country, acquiring thus a special value. The main aspects to be underlined are the following:

1. the status of the prosecution as a component of the judiciary;
2. the independence of the judiciary vis-à-vis the other powers of the state; and
3. a special body to guarantee this independence.

At the same time the elements of continuity with the past are not to be underestimated. The model of the judiciary as a bureaucratic and professionalized body, which had become increasingly clear in the past, has been maintained and developed. Magistrates, and this means members both of the adjudicating and of the prosecuting offices, are to be recruited through a state-wide competitive procedure (*concorso*) and their career is defined by the law. There is no space in this judicial system for elected judges or prosecutors. The only external element is the members of the juries that exist at certain jurisdictional levels and the non-professional judges (*giudici di pace* and *giudici onorari*) who are responsible only for minor judicial cases.

Having maintained, as in most continental legal systems, the great division between administrative law and ordinary civil and penal law (Articles 24 and 28), the constitution confirmed also the distinction between an administrative judicial system and an ordinary one (Articles 100, 103, and 104). To these should be added an accounting jurisdiction (with the *Corte dei Conti* as its central court) (Article 100) and obviously a military one. If we leave aside the very special case of military justice, there are thus three separate judicial bodies—an ordinary, an administrative, and an accounting one. Of the three, however, only the first is defined as an 'autonomous body (*ordine*), independent from the other powers of the state' (Article 104). The ordinary judiciary is not defined as a power of the state, in the same sense as the executive or the legislative, but its position is, however, clearly higher than that of other state institutions and is at the centre of a special system of guarantees directed at ensuring its independence.

The ordinary judicial system is organized into the two branches of civil and penal jurisdiction. These branches have separate courts and prosecuting offices, but their magistrates are all drawn from a common pool and in their career magistrates can move from one to the other. Closer attention is due (also in view of recent reform proposals touching precisely on this aspect) to the relationship between prosecuting and adjudicating components of the judiciary. While the offices and the personnel responsible for these two functions are separate, the recruitment and the status of these two components are essentially the same. Prosecutors share the same selection and career process as judges and enjoy the same independence. This feature puts Italian prosecutors in a rather different position to those in many democratic countries, where their status is that of state bureaucrats dependent on the national or sub-national executives (Guarnieri and Pederzoli 2002). One of the consequences of the adoption of this model is that members of the judiciary can move from the position of prosecutor to that of judge and vice versa without major obstacles.

The organization of courts

Judicial offices are organized according to an internal hierarchy and are territorially distributed more or less following the administrative articulation of the country based on provinces and regions. The hierarchy derives from their role in the judicial process. The tribunals are courts of first instance.

TABLE 8.1 Judicial offices

Territorial and hierarchical level	Adjudicating court	Prosecuting office
Provincial or sub-provincial level	Tribunale or Corte d'Assise	Procura della Repubblica
Regional or sub-regional level	Corte d'Appello or Corte d'Assise d'Appello	Procura generale della Repubblica
National level	Corte di Cassazione	Procura generale della Repubblica presso la Corte di Cassazione
National level	Sezioni riunite della Corte di Cassazione	Procura generale della Repubblica presso la Corte di Cassazione

The courts of appeal will adjudicate when a first-level ruling has been appealed. At the top of the hierarchy there is the Court of Cassation which does not decide on the merit of cases but only on matters of procedure and legitimacy. If its judgment validates an appeal proposed to it with regards to such matters the case is sent back to a lower court for a new judgment on merit. Depending on the nature of the case, it operates through one of its sections or in a joint meeting of all its sections (*a sezioni riunite*). At each level there is a corresponding prosecuting office (Table 8.1).

Over the years the organization of judicial offices has been affected by many important changes, on the one hand, in an attempt to deal with an increasing amount of work, and on the other hand, to reflect changes that have been introduced in the conduct of judicial procedures. It is in particular the prosecuting component of the judiciary which has undergone the most important transformations. Among the most relevant aspects of this change the following deserve to be mentioned: prosecuting offices have acquired an increasingly direct and strong control over police services for the exercise of their role; the hierarchical organization of these offices has been practically dismantled and a much greater autonomy given to their individual components while only a coordination role has been left in the hands of the chief prosecutors; and their autonomy from central political authorities and in particular from the Minister of Justice has significantly increased. These changes have meant that the prosecuting component of the judiciary has to an extent supplanted the executive (Minister of the Interior and Minister of Justice) in the guidance of police actions against crime and the individual initiative of prosecutors has had a significant weight in guiding this action. This evolution together with other aspects of the transformation of the judicial profession played an important role in the events of the 1990s which projected some Italian prosecutors to the centre of the political arena.

Recruitment and career of magistrates

The recruitment of magistrates has been characterized at the entry level by predominantly meritocratic criteria: a very competitive national examination of a mainly theoretical nature has been the gate through which the new recruits have been admitted into the judiciary. Even if the constitution allows, but only for the Court of Cassation, the recruitment of magistrates directly from the legal or the academic professions (the latter limited to the field of law studies), external entries have been extremely rare and have in practice played no role. Not much has changed with regard to the entry mechanism except that competition has significantly increased over the years, as the number of candidates has risen enormously with the expansion of university education and with the attractiveness of the salaries earned by magistrates (who nowadays are in Italy among the best-paid civil servants). The number of applications to take this exam has, however, reached a level that induces many observers to raise doubts about the ability of this process effectively to evaluate the quality of the candidates.

More relevant is what happens at later stages in this career, where in fact important changes have occurred. Originally advancement in a very vertically structured career, from the lower posts to the top in the Court of Cassation, was achieved through a system of internal exams and evaluations where the role of the higher grades of the judiciary (and to an extent of the Minister of Justice) in deciding promotions was paramount. This, together with other factors, contributed to reinforcing the hierarchical character of the judicial body and enhanced the pre-eminence of the top level, that of the *Magistrati di cassazione*. The prestige of the higher ranks was in many material and symbolic ways underlined.

Since the late 1960s a series of reforms have progressively dismantled this model (Law 570 of 25 July 1966; Law 831 of 20 December 1973). In the name of the principles of equality and with the idea of enhancing the autonomy of magistrates from the external influence of political power, which was thought to be more easily channelled via the high grades of the judiciary, it was decided to abolish intermediate exams and to extend to all magistrates a career progression based essentially on age. This has meant that after a given number of years all magistrates reach the upper levels and in the end also the career (and salary) level of the highest court, the Court of Cassation. Of course this does not mean that all will effectively occupy the higher positions for the very simple practical reason that positions at the top are more limited in numbers. The assignment of a specific position is now made through a decision of the Higher Council of the Judiciary. This institution, or rather one of its sub-committees, decides on the allocation of all judicial positions on the basis of a broad evaluation of the professional qualifications of the different candidates. Given the political nature of this body, based on competitive elections among the 'parties' of the judicial body, these decisions are significantly affected also by the affiliations of the magistrates.

Development of the judicial corporation

In the transformation of the judiciary and of its role in society and political life, a crucial role has been played by the Higher Council of the Judiciary (the *Consiglio superiore della magistratura*), the new body to which the constitution assigned its governance. To this should be added also the mobilization of magistrates through their professional association (the ANM, *Associazione Nazionale Magistrati*) and its internal factions, which have progressively become real judicial 'parties' (Vauchez 2007). This institutional innovation, coupled with associational mobilization, has over the years transformed the judiciary from a rather passive component of the establishment, fundamentally dominated by a hierarchical principle and politically rather timid, into a strong corporation guided by an internal political leadership, ready to fight for its corporative rights and with an extremely independent and sometimes even aggressive attitude towards the executive and elected politicians in general.

The Higher Council was conceived by the constitution as an instrument for regulating and disciplining the internal working of the judiciary. In particular it was given the power to nominate and assign magistrates to their places, to promote them, and to remove or punish them for disciplinary reasons. With this institution the judiciary was to be preserved from external interventions that would have endangered its autonomy (Articles 105–6). By the creation of this body the power of the Ministry of Justice over magistrates was significantly reduced. It is now confined to promoting disciplinary action, but any decision will then be taken by the Higher Council: in practice the minister acts as a prosecutor, but the judge is the Higher Council (thus, to a great extent, the magistrates).

In the constitutional design the Higher Council was supposed to represent the magistrates, but at the same time a link was to be maintained with the representative system. For this purpose its presidency was given *de jure* to the President of the Republic; as for its membership, it was to be composed of members elected by all the magistrates and of other lay members elected by parliament; the two highest magistrates were added as further *de jure* members (Box. 8.1). The lay members elected by parliament have typically represented the majority and opposition in government in a proportional way and have often had also a political background.

BOX 8.1 **Higher Council of the Judiciary**

de jure members

- President of the Republic (president of the Higher Council)
- First president of the Court of Cassation
- General prosecutor at the Court of Cassation

Elected members

- 16 elected by all magistrates (judges and prosecutors)
- 8 elected by parliament from among university law professors and lawyers with more than 15 years of professional experience

As the President of the Republic can only rarely preside over the Higher Council and the workload of this institution has increased significantly over the years, the deputy president, elected from among the lay members but by all the Higher Council members, has become a very important figure. Particularly in recent years his or her role has also been to mediate between the judiciary and the political world in the event of conflict between the two.

In the early years the Higher Council, thanks to the electoral system adopted (of a majoritarian type) and the prevailing deferential culture within the ranks of the judiciary, was dominated by the highest magistrates of the Court of Cassation, which at that time had a close relationship with the Minister of Justice and with the government. Given its powers of nomination and promotion and the original career mechanisms, the Higher Council tended to reproduce the existing equilibrium. But its success in preserving the status quo was progressively eroded as the lower ranks became increasingly impatient towards this conservatism and there began a process of politicization of some sectors of the judicial body. The authority of the higher ranks was challenged also by criticisms of their involvement (or in any case their acquiescence) in the past regime. The higher magistrates became increasingly isolated, while the ANM, counting upon the much larger numbers of lower-level members, was able to push for a change to a more proportional electoral system for the Higher Council, and through this gradually overturned the internal equilibrium of the corporation. The different groups within the ANM, defined by their broad political orientation, but also by somewhat different conceptions of the role of the judiciary and magistrates in society and of the internal organization of the judicial body, became the central actors of the Higher Council, introducing in its workings a sort of 'parliamentary logic'. The left–right dialectics within these currents (and particularly between the leftist *Magistratura democratica* and the conservative *Magistratura indipendente*) had an important role in defining the Higher Council's policies; but the internal components were also ready to present a common front in defence of corporative privileges and against reforms promoted by the executive or the parliament that they disliked.

The associations of magistrates individually and acting together with the Higher Council contributed significantly to shape and define the corporative identity of the judiciary. They were promoters of discussions about the functioning of the judicial system and played a major role in designing reforms (and opposing those coming from outside). This role was further increased by the fact that the largest proportion of the experts working within the Ministry of Justice on the same themes were magistrates temporarily attached to its central offices.

The judicial system at the centre of political conflict

The growing autonomy and corporative identity of the judiciary and the increased activism of individual magistrates were among the preconditions for the important phenomena of the 1990s that journalists dubbed 'clean hands' (*mani pulite*). In 1992, what had started as a minor case of local political corruption, quickly developed into a large-scale operation of judicial prosecution involving almost the entire national leadership of all the parties traditionally in government (Christian Democrats, Socialists, Social Democrats, Republicans, and Liberals), a limited component of the opposition parties, and a significant group of private businessmen and of state company managers. The judiciary, but more specifically a group of Milanese prosecutors, uncovered simultaneously the diffuse system of illegal financing of the parties, and the pervasive presence of corruption in public works tenders and in state procurements. While in the past individual magistrates had accused individual politicians, this time groups of prosecutors operating as teams moved against a whole section of the political elite. The fact that a specific case could take this turn had a great deal to do, not only with the preconditions mentioned above, but also and perhaps even more with the internal crisis of this political elite (see Chapter 2), which had become increasingly dependent on these illegal means to support itself and to pay for the costs of politics (which had grown in the age of TV), and at the same time was increasingly unable to legitimate itself in the face of public opinion through its policy accomplishments (which were poor). The role of the media and of public opinion in providing support and encouragement for the judiciary was certainly decisive, but was also the root of some of the problems which ensued. A number of prosecutors in particular, having suddenly become media stars (the processes began to be televised), were encouraged to make exaggerated use of some extraordinary judicial means, such as preventative incarceration, to stimulate confessions from the defendants, and to adopt the posture of societal reformers. In this way they were, on the one hand, treading legally dubious ground and, on the other, entering into the dangerous arena of politics. This border between judicial action and politics was frequently crossed during the early

1990s, for instance when, following the Amato government's attempt in 1993 to find a way to reach a settlement in this judicial storm by way of a parliamentary act, the Milanese prosecutors issued a public stop to the government and parliament action, or when, later on, the most prominent of these prosecutors, and at that time probably the most popular person in Italy, Antonio Di Pietro, decided to become a political leader.

With the victory of Berlusconi in the 1994 election and his rise to prime ministerial power the relationship between judiciary and elective institutions took a new turn. It is true that Berlusconi had dissociated himself from the old political elites, when they were under attack from the prosecutors of *mani pulite*, presenting himself as something new with respect to the old politicians, and even more so had his television channels, which had ridden the wave of anti-politics and anti-partyism of these days. It cannot be forgotten, however, that Berlusconi and his media company had been very close to the governing politicians of the recent period—in particular, Craxi of the PSI and Forlani of the DC. Moreover Berlusconi shared with many Italian entrepreneurs a strong propensity to evade taxes through a variety of legal, semi-legal, and possibly fully illegal means, and as many of them, had entered into dubious exchanges with the politicians, providing illegal resources to the ever-hungry financial managers of the parties. After having pursued the politicians of the first republic, the magistrates found in front of them, as the Prime Minister, a person who combined, the two positions of entrepreneur and politician. There were attempts from Berlusconi's side to find an agreement with the judicial activists by offering Di Pietro a position as minister. But in the end this encounter failed. Very soon Milanese prosecutors began to put under scrutiny the national and international financial empire of the Prime Minister, easily finding a good number of dubious operations conducted by his collaborators. Inquiries and trials involving him and his firms would continue throughout the next twelve years, creating (especially whenever Berlusconi was in power) a 'judicial war' which had inevitably the tones also of a political and institutional conflict. On one side, the prosecutors could adduce significant evidences of illegal behaviours; on the other, the leader of the government, or at other moments of the largest party of the opposition, would accuse them of discriminatory conduct as they were concentrating all their attention on his firms while leaving other important economic centres unaffected.

It is not possible here to evaluate accurately the reasons and the wrongs of the two sides. It is sufficient for the purpose of this book to underline the fact that this conflict has significantly poisoned the relationship between representative politics and the judiciary. While the judiciary continued its action against Berlusconi, the political leader together with his parliamentary majority counteracted with special legislative measures directed at protecting the defendants (and thus also himself) in different stages of the trial.

What is perhaps more relevant is that this conflict had a serious impact on attempts to reform the judiciary. The view that the judicial system required some significant reforms, mainly with reference to the too close relationship between judges and prosecutors, the career and the formation of magistrates, the relationship between Ministry of Justice and Higher Council, had become, after the end of the hot years of *mani pulite*, widely shared among elected politicians (more perhaps of the centre-right but to an extent also of the centre-left) and experts on these matters. The fact that this reform could appear connected with the Berlusconi case, however, made things more difficult. When the centre-left was in government between 1996 and 2001 its intention to propose a reform was in the end shelved: any reform would have probably antagonized either the judiciary or the opposition leader. It was then left to the next centre-right government (the second and third Berlusconi cabinets) after 2001 to make a move. After long internal discussions particularly on the issue of the separation between prosecutors and judges, the then Minister of Justice, the Lega Nord politician Castelli, proposed a wide-ranging reform touching all the critical aspects (see Box 8.2).

BOX 8.2 **The centre-right reform of the judiciary (L. 150/2005)**

Higher offices appointments: Introduction of special requisites of professional experience.

Separation of careers between prosecutors and judges: Common initial selection procedure, followed by separation of the two careers. Later passages from one career to the other more difficult and linked to internal exams and ad hoc courses.

Career progression: Introduction of exams and evaluation procedures.

Disciplinary sanctions: Obligatory procedure when requested by the Minister of Justice.

continues

Box 8.2 continued

Organization of local prosecuting offices: Greater directive powers for the local offices' chiefs.
Powers of the Minister of Justice: The minister can appeal to the administrative justice against decisions of the Higher Council of the Judiciary concerning appointments of magistrates. The minister is also requested to transmit an annual report to the parliament on government policy concerning matters of justice.

Inevitably these proposals were perceived by a significant part of the judiciary as an attempt to put the reins on the judiciary: a strong mobilization of magistrates followed with strikes and other forms of opposition. The eruption of this conflict made also any agreement between the two parliamentary fronts practically impossible. In the centre-left even those who supported a reform (and also some of the points proposed by the centre-right) could not accept being seen as aligned with the government and Berlusconi. The reform, after a presidential veto, was in the end approved only by the parliamentary majority and with strong opposition from almost the entire judicial body. After the electoral defeat of the Berlusconi coalition in 2006 the implementation of the reform is now the responsibility of the centre-left government. The new government and its tiny majority have to face the diverging pressures of the judiciary and parts of the majority coalition that have fiercely opposed the reform and of the moderate wing of its supporters that want to continue (with some corrections) the reform begun by the previous government. It is clear that this debate and the problems of the judiciary will continue to be a significant theme in the coming years.

The Constitutional Court

The institutional design

The creation of a Constitutional Court was the third important innovation of 1948. Constitutional courts are not strictly part of the judiciary, yet they have important things in common with the latter (in particular many elements of the functioning logic and style of other courts), and their activity is in many ways connected with that of the judicial bodies. In fact they are a sort of *genre mixte* combining in a delicate way political and jurisdictional elements. In the Italian case this institution, which, as in most European cases, had not existed under the previous constitution, was introduced under pressure from Christian Democracy and other small centrist parties, and against the wishes of the Socialist and Communist left, which was suspicious of any obstacle to a fuller assertion of parliamentary sovereignty.

The arguments militating in favour of this institution had to do with the intention of ensuring the superiority of the constitution over ordinary laws (which was already implicit in the choice of a rigid constitution), to enforce the bill of rights effectively, and to solve possible conflicts between powers and institutions of the state. It was also coherent with a conception of democracy more centred on the principle of division of powers than on the absolute supremacy of electoral and parliamentary sovereignty (Pederzoli 2007).

The constitutional text assigned three fundamental powers to this institution:

1. to decide on the constitutionality of national and regional laws;
2. to adjudicate on matters of conflict of competency between powers of the state, between state and regions, and between regions; and
3. to act as a judge in the case of an impeachment of the head of state.

Later on, as a fourth competence, it was allotted to the Court also:

4. to decide on the admissibility of referendum proposals.

With regard to its composition the Constituent Assembly decided to combine technical competence and non-partisanship, but at the same time to maintain an important link with the democratic process and its institutions. To reach this goal it was agreed that of its fifteen members, one-third would be nominated by the head of state, one-third elected by the parliament in a joint session of its two chambers, and the final third elected by the highest offices of the different branches of the judiciary (three of them are elected by Cassation magistrates, one by the magistrates of the Council of State, and one by those of the Court of Accounts). The nominees must have a juridical background: to ensure this they must be either university professors in the legal disciplines, or lawyers with at least twenty years of professional experience, or magistrates from the highest levels of the judiciary. The mandate of constitutional judges lasts nine years and cannot be renewed. The renewal of judges is staggered in time. Judges elect a president for a term of three years (or less if the mandate of the president as a judge ends before that term).

In order to ensure their non-partisanship, the judges chosen by the parliament must be elected by a two-thirds majority (and if this is not reached, by a three-fifths majority after the third ballot). In practice an agreement has prevailed to assign them proportionally to the main political currents of the parliament. This means that majority and opposition first reach an internal agreement on their proposal, which is then submitted to the other side and normally accepted unless there are special political and personal problems. In the latter case the substitution of a retiring judge can be delayed also for many months and the court works with an incomplete membership.

The working of the Constitutional Court

The constitution left to a further constitutional law and to ordinary laws the regulation of access to the Constitutional Court for procedures concerning the constitutional legitimacy of bills and definition of other aspects required to implement this institution. As with other aspects of the constitution the governments in office in the following years, despite being dominated by the same parties (and in particular by the DC) which had more strongly supported this innovation, dragged their feet in the implementation of the new institution. As for the other cases the explanation can be easily found in a combination of the asperities of the conflict with the opposition and the changed perspective of parties which had come to power and expected to maintaining this position for a long time. All this made the parties in government less interested in implementing aspects of the constitution which would have inevitably weakened the executive, while the strengthening of the government seemed in that period the most important priority.

Only in 1956 was the Constitutional Court formed and able to start operating. Being an entirely new institution for the Italian legal and political system, it had to learn from scratch, or even to invent, its own modus operandi and was to find only slowly its place within an already dense and more established institutional network. This inevitably entailed some tensions with other organs which, up to that time, had in some way performed some of its functions. On the side of the judiciary this had been the case with the highest court, the *Corte di cassazione* which, in the first years of the republic, had, albeit in a less explicit way, decided on matters of constitutional legitimacy with regard to laws of the previous regime. On the other side, there were obviously tensions with the democratic decision-making institutions—parliament and executive—which had to come to terms with the fact that another public body could nullify their decisions.

Since its beginning the Constitutional Court has been predominantly composed of prestigious academics and magistrates and has acquired a significant degree of authority. From time to time, however, completing its composition in terms of the component elected by parliament has proved difficult. As a large majority, and thus an agreement extending beyond the governing majority, is required, finding an individual who is largely accepted has sometimes proved difficult.

As regards the components of the court elected by the president and by parliament, the principle of proportionality has been rigorously applied so that the main political currents would be represented. It has not been uncommon therefore to ascribe to this or that judge the label 'Socialist', 'Catholic', or 'Communist'. It has been much more rare for small parties to have their supporters elected.

The work of the Constitutional Court has concentrated mainly on decisions concerning the legitimacy of laws. In this field it has progressively widened its activity, moving from the simple rejections of laws (or of articles of a law), judged illegitimate for procedural or substantial reasons, to subtler interventions which, without rejecting the law or parts of it, establish the constitutionally correct interpretation of a law (Figure 8.1).

Access to the court is regulated in such a way that only from within a pending judicial proceeding can one or more of the parts involved ask the judge to provoke a court judgment. Whenever the point raised either by the defence or by the prosecution is not manifestly ungrounded in the constitution, the judge of the proceeding must grant access to the Constitutional Court. To this means of access must be added a direct one when the government asks of the court that a regional law be examined to

FIGURE 8.1 **Decisions and rulings of the Constitutional Court, long-term trends**

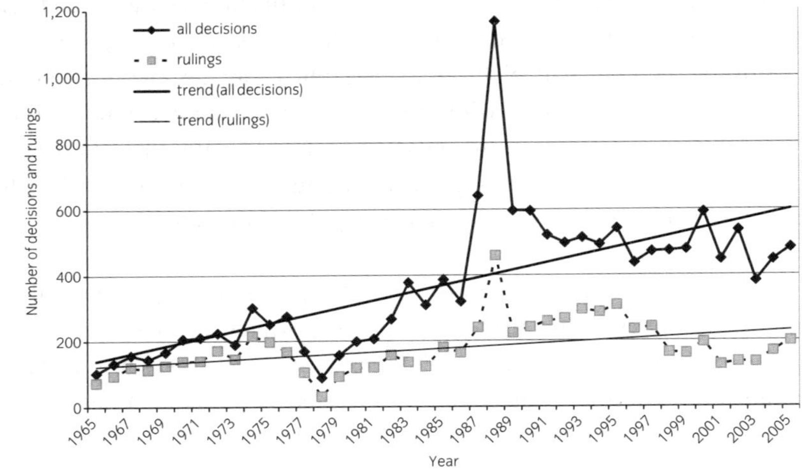

Note: Decisions include both rejections of requests judged to be ungrounded in the constitution and rulings on a specific point.

Source: Constitutional Court.

establish its compatibility with constitutional principles. In both cases it is then the responsibility of the Constitutional Court to decide whether the request submitted can be admitted or not.

The second area in which the Court has an important role is in decisions on conflicts between the powers of the state. To this should be added relations between the central state and regions and between regions. Conflicts of competencies of both types have burgeoned particularly in more recent years (Figure 8.2).

The Constitutional Court has also acquired a not irrelevant role in referendum procedures: as the constitution excluded certain matters from being the subject of a referendum, the law has stated that it is left to the Constitutional Court to rule whether a referendum is admissible (Figure 8.3). The court has used this power with some freedom, even excluding referenda on matters not mentioned in the constitution on the grounds that their effects might endanger the functioning of democratic institutions. For this

FIGURE 8.2 **Rulings on matters of conflict of competency**

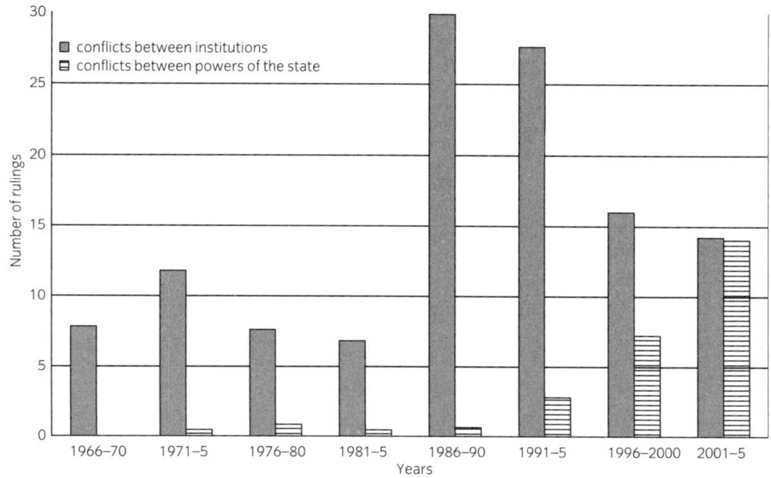

Source: Constitutional Court

reason, for instance, it prohibited in 1991 a referendum on the electoral system that would have abolished the entire existing regulation.

Overall the Constitutional Court has expanded its powers with time, but by operating with some prudence has so far escaped criticism. In fact it is one of the few Italian institutions that has never been at the centre of open controversies. Recent proposals to change its composition in order to give a say to the regions in the nomination of its members have so far failed.

Conclusion

The judicial side of the Italian political system has undoubtedly gone through important changes over the years. Some of these changes are rooted in a fairly long and gradual process of innovation, adaptation, and institutionalization that started with the beginning of the democratic republic of 1948. Other changes of a more recent nature are linked in part to the cumulative effects of this long-term process and to the consequences it

FIGURE 8.3 **Rulings on the admissibility of referendums**

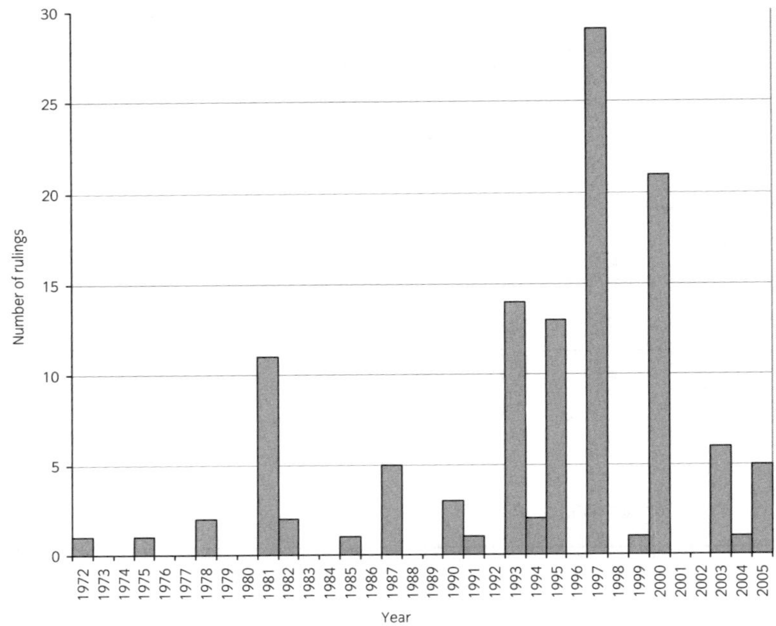

Source: Constitutional Court

has had, but depend in part also on the interactions between the renovated judicial institutions and other political institutions or actors which have also undergone significant transformations in recent years. These interactive effects have also produced some very tense conflicts, the solution of which is still uncertain.

There is no doubt that the protection of the different civil, political, and social rights of citizens has been expanded and improved significantly thanks to the combined effects of the Constitutional bill of rights, of a more active and independent judiciary, and of a strongly institutionalized Constitutional Court.

Among Italian institutions the Constitutional Court has probably been the least publicly debated and the one least involved in political conflicts.

Its decisions have been in general accepted without major contestations. Whether this will continue in the future is, however, less sure. Its role in deciding on conflicts between powers of the state and between state and regions puts it in a position which may become increasingly contentious in view of the more adversarial nature of political life and of the complicated sub-division of competencies between different levels of the state.

The judiciary, in contrast, has been constantly close to the centre of the political storms of the past fifteen years. Its evolution has undoubtedly transformed it into a more independent and self-conscious body capable of resisting external influences and challenging political power. At the same time its changed configuration and activism cannot but raise a number of relevant questions. There are at least three main aspects at the centre of the debate. First, the integration of judges and prosecutors in the judicial 'corporation' runs the risk of putting the third party in the process, the defendants and the lawyers, in a position of weakness vis-à-vis the two other parties that share the same background and career (and possibly the membership of the same associational 'party'). Second, the independence acquired by prosecutors has made them fundamentally inaccountable to any democratic authority. Their decisions in choosing which crimes to prosecute (in theory, they are obliged to prosecute all; in practice, for obvious reasons they make drastic selections) are in the end theirs alone and are often seen as arbitrary. This of course acquires a particularly critical significance when the defendants are major political figures. Is the decision of whether to start a judicial action an act of justice or a political act? Third, given the considerable power acquired by the judiciary, the lack of a more serious process of internal selection and promotion raises questions about the qualifications of judges and prosecutors. Finding a satisfactory solution to these issues has so far proved difficult.

KEY TERMS

- access to the Constitutional Court
- adjudicating magistrates
- conflict of competency among powers of the state
- Higher Council of the Judiciary
- judicial career
- judgment of constitutional legitimacy
- prosecutors

GUIDE TO FURTHER READING

CAZZOLA, F., and MORISI, M. (1996) *Magistratura e politica in Italia* (Milan: Feltrinelli).

Interesting information on and interpretations of the phenomenon of legal procedures against members of parliament.

DELLA PORTA, D. (2004) 'A Judges' Revolution? Political Corruption and the Judiciary in Italy', *European Journal of Political Research*, 39, 1: 1–21.

A study of the processes determining the emergence of *mani pulite*.

GUARNIERI, C. (2001) *Giustizia e politica. I nodi della Seconda Repubblica* (Bologna, Il Mulino).

A useful overview of the transformation of the Italian judiciary.

GUARNIERI, C., and PEDERZOLI, P. (2002) *The Power of Judges: A Comparative Study of Courts and Democracy* (Oxford, Oxford University Press).

Offers a useful comparative overview and interpretation of the main judicial systems.

PEDERZOLI, P. (2007) *La corte Costituzionale* (Bologna: Il Mulino).

VAUCHEZ, A. (2007), *Il consiglio superiore della magistratura* (Bologna, Il Mulino).

Two up-to-date textbooks dedicated to the crucial actors of the Italian judiciary system.

VOLKANSEK, M. (2000) *Constitutional Politics in Italy: The Constitutional Court* (London, Macmillan).

Detailed research on the role of the Italian Constitutional Court in the broader institutional environment.

9

Conclusion

In the 1990s the Italian political system went through a political and institutional crisis which has had no parallel among European countries with an established democratic regime since the Second World War. Only the crisis of the French Fourth Republic of 1958—which, however, happened only twelve years after the restoration of democracy in that country—could in some way be compared to the Italian one. This political earthquake, which during its most heated phase induced some observers to raise doubts about the future of Italian democracy, has triggered a number of significant and sometimes tumultuous changes to an institutional landscape that had previously been perceived as unchangeable.

Table 9.1 offers a synthetic view of what has been analyzed in greater detail in the chapters of this book. For each of the main institutional sectors of the Italian political system it provides a brief summary of the most important features that characterized the long period of continuity, of what has changed since 1992, and of the main problems still pending, or the solutions that are being currently debated.

This synoptic picture confirms the significance of the transformations which have occurred since the crisis years of 1992–4. A number of changes had, of course, taken place even before that period, but they had been of a lesser relevance, of a basically incremental nature, and they had been less simultaneous in their timing. On the contrary, most of the institutional reforms that, especially during the 1980s, had been explicitly at the centre of political discussions, failed in the end to be adopted. From this point of view the 1980s had closed with an essentially negative record. The novelty of the more recent period is that significant changes have taken place in all the sectors examined here during a relatively short time span. It is true that, contrary to what happened in the French case, the 'big reform', entailing

TABLE 9.1 Main institutional features and changes

Institutional areas	Phase of continuity (consolidated institutions of first republic) 1950s–1992	Phase of change (institutions in crisis/transition/partial consolidation) 1992–2006	Problems and perspectives of the current phase
Parties/party system	Limited electoral fluctuations. Long-term decline of DC	Collapse of old parties (DC, PSI). Birth and success of new parties (LN, FI, Margherita); renewal of old parties (PCI-DS; MSI-AN)	Persisting fragmentation of parties
	Birth of new minor parties (after 1976)	Consolidation of two left and right coalitions. Bipolar competition	Projects of large unified left and right parties
	Organizational decline of major parties (1980s)	Innovations in party organization	
Elections and electoral systems	Predominance of PR rule	Pro-majoritarian twist (1991–3) Mixed-majority system (for both chambers)	Permanent electoral campaign
	Predictability and stability of electoral outcomes	Alternation of 'winners'	Excessive tensions between the two coalitions
	Sub-cultural areas of vote	Increasing differences between local and general elections	Strategic use of electoral reforms
	First claims for change (1980s)	Voter begins to choose? Personalization and decline of identification vote	A new reform of the electoral system (general elections)?
		Return to PR with thresholds and majority bonus(es) for coalitions (2006)	
Parliament	Polycentric parliament	Delegitimation of old parliamentary elite via judicial proceedings (1992–4); large renewal	High fragmentation of parliamentary groups.

Table 9.1 continued

Institutional areas	Phase of continuity (consolidated institutions of first republic) 1950s–1992	Phase of change (institutions in crisis/transition/partial consolidation) 1992–2006	Problems and perspectives of the current phase
	Limited control of government over parliamentary agenda	Relatively clear borders between majority and opposition; more adversarial style of parliamentary workings	Difficult coordination of majority
	Limited discipline of majority		Reform of bicameralism on the agenda
	Legislative activism of parliament	Adaptation of rules of procedure	
	Attempts to increase government weight (1980s)		
Executive	Coalition governments	Pre-electoral formation of coalitions	Tensions between stronger leaders and fragmented coalitions
	Only peripheral alternation; DC permanently in government	De facto direct electoral investiture of PM (after 1994)	
	Instability of cabinets	Greater stability of cabinets	Big reform (stronger premiership, powers of parliamentary dissolution, etc.)
	Proliferations of government posts	Greater weight of Prime Minister within the cabinet	
	First reform of Prime Minister's Office	Increasing role of the executive in the supra-national arenas	
Sub-national governments	Slow implementation of constitutional rules	Direct election of chief executives (1993–9)	Tensions between central state and regional governments over financial resources and allocation of legislative responsibilities

continues

Table 9.1 continued

Institutional areas	Phase of continuity (consolidated institutions of first republic) 1950s–1992	Phase of change (institutions in crisis/transition/partial consolidation) 1992–2006	Problems and perspectives of the current phase
	Birth of ordinary regions (1970)	Constitutional reform and introduction of temperate federalism (2001)	Fiscal federalism?
	Institutionalization of regional governments	Failure of new reform (2006)	
	Weak executives	Organizational change and development of executive-centred local governance (neo-parliamentary system)	
Public administration	Adaptation and expansion of previous order	Rationalization, new management reforms; Bassanini laws and their controversial implementation (1996–2006)	Persisting inadequacy of performance
	Proliferation of parallel administrations	Dismantling of state holdings and privatizations	Contrasting mix of old and new principles in administrative management
	Attempts at reform (particularly after 1980)	Development of independent authorities	
Judiciary	Slow implementation of constitutional rules	*Mani pulite* and conflicts between judiciary and political actors	Persistence of slow and inadequate functioning of justice
	Growing corporate identity and autonomy of judicial class	Reform of the judiciary (separation of careers between judges and prosecutors; meritocratic selection of magistrates) (2005)	Conflicts between judiciary and political authorities
	Institutionalization of Constitutional Court		

a comprehensive redrafting of the parts of the constitution concerning the crucial democratic institutions, has not taken place. As it had failed to materialize during the last decade of the first republic, so it continued to fail despite the renewed attempts in the following years. In the absence of a 'big reform', changes have been of a more piecemeal character and they have not been orchestrated by the same hands. Some of them were the result of popular referendums, others of ordinary laws, or of limited constitutional corrections adopted by different majorities, or of de facto transformations of political actors and of their behaviours. In some cases, as in that of electoral reform, a change has been soon followed by another change.

The transformations affecting the central actors and institutional mechanisms of representative democracy have been particularly visible, as during recent years they have continuously occupied the headlines of the media. The crisis of the old parties and of their political leadership, the change in electoral rules, the birth of new parties, and the new shape of electoral competition have gone hand in hand with (and have produced) significantly different political dynamics having important consequences for the lives of democratic institutions. After forty years of elections without alternation of winners, the years after 1994 have seen a regular substitution of majorities and minorities at each electoral turn. These mutations in the central processes of political competition have had important effects upon the working of governments and for the relations between cabinet and parliament. The stabilization of governmental coalitions and the diminished volatility of cabinets, a greater prominence of the Prime Minister vis-à-vis the other governmental actors, a more balanced equilibrium between the executive and parliament, with the first taking more clearly the lead of legislative production and the latter developing its oversight prerogatives, have been among the most noticeable effects.

While these changes were taking place in the central institutions, other aspects of the political system were also giving way to multiple transformative pressures. In a few years, the whole system of territorially decentralized governance, in its different levels, has gained a greater political prominence, effectively claiming new powers from the central state, and its executive institutions have acquired a more majoritarian character. Even though the allocation of resources and responsibilities between central state and peripheral authorities has not yet found a stable definition, the quite recent idea of the need to transform Italy into a quasi-federal system has become largely acceptable.

As for the public administration in its different forms and dimensions, the season of supra-nationally constrained budgets, of privatizations, and of new models of public management has significantly altered its borders, internal composition, and, to a far from irrelevant degree, its ways of operating. While the traditional bureaucracy has become leaner and the state ownership of economic assets has been to a large extent dismantled, institutions of a new type, such as the independent authorities, have acquired a number of traditional functions of state administration but also introduced new models of administering the important social and economic problems concerned.

Finally, a crucial body of the state, the judiciary, has become an increasingly active participant in public life, to the point of acquiring some features of a new 'opposition' to the executive (and perhaps even to representative institutions). This has opened a sometimes harsh conflict which, even when starting from very practical matters and interests, has in the end revolved around rather fundamental issues related to the legitimacy of power and ultimately the conceptions of democracy.

The changes that have erupted during recent years stimulate some reflections on the vicissitudes of Italian democracy after the Second World War and on this peculiar sequence in which a long period of stagnation and immobility was succeeded by one of rather tumultuous change. On a closer look the connection between the two probably becomes more understandable. The period of continuity and lack of institutional innovation has its origins in the peculiar political configuration that had emerged from the fall of the authoritarian regime and its conjuncture with the international system which followed the Second World War. A deep ideological divide combining internal and international aspects and a fragmented party system, together with a consensus-orientated constitution, had led to the freezing of the institutional framework and of political alternatives as the most practicable solution to the problems of a difficult, divided democracy. The tensions of this political system had been tackled with slow processes of adaptation (and limited inclusion) which, on average, increased the polycentric character of the institutional system. This was the price paid for ensuring a measure of consensus.

This defensive and prudent adaptation proved effective in containing and managing the political tensions of the system, but at the same time made the performance of the institutional system increasingly unsatisfactory. Surviving without governing (Di Palma 1977) was probably the formula which best captured the logic of the system. New external challenges, new needs and claims from society and individuls, and the growing dissatisfaction with performance were increasingly bound to erode the support of the public and to stimulate demands for change. But the polycentrism of the institutional system and the fragmentation of political actors by multiplication of the veto turned into failure any attempt to reform the system.

Change could only come after a serious crisis of the existing establishment, which under attack from multiple challengers, produced the shattering of the existing political and institutional equilibrium. At that point the collapse of traditional political elites opened new opportunities for innovation. The absence, however, of a dominant new actor (as in the French case), or of a coherent coalition of reformers (as in the Spanish transition to democracy), determined a situation where change could take the form not of a comprehensive and systematic 'big reform', but rather that of multiple, non-coordinated transformations affecting different sectors of the institutional system. The lack of coordination has meant that some of these changes still require a reciprocal adaptation and may generate conflicts and tensions among sections of the institutional system. A good example is the tension between sub-national governments and central government, or between executive and judiciary. In the end this means also that the full stabilization of the new political and institutional landscape may require still more time. But in contrast to the past, the Italian political system seems to have acquired a somewhat greater dynamism and ability to respond to the challenges, and to be readier to explore new paths of change.

REFERENCES

ACQUARONE, A. (1965) *L'Organizzazione dello Stato Totalitario* (Torino, Einaudi).

ALLUM, P. (1973) *Italy: A Republic Without Government?* (London, Sage).

AMATO, G. (1976) *Economia, Politica e Istituzioni in Italia* (Bologna, Il Mulino).

AMMENDOLA, T., and ISERNIA, P. (2005) 'L'Europa vista dagli italiani. I primi venti anni', in COTTA, ISERNIA, and VERZICHELLI (2005), 117–70.

ANDERSEN, S., and BURNS, T. (1996) 'The European Union and the Erosion of Parliamentary Democracy: A Study of Post-Parliamentary Governance', in S. ANDERSEN and K. A. ELIASSEN (eds.), *European Union–How Democratic is it?* (London, Sage), 227–52.

BAGNASCO, A. (1977) *Le Tre Italie. La Problematica Territoriale dello Sviluppo Italiano* (Bologna, Il Mulino).

BALDI, B. (2006) 'Le regioni', in CAPANO and GUALMINI (2006), 147–70.

BALDINI, G. (2002) 'The Direct Election of Mayors: An Assessment of the Institutional Reform Following the Italian Municipal Elections of 2001', *Journal of Modern Italian Studies*, 7, 3:364–79.

BANFIELD, E. C. (1958) *The Moral Basis of a Backward Society* (Glencoe, IL, Free Press).

BARDI, L. (2006) 'Arena Elettorale e Dinamiche Parlamentari nel Cambiamento del Sistema Politico Italiano', in BARDI (ed.), *Partiti e Sistemi di Partito* (Bologna, Il Mulino), 265–86.

BEST, H., and COTTA, M. (eds.) (2000) *Parliamentary Representatives in Europe 1848–2000* (Oxford, Oxford University Press).

BERGMANN, T., STRØM, K., and MÜLLER, W. C. (eds.) (2003) *Delegation and Accountability in Parliamentary Democracies* (Oxford, Oxford University Press).

BLONDEL, J., and MUELLER ROMMEL, F. (eds.) (1998) *Cabinets in Western Europe* (London, Palgrave).

BOBBIO, L. (2005) 'Italy: After the Storm', in B. DENTERS and L. E. ROSE (eds.), *Comparing Local Governance* (London, Palgrave), 29–46.

BUFACCHI, V., and BURGESS, S. (2001) *Italy After 1989: Events and Interpretations* (London, Palgrave).

BULL, M. (2004) 'Parliamentary Democracy in Italy', *Parliamentary Affairs*, 57, 3:550–67.

——, and NEWELL, J. (2005) *Italian Politics: Adjustment under Duress* (Cambridge, Polity Press).

BULL, M., and RODHES, M. (eds.) (1997) *Crisis and Transition in Italian Politics* (London, Frank Cass).

CALANDRA, P. (1996) *Il Governo della Repubblica* (Bologna, Il Mulino).

CALISE, M. (1994) 'The Italian Particracy: Beyond President and Parliament', *Political Science Quarterly*, 109, 3:441–60.

——(2005) 'Presidentialization Italian Style' in T. POGUNKTE and P. WEBB (eds.), *Presidentialization of Politics: A Comparative Study of Modern*

Democracies (Oxford, Oxford University Press), 88–106.

——(2006) *La Terza Repubblica. Partiti Contro Presidenti* (Rome and Bari, Laterza).

CALISE, M., and MANNHEINMER, R. (1983) *Governanti in Italia. Un Trentennio Democristiano* (Bologna, Il Mulino).

CAPANO, G. (2000) 'Le Politiche Amministrative. Dall'improbabile Riforma alla Riforma Permanente', in G. Di PALMA, S. FABBRINI, and G. FREDDI (eds.), *Condannata al Successo? L'Italia nell'Europa Integrata Degli Anni Novanta* (Bologna, Il Mulino), 153–98.

——(2005) 'Legislative Institutionalization and Change: The Case of Italian Parliament Viewed from a Diachronic Perspective', *Quaderni di Scienza Politica*, 12, 2:255–92.

——, and GIULIANI, M. (2001a) 'Governing without Surviving? An Italian Paradox: Law-making in Italy 1987–2001', *Journal of Legislative Studies*, 7, 4:17–36.

——, and ——(eds.) (2006) *Parlamento e Processo Legislativo in Italia* (Bologna, Il Mulino).

——, and ——(2003) 'The Italian Parliament: In Search of a New Role?', *Journal of Legislative Studies*, 9, 2:8–34.

——, and GUALMINI, E. (eds.) (2006) *La Pubblica Amministrazione Italiana* (Bologna, Il Mulino).

——, and VASSALLO, S. (eds.) (2003) *La Dirigenza Pubblica. Il Mercato e le Competenze dei Ruoli Manageriali* (Soveria Mannelli: Rubettino).

CARTOCCI, R. (1985) *Elettori in Italia* (Bologna, Il Mulino).

CASSESE, S. (1981) 'Is There a Government in Italy? Politics and Administration at the Top', in R. ROSE and E. N. SULEIMAN (eds.), *Presidents and Prime Ministers* (Washington, DC, American Enterprise Institute), 171–202.

——(1993) 'Hypotheses on the Italian Administrative System', *West European Politics*, 16, 3:316–28.

——(1994) 'Italy: Privatizations Announced, Semi-Privatizations and Pseudo-Privatisations', in V. WRIGHT (ed.), *Privatizations in Western Europe: Pressure, Problems and Paradoxes* (London, Pinter).

——, and FRANCHINI, C. (1994) *Il Sistema Amministrativo in Italia*, (Bologna: Il Mulino).

CAVATORTO, S. (2006) 'Le Autorità Indipendenti', in CAPANO and GUALMINI (2006), 87–118.

CENTO BULL, A. (2002) 'Towards a Federal State? Competing Proposals for Constitutional Revision', in P. BELLUCCI and M. BULL (eds.), *Italian Politics 2001: The Return of Berlusconi* (New York, Berghahn), 85–104.

——, and GILBERT, M. (2001) *The Lega Nord and the Northern Question in Italian Politics* (London, Palgrave).

CHABOD, F. (1951) *Storia della Politica Estera Italiana dal 1870 al 1914* (Bari, Laterza).

CHIARAMONTE, A. (2007) 'How Prodi's Unione Won, for a Handful of Votes', in J. NEWELL (ed.), *The Italian General Election of 2006* (Manchester, Manchester University Press).

CHIARAMONTE, A., and D'ALIMONTE, R. (2007) (eds.), *Proporzionale e Non Solo* (Bologna, Il Mulino).

CLARK, M. (1996) *Modern Italy, 1871–1995* (London, Longman).

CONTI, N. (2006) 'Party Conflict over European Integration in Italy: A New Dimension of Party Competition?',

Journal of Southern Europe and the Balkans, 8, 2:217–34.
——, Cotta, M., and Tronconi, F. (2007) *The Cartelisation of the Italian Party System: One Step Forward and One Step Backward* (Siena, CIRCaP Occasional Paper).
Cotta, M. (1979) *Parlamento e Classe Politica in Italia* (Bologna, Il Mulino).
——(1990) 'The Centrality of Parliament in a Protracted Democratic Consolidation: The Italian Case', in U. Liebert and M. Cotta (eds.), *Parliament and Democratic Consolidation in Southern Europe* (London, Pinter), 55–91.
——(1991) 'Conclusion', in J. Blondel and J. L. Thiebault (eds.), *The Profession of Government Minister in Western Europe* (London, Macmillan), 174–98.
——(1994) 'The Rise and Fall of the "Centrality" of the Italian Parliament: Transformations of the Executive–Legislative Subsystem after the Second World War', in G. Copeland and S. Patterson (eds.), *Parliaments in the Modern World: Changing Institutions* (Ann Arbor, University of Michigan Press), 59–84.
——(1998) 'Italy: A Fragmented Government', in J. Blondel and F. Mueller Rommel (eds.), *Cabinets in Western Europe* (London, Macmillan), 120–37.
——, and Isernia, P. (eds.) (1996) *Il Gigante dai Piedi d'Argilla* (Bologna, Il Mulino).
——, and Verzichelli, L. (1996) 'Italy: Sunset of a Partitocracy', in J. Blondel and M. Cotta (eds.), *Party and Government* (London, Macmillan), 180–201.
——, and ——(2003) 'Ministers in Italy: Notables, Partymen, Technocrats and Mediamen', *South European Politics and Society*, 4:117–52.
——, Isernia, P., and Verzichelli, L. (eds.) (2005) *L'Europa in Italia. Elites, Opinione Pubblica e Decisioni* (Bologna, Il Mulino).
——, Mastropaolo, A., and Verzichelli, L. (2000) 'Italy: Parliamentary Elite Transformations along the Discontinuous Road of Democratization', in H. Best and M. Cotta (eds.), *Parliamentary Representatives in Europe, 1848–2000* (Oxford, Oxford University Press), 226–69.
Criscitiello, A. (1996) 'Alla Ricerca della Collegialità di Governo: I Vertici di Maggioranza dal 1970 al 1994', *Rivista Italiana di Scienza Politica*, 26, 2:365–90.
D'Alimonte, R. (2005) 'Italy: A Case of Fragmented Bipolarism', in M. Gallagher and P. Mitchell (eds.), *The Politics of Electoral Systems* (Oxford, Oxford University Press), 253–76.
——, and Bartolini, S. (2002) (eds.) *Maggioritario Finalmente. La Transizione Elettorale in Italia, 1994–2001* (Bologna, Il Mulino).
D'Onofrio, F. (1979) 'Committees in the Italian Parliament', in John D. Lees and Malcolm Shaw (eds.), *Committees in Legislatures: A Comparative Analysis* (Durham, NC, Duke University Press), 186–211.
D'Orta, C., and Talamo, V. (1996) 'Italy', in D. Farnham, S. Horton, J. Barlow, and A. Hondeghem (eds.), *New Public Managers in Europe: Public Servants in Transition* (Basingtoke, Macmillan), 215–39.
De Micheli, C., and Verzichelli, L. (2004), *Il Parlamento* (Bologna, Il Mulino).

De Winter, L. (1995) 'The Role of Parliament in Government Formation and Resignation', in H. Döring (ed.), *Parliament and Majority Rule in Western Europe* (New York, St. Martin's Press), 115–51.

Della Porta, D. (2004) 'A Judges' Revolution? Political Corruption and the Judiciary in Italy', *European Journal of Political Research*, 39, 1: 1–21.

Della Sala, V. (1997) 'Hollowing out and Hardening the State: European Integration and the Italian Economy', *West European Politics*, 20, 1:14–33.

Di Palma, G. (1977) *Surviving without Governing: The Italian Parties in Parliament* (Berkeley, University of California Press).

Di Virgilio, A. (2002) 'L'offerta Elettorale. La Politica delle Alleanze si Istituzionalizza?', in R. D'Alimonte and S. Bartolini (eds.), *Maggioritario Finalmente. La Transizione Elettorale in Italia, 1994–2001* (Bologna, Il Mulino), 79–130.

——(2005) 'The Italian Regional Elections of April 2005: Does the Triumph of the Union Signal the End of the Berlusconi Era?', *South European Society and Politics*, 10, 3:477–90.

——(2006) 'Forza e Debolezza delle Coalizioni Dopo le Politiche di Aprile', *Il Mulino*, 3:443–52.

Diamanti, I. (2003) *Bianco, Rosso, Verde e . . . Azzurro. Mappe e Colori dell'Italia Politica* (Bologna, Il Mulino).

Dogan, M. (1989) 'How to Become Ministers in Italy', in M. Dogan (ed.), *Pathways to Power: Selecting Rulers in Western Democracies* (Boulder, Westview Press), 99–129.

Fabbrini, S. (2000) *Tra Pressioni e Veti. Il Cambiamento Politico in Italia* (Rome and Bari, Laterza).

——(2001) 'Features and Implications of Semi-parliamentarism: The Direct Election of Italian Mayors', *South European Society and Politics*, 6, 2:44–70.

——(2006) 'The Italian Case of a Transition within Democracy', *Journal of Southern Europe and the Balkans*, 8, 2:145–62.

Fargion, V., Morlino, L., and Profeti, S. (eds.) (2006) *Europeizzazione e Rappresentanza Territoriale. Il Caso Italiano* (Bologna, Il Mulino).

Farneti, P. (1978) 'Social Conflict, Parliamentary Fragmentation, Institutional Shift and the Rise of Fascismo', in J. Linz and A. Stepan (eds.), *The Breakdown of Democratic Regimes* (Baltimore, The Johns Hopkins University Press), 3–33.

——(1985) *The Italian Party System (1945–1980)* (London, Pinter).

——(1989) *La Classe Politica dal Liberalismo alla Democrazia* (Genoa, ECIG).

Farrell, D., and Webb, P (2000) 'Political Parties as Campaign Organisations' in R. J. Dalton and M. P. Wattenberg (eds.), *Parties without Partisans? Political Change in Advanced Industrial Democracies* (Oxford, Oxford University Press), 102–28.

Fella, S. (2006) 'Introduction: One Step Forward or Two Steps Back? Assessing the Italian Transition', *Journal of Southern Europe and the Balkans*, 8, 2:133–44.

Ferrera, M. (1985) *Il Welfare State in Italia* (Bologna, Il Mulino).

——, and Gualmini, E. (2004) *Rescued by Europe? Italy's Social Policy Reforms from Maastricht to Berlusconi* (Amsterdam, Amsterdam University Press).

FOOT, J. (2003) *Modern Italy* (London, Palgrave).

GALLI, G. (ed.) (1966) *Il Bipartitismo Imperfetto* (Bologna, Il Mulino).

____(1968) *Il Comportamento Elettorale in Italia* (Bologna, Il Mulino).

GILBERT, M. (2000) 'The Bassanini Laws: A Half-way House in Local Government Reform', in D. HINE and S. VASSALLO (eds.), *Italian Politics 1998: The Return of Politics* (New York, Berghahn), 139–56.

GINSBORG, P. (1990) *A History of Contemporary Italy: Society and Politics, 1943–1988* (London, Penguin).

____(2003) *Italy and its Discontents: Family, Civil Society and State, 1980–2001* (London, Penguin).

GIULIANI, M. (1996) 'Italy', in D. ROMETSCH and W. WESSELS (eds.), *The European Union and Member States: Towards Institutional Fusion?* (Manchester, Manchester University Press), 105–33.

GUALMINI, E. (2006), 'I Ministeri' in CAPANO and GUALMINI (2006), 57–86.

GUARNIERI, C., (2001) *Giustizia e Politica. I Nodi della Seconda Repubblica* (Bologna, Il Mulino).

____, and PEDERZOLI, P. (2002) *The Power of Judges: A Comparative Study of Courts and Democracy* (Oxford, Oxford University Press).

GUNDLE, S., and PARKER, S. (eds.) (1996) *The New Italian Republic: From the Fall of the Berlin Wall to Berlusconi* (London, Routledge).

HELMS, L. (2000) 'Parliamentary Party Groups and their Parties: A Comparative Assessment', *Journal of Legislative Studies*, 6, 2:104–20.

HINE, D. (1993) *Governing Italy: The Politics of Bargained Pluralism* (Oxford, Clarendon Press).

____(2005) 'Codes of Conduct for Public Officials in Europe: Common Label, Divergent Purposes', *International Public Management Journal*, 8, 2:87–103.

IGNAZI, P. (2002) *Il Potere dei Partiti. La Politica in Italia dagli Anni Sessanta ad Oggi* (Rome and Bari, Laterza).

ITANES (2006) *Dove è la Vittoria? Il Voto del 2006 Raccontato dagli Italiani* (Bologna, Il Mulino).

KALYVAS, S. N. (1996) *From Pulpit to Party: The Rise of Christian Democracy in Europe* (Ithaca, Cornell University Press).

KATZ, R. S. (2003) 'Reforming the Italian Electoral Law, 1993', in M. S. SHUGART and M. P. WATTENBERG (eds.), *Mixed-Member Electoral Systems–The Best of Both Worlds?* (Oxford, Oxford University Press), 96–122.

____, and MAIR, P. (1995) 'Changing Models of Party Organization and Party Democracy', *Party Politics*, 1, 1:5–28.

____, and WESSELS, W. (eds.) (1999) *The European Parliament, National Parliaments, and European Integration* (Oxford, Oxford University Press).

KOFF, S. Z., and KOFF, S. P. (2000) *Italy: From the First to the Second Republic* (London, Routledge).

LA PALOMBARA, J. (1964) *Interest Groups in Italian Politics* (Princeton, Princeton University Press).

____(1987) *Democracy Italian Style* (New Haven, Yale University Press).

LEGNANTE, G. (2004) *Alla Ricerca del Consenso* (Milan, Angeli).

LEONARDI, R., NANETTI, R. and PASQUINO, G. (1978) 'Institutionalisation of Parliament and Parliamentarization of Parties in Italy'. *Legislative Studies Quarterly*, 3, 1:161–86.

LESTON BANDEIRA, C. (ed.) (2005) *Southern European Parliaments in Democracy* (London, Frank Cass).

Levy, C. (ed.) (1996) *Italian Regionalism: History, Identity and Politics* (Oxford, Berg).

Lijphart, A. (1968) *The Politics of Accommodation: Pluralism and Democracy in the Netherlands* (Berkeley, University of California Press).

——(1999) *Patterns of Democracy: Government Forms and Performance in Thirty-Six Countries* (New Haven, Yale University Press).

Linz, J. J. (1975) 'Authoritarian and Totalitarian Regimes', in F. I. Greenstein and N. Polsby (eds.), *Handbook of Political Science,* vol. III (Reading, MA, Addison Wesley), 175–357.

Loughlin, J. (2001) *Subnational Democracy in the European Union* (Oxford, Oxford University Press).

Mannheimer, R., and Sani, G. (2001) *La Conquista degli Astenuti* (Bologna, Il Mulino).

Marradi, A. (1982) 'Italy: From "Centrism" to Crisis of Centre-Left Coalition', in E. C. Browne and J. Dreijmanis (eds.), *Government Coalitions in Western Democracies* (New York: Longman), 33–70.

Mattson, I. (1995) 'Private Members' Initiatives and Amendments,' in H. Döring (ed.), *Parliaments and Majority Rule in Western Europe* (New York, St Martin's Press), 448–87.

Melis, G. (1993) *Storia dell'amministrazione Italiana* (Bologna, Il Mulino).

——(1998) *La Burocrazia* (Bologna, Il Mulino).

Merlini. S. (1995) 'Il Governo', in R. Romanelli (ed.), *Storia dello Stato Italiano* (Rome, Donzelli).

Merusi, F. (1977) 'I Comitati Interministeriali nella Struttura di Governo', in S. Ristuccia (ed.), *L'Istituzione Governo* (Milano, Comunità).

Morlino, L. (ed.) (1991) *Costruire la Democrazia. Partiti e Gruppi in Italia* (Bologna, Il Mulino).

——, and Tarchi, M. (1996) 'The Dissatisfied Society: Protest and Support in Italy', *European Journal of Political Research*, 30:41–63.

——(2006) *Partiti e Caso Italiano* (Bologna, Il Mulino).

Müller, W. C., and Strøm, K. (eds.) (2000) *Coalition Governments in Western Europe* (Oxford, Oxford University Press).

Nanetti, R. (1988) *Growth and Territorial Policies: The Italian Model of Social Capitalism* (London, Pinter).

Newell, J. (ed.) (2002a) *The Italian General Election of 2001: Berlusconi's Victory* (Manchester, Manchester University Press).

——(2002b) *Parties and Democracy in Italy* (London, Ashgate).

——(2004) 'Interpretative Approaches and the Study of Italian Politics', *Modern Italy*, 9, 2:241–62.

——(2006) 'The Italian 2006 Elections: Myths and Realities', *West European Politics*, 29, 4:802–13.

—— (ed.) (2007), *The Italian General Election of 2006* (Manchester, Manchester University Press).

Norris, P. (ed.) (1997) *Passages to Power: Legislative Recruitment in Advanced Democracies* (Cambridge, Cambridge University Press).

Norton, P. (1998) *Parliaments and Governments in Western Europe* (London, Frank Cass).

Pajno, A., and Torchia, L. (2000) *La Riforma del Governo* (Bologna, Il Mulino).

Papavero, L., and Verzichelli, L. (2007) 'The Election and the XV Legislature', in J. Newell (ed.), *The Italian General Election of 2006* (Manchester, Manchester University Press).

Parisi, A., and Pasquino, G. (1979) 'Changes in Italian Electoral Behavior: The Relationships between Parties and Voters', *West European Politics*, 2, 3:6–30.

Pasquino, G. (1986) 'The Demise of the First Fascist Regime and Italy's Transition to Democracy', in G. O'Donnell, P. C. Schmitter, and L. Whitehead (eds.), *Transition from Authoritarian Rule: Southern Europe* (Baltimore, MD, The Johns Hopkins University Press), 45–70.

____(1987) 'Party Government in Italy: Achievements and Prospects', in Richard S. Katz (ed.), *Party Governments: American and European Experiences* (Berlin, De Gruyter), 202–42.

____(2001) 'Partiti, Gruppi Sociali, Lobby e Singoli Parlamentari nella Vita di Camera e Senato', in L. Violante (ed.), *Il Parlamento. Annali della Storia d'Italia, vol. 17, Il Parlamento* (Turin, Einaudi), 659–82.

____(2007) 'The Electoral Context', in J. Newell (ed.), *The Italian General Election of 2006* (Manchester, Manchester University Press).

Perderzoli, P. (2007) *La Corte Costituzionali* (Bologna, IL Mulino).

Pierson, P. (2004) *Politics on Time: History, Institutions and Social Analysis* (Princeton, Princeton University Press).

Poli, E. (2001) *Forza Italia* (Bologna, Il Mulino).

Polsby, N. W. (1975) 'Legislatures', in F. L. Greenstein and N. W. Polsby (eds.), *Governmental Institutions and Processes: Handbook of Political Science, vol. 3* (Reading, Addison-Wesley).

Putnam, R. D. (1993) *Making Democracy Work: Civic Traditions in Modern Italy* (Princeton, Princeton University Press).

____, Leonardi, R., and Nanetti, R. (1985) *La Pianta e le Radici* (Bologna, Il Mulino).

Recchi, E., and Verzichelli, L. (2003) 'Italy: The Homeland of Political Class', in J. Borchert and J. Zeiss (eds.), *The Political Class in Western Democracies* (Oxford, Oxford University Press), 223–45.

Rokkan, S. (1970) *Citizens, Elections, Parties* (Oslo, Universitetsforlaget).

Rose, R. (1985) *Employment in Western Europe* (Cambridge, Cambridge University Press).

Rugge, F. (2003) 'Administrative Traditions in Western Europe', in G. Peters and J. Pierre (eds.), *Handbook of Public Administration*, (London, Sage) 177–91.

Sartori, G. (1976) *Parties and Party Systems: A Framework for Analysis* (Cambridge, Cambridge University Press).

____(1982) *Teoria dei Partiti e Caso Italiano* (Milano, Sugarco).

Strøm, K. (1995) 'Parliamentary Government and Legislative Organization' in H. Döring (ed.), *Parliaments and Majority Rule in Western Europe* (New York, St Martin's Press), 51–82.

____(2000) 'Delegation and Accountability in Parliamentary Democracies', *European Journal of Political Research*, 37:261–89.

Tebaldi, M. (2005) *Il Presidente della Repubblica* (Bologna, Il Mulino).

Trigilia, C. (1992) *Sviluppo Senza Autonomia* (Bologna, Il Mulino).

Vandelli, L. (2005) *Il Sistema delle Autonomie Locali* (Bologna, Il Mulino).

Vassallo, S. (1994) *Il Governo di Partito in Italia* (Bologna, Il Mulino).

____(2001) 'Le Leggi del Governo'. Come Gli Esecutivi della Transizione Hanno Superato i Veti Incrociati', in Capano and Giuliani (2001b), 85–126.

____(2006) 'The Constitutional Reforms of Centre-Right', in C. Guarnieri and J. Newell (eds.), *Italian Politics, ed. 2005* (New York, Berghahn), 141–61.

Vauchez, A. (2007) *Il Consiglio Superiore della Magistratura* (Bologna, Il Mulino).

Verzichelli, L. (1998) 'Parliamentary Elites in Transition', *European Journal of Political Research*, 34:121–50.

____(2001) 'La Distribuzione delle Spoglie Ministeriali. Proposte per L'analisi Comparata con una Indagine sul Caso Italiano', *Quaderni di Scienza Politica*, 1:53–100.

____(2002). 'Da un Ceto Politico All'altro. Il Mutamento nel Personale Legislativo Italiano (1992–2001)', in R. D'Alimonte and S. Bartolini, (eds.), *Maggioritario Finalmente. La Transizione Elettorale in Italia, 1994–2001* (Bologna, Il Mulino), 319–62.

____(2003a) 'Italy: Delegation and Accountability in a Changing Parliamentary Democracy', in T. Bergmann, W. C. Müller, and K. Strøm (eds.), *Delegation and Accountability in Western Democracies* (Oxford, Oxford University Press), 445–73.

____(2003b) 'Much Ado about Something? Parliamentary Politics in Italy amid the Rhetoric of Majority Rule and an Uncertain Party System', *Journal of Legislative Studies, Special Issue Parliaments in Southern Europe*, 9, 2:35–55.

____, and Cotta, M. (2000) 'Italy: From "Constrained" Coalitions to Alternating Governments?' in W. Müller and K. Strøm (eds.), *Coalition Governments in Western Europe* (Oxford, Oxford University Press), 433–97.

Volkanšek, M. (2000) *Constitutional Politics in Italy: The Constitutional Court* (London, Macmillan).

Wertman, D. (1988) 'Italy: Local Involvement, Central Control', in M. Gallagher and M. Marsh (eds.), *Candidate Selection in Comparative Perspective* (London, Sage), 145–68.

____(1994) 'L'ultimo Anno di Vita della Democrazia Cristiana', in C. Mershon and G. Pasquino (eds.), *Politica in Italia. I Fatti dell'anno e le Interpretazioni.* (Bologna, Il Mulino), 289–307.

Wiberg, M. (1995) *Parliamentary Questioning: Control by Communication?*' H. Döring (ed.), *Parliaments and Majority Rule in Western Europe* (New York, St Martins Press), 179–222.

Zamagni, V. (1998) *The Economic History of Italy (1860–1990): Recovery after Decline* (Oxford, Clarendon Press).

Ziblatt, D. (2006) *Structuring the State: The Formation of Italy and Germany and the Puzzle of Federalism* (Princeton, Princeton University Press).

INDEX